TWO RIDERS WERE APPROACHING

Also by Mick Wall:

Like a Bat Out of Hell: The Larger than Life Story of Meat Loaf
Last of the Giants: The True Story of Guns N' Roses
Prince: Purple Reign
Lemmy: The Definitive Biography
Foo Fighters: Learning to Fly
Getcha Rocks Off
Love Becomes a Funeral Pyre: A Biography of The Doors
Lou Reed: The Life
Black Sabbath: Symptom of the Universe
AC/DC: Hell Ain't a Bad Place to Be
Enter Night: Metallica – The Biography
Appetite for Destruction
W.A.R: The Unauthorised Biography of William Axl Rose
Bono: In The Name of Love
John Peel: A Tribute to the Much-Loved DJ and Broadcaster
XS All Areas: The Autobiography of Status Quo
*Mr Big: Ozzy, Sharon and My Life as the Godfather of Rock, by
Don Arden*
Paranoid: Black Days with Sabbath & Other Horror Stories
Run to the Hills: The Authorised Biography of Iron Maiden
Pearl Jam
Guns N' Roses: The Most Beautiful Band in the World
Diary of a Madman: The Official Biography of Ozzy Osbourne

TWO RIDERS WERE APPROACHING

The Life and Death of Jimi Hendrix

MICK WALL

First published in Great Britain in 2019 by Trapeze
an imprint of The Orion Publishing Group Ltd
Carmelite House, 50 Victoria Embankment,
London EC4Y 0DZ

An Hachette UK company

3 5 7 9 10 8 6 4

A CIP catalogue record for this book is
available from the British Library.

ISBN (Hardback): 978 1 409 16029 8
ISBN (Trade Paperback): 978 1 409 16030 4
ISBN (eBook): 978 1 409 16032 8

Typeset by Input Data Services Ltd, Somerset

Printed and bound in Great Britain by Clays Ltd, Elcograf S.p.A.

www.orionbooks.co.uk

CONTENTS

CHAPTER ONE

Two Riders

Said the joker to the thief . . .

Jimi drowning in cheap red wine. Red in his hair, his lungs, his eyes . . . Jimi washed clean in wine. Jimi swept away.

'He's done.'

'Are you sure? Make fuckin' sure.'

'Naw, he's fuckin' done.'

The men, CIA, MI6, ex, current, part-time, London crims, New York mob, Geordie fixers, final scorers, English-sounding, American-sounding, very heavy trip. The two riders moved away from the bed, from the mess they had made of it. Red wine and cold blood, a tangle of sweaty sheets and bed-spin. Coughed up. Yucked out. Shitted up. Testing the witchiness of witches.

'When's blondie coming back?'

'Doesn't matter.'

'What you wanna do about that?'

'Nothing. She knows what to do.'

Jimi limp – zedded-out. Jimi X-ed. The past no longer close behind.

Earlier . . .

Making the scene. Hanging with Posh Phillip, groovy son of Lord Harvey. Some chick in pearls and an English-money accent, others like that too: red-lipstick cigarettes, short skirts, look-see panties. Jimi smiling, high, coasting, showing good times; baby, you know I dig you special.

Jimi partying. Playing grab-ass with the bell-bottomed well-wishers. High fives. Low numbers. Just got back, you know, in town for a few days, catch up with some *gooood friends*. Cool on the outside, feverish on the inside. Jimi mouldering. Looking for a place to hide.

'Didja see *Monty Python* the other night, man? So funny! The Ministry of Silly Walks.' Jimi jiving his own version. 'Oh man, *so* funny! We'd been smoking that Red Leb. Oh man, I nearly *died!*'

Everyone: HA-HA-HA-HA-HA!

Smashed hippy cats kicking their legs, doing silly walks, Cleese-style. Jimi doubled over laughing, smoke pluming from him. Dunhill in hand, joint in hand, glass in hand. Nice pad. Laying back a cushioned kasbah vibe, all Saturn smoke rings and storied gold-thread rugs on the ceiling. On the record player, Smokey Robinson . . . '*But don't let my glad expression / Give you the wrong impression . . .*' Jimi the only black face, the only cat in the room really grooving on it. Jimi digging that too; Jimi *comfortable* in this scene. Groovy London white cats soft with daddy-money and cool class-connections, digging on the freaky minstrel *nee-gro*. The no-strings honorary white man.

Then the blonde chick hassling Jimi, a bringdown, crying that she wants to leave. The one with the heavy German accent, all whey face and train-track eyeliner. Jimi shaking her off but that chick losing it, running out, door slamming behind her.

Jimi going after her, vexed. 'You fucking pig!' she yells at him. Jimi yelling too, man, threatening to beat her ass. Posh Phil runs outside, begging them to stop, worried someone might summon the pigs. But Jimi has blood in his eyes. The blonde – Monika – has put it there. That chick is burning, man. After half an hour of this shit he gives in, apologises to everyone then leaves, taking Monika with him, hunting down a cab.

Back to the Samarkand – to Monika's little pad, the place too small for Jimi to settle. Monika suggests a bath, something to eat. Jimi wants to use the phone. Tells her Pete Kameron needs to see him at his pad. Pete helped kick-start Track Records. Jimi likes talking to him about his problems. Biz stuff. Serious shit. Dig?

Jimi explains, acting plausible: Pete is having like a dinner party, private. Monika can drive Jimi, drop him off, but Monika can't come in. It's not that kind of scene. You understand, doncha, baby?

Monika is down with that. She sees, she says. Around midnight she drops Jimi off. Jimi mighty relieved to be away from her, that bummer German chick, man, too goddamn much! Jimi needs to breathe. Besides, Devon Wilson – Dolly Dagger – is at Pete's, acting junkie coy. Stella Douglas and Angie Burdon too – chicks that *know* Jimi. Know his scene. Don't come on to it all so heavy. *Dig?*

It's a cool vibe. Jimi is happy to see Devon. He'd bitched and moaned when she told him she was coming all the way from New York. 'Christ's sake, Devon – get off my fucking back!'

But that was when he was still with Kirsten. Now Kirsten is gone, and the heavy German chick is on the scene, all of them claiming to be Jimi's bride to be. All of them pretending not to know when Jimi is just jiving, just saying love words, man, can't you see?

Now here in this place in the flesh, Jimi is digging on Devon again, drinking blood from the jagged edge. Only now Devon is the one playing it *coool*. On a Jagger trip still; knowing it smokes Jimi's mind.

But Stella is here – Alan Douglas's old lady. Alan is Jimi's new best friend. The one who's going to help lead him out of the sea of shit he is swimming in, towards the promised land of million-dollar smiles and other bullshit friends of mine.

Jimi *trusts* Alan. Jimi doesn't trust anyone. So he trusts his old lady too. Stella with her bindi and ultra-cool threads, her wise face and features open. Stella is not just another rock 'n' roll hang chick. You can talk to Stella. Stella knows the scene. No sex trips. Just love, l-u-v.

Same for Angie – Eric's old lady – only different in that Angie is on a smack trip. Angie and Devon. White-horse witches. Angie has had Jimi before, plenty of times. Like Devon, except Devon felt like a keeper; Angie was a one-off, repeat to fade. But now that chick don't wanna know 'less you got that sweet-brown-sugar jive.

Mainline time. Next stop: nowhere.

Jimi swerves Angie, fixes on Devon, fast-chats Stella. There is Chinese food on the table. He swallows a couple of black bombers and rolls another joint. Has a little taste of the chicken and rice.

Then the intercom buzzing ... Jimi flinching. 'Oh, man, please, you gotta tell that chick. Man, you know, leave me alone ...'

Stella, taking charge, picking up the intercom, telling the put-upon blonde, 'Come back later.'

'But I am Jimi's fiancée. You understand, *ja*?'

No tea and sympathy here, though. 'Go home.'

'*Nein*. No. You must understand—'

Stella hangs up.

Monika left standing alone outside. Monika crying. Monika freaking out.

Ten minutes later, the buzzer again. *Shit* ... Jimi losing it now. Stella, uptight, back on the phone telling the chick, 'No, man.'

Monika crying, yelling, noises off. Jimi apologising to the room, embarrassed. Jimi outside on the street again, so tired of this scene.

Taxi ride back to the Samarkand. Jimi bugged-out, vibing, bad-scene motherfucking chick, man. Monika silent, lights a cigarette. London skidding past, pre-dawn, yellow tobacco eyes watching from the Jag idling outside, waiting for them to return.

Mike stubs out his ciggie and pushes open the car door. The others follow. Big lads, *Get Carter* extras, Mob imports. Laughing and joking: under order of the thief.

Straight in behind the unhappy couple as they push open the door, straight into the cunt before he knows what's hit him. Knee him in the balls. He goes down gasping. Tell the blonde slag, 'Fuck off while we talk to your boyfriend.'

Give her the look. *Fuck – off – now.*

'I get cigarettes, Jimi, okay? From the garage I get cigarettes . . .'

The lads smile. Shove her out the door.

'Hey, Mike, what the hell, you know?'

Mike silent, his mind's eye hovering. Jimi pleading. 'Mike, come on, man—'

Then the lads are on him. Force the head down onto the pillow. Swing a couple of good ones to the gut. Jimi on all fours gasping, yowling, spluttering, Jimi frightened now, really hurt, man . . .

Another couple. Fold him over onto his back, yank his head back by the corkscrew hair; two hold him, another sets down the shopping bag, pulls out the first couple of bottles, pushes in the cork with his thumb. Tough guy. The wine sloshes over his hand. He wipes it on the golliwog's shirt. Then forces the bottle into his mouth. Glug, glug, glug, glug, glug . . .

'The boy's thirsty,' says one. The others jeer. 'Good job we brought more,' says one. The boys jeer.

Thumbs the cork. Wipes his hand. Forces the bottle in.

Wine *everywhere*. Jimi's eyes popping out, hands grasping, unable to breathe, wine pouring from his nose, into his hair, onto the bed, over the hands holding him down.

Thumbs the cork. Wipes his hand. Forces the bottle in.

Over his chest and arms, his mouth, his eyes. This scene is *real*. Impossible. This shit is *happening*. No way. The boys jeer.

Then the screen shuts off, little white dot ... quickly then slowly ... slowly ... shrinking into ...

Nothing. Deep, black, heavy ...

Nothing.

CHAPTER TWO

Lucille and Al

The night he was born, the moon was in shadow, on the wane, slipping from Cancer to Leo, stomach to heart, mucus to blood.

Mama was sugar-sweet, just turned seventeen. Daddy was all snafued, in army jail.

Lucille Jeter had married twenty-three-year-old US Army private James Allen Ross Hendrix eight months before. Three days later Al had shipped out to Fort Rucker, Alabama. When the baby was born, Al had been denied paternity leave and imprisoned. The CO said it was for his own good, knowing the boy would likely go AWOL instead. Al was pissed. All the white grunt fathers were given leave.

Like all Americans, the bloodlines were tangled, chewed up, faithfully ignored. African slaves, white slave owners, Red Indian tribes, the long line products of rape, murder, race hate, religious perversion, expulsion of expectation and the unsought prevailing of tough field grass in the cracks of centuries-hardened rockface.

On Lucille's side a white slave-owner grandfather and a black slave grandmother. Captain and concubine, odd couples made complete in the nineteenth-century Deep South. From them a boy, Preston Jeter: born 1875, classic mulatto. Fled Virginia after witnessing a lynching, headed for the Northwest where blacks were said to have it easier.

Yeah-yeah-yeah.

Mining in Roslyn, Washington, then Newcastle, anyplace a young black could earn a dollar. In his forties by the time he reached Seattle – but above ground in sunlight at least now, working in gardens – where he met Lucille's mama, Clarice Lawson. From Confederate, segregated Arkansas, Clarice came from the Cherokee, who'd been cattle-rounded there under the Indian Removal Act of the 1830s. Sheltered by slaves, intermarried, poor, Clarice was nineteen years younger than Preston and already pregnant after being raped in the cotton fields of the Louisiana Delta.

When her older sisters offered Preston the loot to marry Clarice, he called bullshit and made a run for it. She had the child, put it up for adoption and nearly died of grief. So the sisters went back to Preston, upped their offer, and this time he said, 'I do.' They were married in 1915 and stayed married until the old man died thirty years later. Though never truly happy, who is?

They lived in Seattle's Central District – four square miles of black street ghetto, home to jigs, chinks, redskins, nips, krauts, wops, kikes, flips – all the unwanted white negated trampled underfoot. Give 'em their own newspapers, schools, storefronts, juke joints and barrelhouses. *Give 'em anything they want, just don't put 'em next door to good God-fearing white folks like us.*

Jackson Street was where the action was, the mainline to the good-times night-time. The daylight hours mainly given over to cleaning up after the rich folks living high outside the District.

Preston and Clarice had eight kids, six of whom survived childhood. Lucille was the baby. Preston was old by then, past fifty, and Clarice was diagnosed with a tumour. She survived but was a long time gone in hospital. Lucille's sisters raised her. When things got too bad they were all fostered out to a good-hearted German family on a farm in the whites-only area of Greenlake, where the gun-toting locals assumed they were just the filthy off-spring of gypsies.

Lucille was light-skinned and pretty, a coffee-coloured doll turning heads on the street as she trilled on by. Lucille was so light and easy she could pass if she wanted. But she never did. Instead, living back in Central as a teenager, she loved to dance and had just turned sixteen, still in junior high, when she went with school friends to Washington Hall to see Fats Waller, the black Horowitz, perform. Where she met Al Hendrix, a short, hand-some iron-foundry worker with ideas above his station. Al could really dance. And he was older, had been around and earned a little spending money. Al was *fun*.

Like his eventual teenage bride, Al's background was from all over. Daddy was born a year after the Civil War ended. His mama, Fanny Hendricks, a recently freed slave recently divorced from Jefferson Hendricks; his papa an unreconstructed white slave owner who wanted nothing to do with the boy, even though his mama ensured he bore all his names – Bertran Philander Ross.

Ross, as he preferred to be known, was forty-six when he changed his surname to Hendrix. He'd been a 'special' police officer in Chicago for a spell, been married and split, and was now in showbiz, a stagehand for a Dixieland vaudeville troupe that travelled the Pacific Northwest. He was about to marry again.

Zenora 'Nora' Moore was a dancer and chorus girl, a real looker. Her mama, also named Fanny, was half-Cherokee, half-African. Her daddy Robert was a freed slave from Georgia. They lived as best they could on Tennessee time.

Nora had bigger dreams, though. She'd toured with her sister Belle as a hoofer, meeting Ross when she joined the same troupe of actors, musicians, comedians and dancers. When the money-pipe ran dry and the troupe disbanded, they were left stranded in Seattle. Stage-work prospects: zero.

To save rent on a shared room – no white-owned boarding

house was going to let to an unwed black couple – they married. When someone suggested Canada as a good place that people of colour might find jobs, they scrambled. On the recommendation of a patron, Ross got a gig in Vancouver, working as a steward at the American Club.

Nora swapped showbiz for housewife and five kids. Two died – the eldest, Leon, when he was twenty, and the youngest, Orville, when he was just two months old. That left Patricia Rose, Frank and, in 1919, James Allen Ross – Al to everyone else.

Three years after that the family were officially naturalised and became Canadian citizens. Life bumped along. Ross was active in the African Methodist Episcopal Church and became first porter at the newly opened Quilchena Golf and Country Club, at King Edward and 33rd Avenue, on the former First Peoples edge of Vancouver.

When the old man's aorta ruptured spontaneously, causing rapid exsanguination and death, he was sixty-nine. The Hendrix family ruptured likewise. Nora froze. The kids flew. The Great Depression hit and the world turned wrong. Any thoughts of Al making college died with his dad. Leaving school to look for work. But jobs were bum or no-count. Waiting tables at after-hours chicken joints.

Encouraged by his mother, he took to tap-dancing. He had the biz in his blood, she said. His older brother Leon had been like a gazelle, showed him all the cool steps, tap, Charleston, the Lindy Hop, Ballin' the Jack, the Eagle Rock and the Georgia Grind. Al got low-rent gigs off it. Added some steps of his own. Got an agent. Moved up to the clubs.

The jitterbug came in and Al got good at that too. Nora laughed and told him that when she'd dance it twenty years before it was called the Texas Tommy, from the all-black musical *Darktown Follies*. But the dances were segregated, to give the whites a chance, and Al went sour on it.

When his pal Al Ford told him about the amateur prizefights, twenty-five bucks a round for three rounds, Al Hendrix nearly shit. Short but strong and stocky, he talked his way into a Golden Gloves competition in Seattle, at the Crystal Pool, where he fought his first bout as a 147-pound welterweight. He won and won again. Then lost in the final. So what? The paycheck would cover the loss. Only he'd been conned. Told that only pros got paid, he walked back to the Moore hotel without the price of a cup of coffee. The topper: being told the pool there was whites only.

Fuck this cracker bullshit.

When Canada declared war on Germany, Al hightailed it to Victoria, where he figured on a railroad job, but the racist gang-buster manager wouldn't hire him, saying he was 'too daggum short'. More bullshit. Al slept on a friend's floor and picked up a couple of dollars shoe-shining. Then headed back to Seattle in 1940, with forty bucks and his dick in his hand.

Al hustled. Cleaned apartments. Got a gig dishwashing at a black ghetto joint on Pike Street. He still danced, still jitterbugged with the ladies, in his zoot suit and stripes. Showing them the hip to hip, the side flip and the over the back. But those Seattle gals were *big*. Al could spin the fat ones around, even slide the tall ones between his legs. But the only gals who seemed the right size for five-foot-six Al were the whiteys, and they only spelt danger for a black boy like him.

Working at the foundry when he met sweet-sixteen Lucille Jeter, Al couldn't believe his luck. This chick was shorter than he. And could really dance. Really keep up. Really show Al a thing or two.

What a team, baby.

CHAPTER THREE

Chas and Kathy

Saturday, 24 September 1966. Jimmy was still on New York time when the plane touched down in London – 9 a.m. local, 4 a.m. for Jimmy. There had been so much to eat on the plane – filet mignon, lobster – and so much to drink – champagne, top-shelf Scotch and brandy – that Jimmy was frazzled. Unused to long-haul travel and being woken at 4 a.m. when he'd only just managed to fall asleep a couple of hours before, he was bad breath, cold sweat, red-eyed unprepared for what was about to happen.

Being in first class, he and Chas and their roadie Terry McVay (borrowed from the Animals) were first off the plane and first into customs, Jimmy smiling but acutely self-conscious. His social unease tainting his aura, making him feel freak-show gawky. His blackness a smear, his showy *American* blackness going against him, he sensed it.

Terry carried Jimmy's guitar case. Jimmy didn't have a work permit. The story Chas had invented for him: that he was a pro songwriter here to collect some royalties. The customs guys didn't like it, knew it was fishy, but the big white guy in the suit seemed to know what he was talking about – they'd heard of the Animals – so they let the dodgy-looking darkie through on a seven-day non-work permit.

Jimmy and his brand-new passport and his jeans and Bob

Dylan hair. Everything else he owned – the borrowed Strat, the one change of clothes, the jar of Valderma antibacterial face soap (those fucking spots, man) and his pink hair curlers – was in the guitar case.

Out on the other side of customs, Jimmy is wired, ecstatic, an unexploded firework. Chas, who has been scheming all the way over on the plane, goes to a phone box and starts plying it with penny pieces. He calls the Animals' office, speaks to Trixie Sullivan, Mike Jeffery's PA. Trixie knows all about Chas leaving the Animals and wanting to go into management with Mike. She likes Chas, sees him for what he is: an honest broker, talented music man and genial company. But she knows he is nothing without Mike. Mike, says Trixie, is 'someone special . . . one tough guy and bloody clever'.

Chas's next phone call is to his new Swedish girlfriend, Lotte. Chas and Lotte have rooms booked at the Hyde Park Towers Hotel in Bayswater, including one for Jimmy. Chas tells Lotte they will arrive later this afternoon, after he and Jimmy make a quick stop-off. Tells her to be ready. They will all be going out tonight to the Scotch of James.

The Scotch – hidden in the cobbled streets around St James's Square, near the Houses of Parliament – is one of a handful of swinging London nightspots catering to the new pop aristocracy, places like the Ad Lib, in Leicester Square, and Blaises and the Cromwellian in Kensington. Boozed-up young bluebloods and glamorous gangsters, pushy snappers in night-time sunglasses, flat-chested fashion queens and pilled-up film-star wannabes. The sort of after-midnight champagne-ghettos Paul McCartney and Mick Jagger showed up in, surrounded by pop-life hierophants like Robert Fraser and David Bailey, Stash and Peter Max, and well-dressed goddess-class girls like Twiggy and Marianne Faithfull, Julie Christie and Jacqueline Bisset.

Chris tells Lotte to call the guys at the Scotch, let them know they will be coming down that night, hold a couple of tables. The Scotch is the most likely Saturday-night happening in London at the moment, a great shop window in which to show Jimmy off, even if he can't legally play anything in public – yet.

Next call is to old mucker Zoot Money.

Zoot is the singer-organist in his own outfit, the Big Roll Band, who have just had a minor hit with 'Big Time Operator'. Though he doesn't know it yet, Jimmy's influence is about to transform Zoot from an average R&B club act – one up from nice-boy square Georgie Fame, one down from wild-man Brian Auger – into a short-lived, summer of love psychedelia-by-numbers outfit called Dantalian's Chariot. (Dantalian being the name of the mytho-logical Great Duke of Hell, who commanded thirty-six legions of demons.)

Zoot has a nice pad in Fulham, a taxi ride from the airport. Chas figures to take Jimmy there first, grab a smoke, a tea, a gentle hang with like-minded cats before going official later that night at the Scotch. It's that or take Jimmy straight to the hotel. Lonely one-window bedroom, no friends, no vibe, no smoke.

Zoot's pad is Grand Central for every passing head and muso in west London. When Chas swings by with Jimmy around eleven Zoot is very cool. When Jimmy sees the Big Roll Band's gear all set up in the lounge, he knows he has come to the right place. That Chas knows things. Jimmy asks, humble-faced, if he can jam on Zoot's white Telecaster, and Zoot gives him the nod, head wreathed in the good smoke.

Jimmy big-grin lets fly.

Zoot takes it in. Tries to. He hears blues, soul, gospel; he hears black, white; he hears pure bright light. Jingle-jangled. Kissing, biting, laughing. He looks over at his wife Ronni and she is vis-ibly turned on. Inside shrieking. She is gunking-gooing.

Jimmy all shy eyes thrusts out his crotch and makes the Tele cry.

Ronni can't believe it, runs upstairs to her friend Kathy's flat.

Kathy Etchingham on the phone to me years and lifetimes later, telling me Ronni shouted: 'Kathy! Come downstairs quick! Chas has brought this bloke from America and he looks like the Wild Man of Borneo!'

Kathy, lying in bed smoking, is in no hurry. She hears the noise, but she didn't get back last night till God knows what time. Zoot and Ronni have a lot of would-be wild men in the house. Kathy is twenty years old, very fashionable and very pretty. Large brown eyes, dark straight hair, Kathy works as a hairdresser. When she's out at night with Ronni, though, she is a DJ, sometimes at the Cromwellian and the Scotch.

Kathy and honey-blonde Ronni are a good double act. Kathy the sexy, free, swinging London chick, Ronni the warm earth mother and hands-off wife of Zoot. They are what's happening wherever they go. Ronnie protective; Derbyshire-lass Kathy in no need of protection. She's already been out with Brian Jones, Keith Moon, that scene. Kathy is a big girl now, lipstick-tipped cigarettes and hash.

Kathy takes her time getting down the stairs and by then it's too late. Chas and Jimmy are leaving. Never mind. They agree to meet at the Scotch that night.

Jimmy wants to see Linda Keith. Linda is the reason Jimmy has made it this far. Jimmy wants to see everything there is to see. But Linda is still Keith's chick, and though she's psyched to see Jimmy finally in London, all her own work, Linda says she'll meet him later at the Scotch.

When Jimmy turns up that night with Chas and Lotte, it is quiet, shy Jimmy that is on display – until he gets his little showcase on the stage and every cat in the place falls about like, What, huh?

This is not Wild Man of Borneo Jimmy, this is serious muso Jimmy, here to show his credentials. A young, black American bluesman, dig? Hear that train a-coming. No show, just blow. In-house hurricane. The sharkskin-suited mods and art-school, post-Beat scruffs can't believe what they're hearing. The pretty mini-skirted chicks all flicking their hair, all aquiver like it's cool to love a black man stranger dude.

Before Jimmy there had been safe old coloureds over from the States playing homespun acoustic blues, like Big Bill Broonzy, already in his fifties and therefore ancient. Or there had been mean-bear electric black dangermen like Muddy Waters, not much younger than Big Bill but infinitely scarier. Crazy old geezers the boys liked but the girls held their noses to.

Now here was Jimmy James, young and pretty and shy and sweet, mumbling soft words into the mic. Magicking with his guitar like Pan playing his pipes on your window ledge after dark when the world is sound asleep dreaming.

Linda Keith watched this from her table with a mixture of delight and dread. She had been right: Jimmy really was a star in the making. Only now did it dawn on her what came next, and she wasn't sure how she felt about that. Jimmy had been Linda's great discovery, Linda's special friend. Now Jimmy would belong to everyone else. Linda who?

When Kathy arrived – perfumed hair, bum-cheek skirt, manic up-north energy – she was late again. Jimmy had already finished his little hot spot. Chas waved her and Ronni and Zoot over to the table where he and Jimmy and the rest of the gang were sitting. Pulled out a chair and sat Kathy right down next to Jimmy.

Jimmy instantly gratified. Gestures for Kathy to come closer, then whispers in her ear, 'I think you're beautiful.' Kisses her ear and smiles. Then tells her some other things. Man-to-girl things, all googly-eyed.

Ronni seeing this: happy for her friend, giggly. This is too goddamned much for Linda, who flips out. Throws her drink at Ronni. Plates start flying. Tables turn over. Jimmy grabs Kathy's hand and they flee. Chas telling them to grab a taxi and meet them back at the hotel. Kathy and Jimmy laughing, running out into the street still holding hands.

Back at the hotel, in the bar, Jimmy gives Kathy the treatment. Shy and sweet, polite and attentive – and American and *fun*. Chas says he's going to be a star. Jimmy all aw shucks, Kathy trying to be cool.

In the morning, in bed with Kathy holding his arms out, looking at the scars on his wrist, cooing. Jimmy nearly shits when the door flies open and Linda Keith bursts into the room.

'Hey, baby . . .'

Linda, not listening, grabs the Strat she'd given him and runs out again.

'*Bastard!*'

Jimmy telling Kathy it's okay, baby, it's Keith Richards's chick. Out-of-her-mind crazy chick, forget her. Kathy okay with it – for now. Everything a big one-night-stand adventure, maybe more, Kathy doesn't know yet, but she'll work on it.

Jimmy simply jazzed on openly being with a white chick. Back home that could still get you lynched in some states. Interracial marriages still a crime in most of them. White-hate protesters with their Race Mixing Is Communism banners still coming out marching whenever the TV news needed them.

Even Frank Sinatra's buddy Sammy Davis Jr., the biggest 'honorary white man' in showbiz, didn't get away with schtupping a white chick. After his marriage in 1960 to hot-tomato Swedish movie queen May Britt, white-hate groups picketed the theatre where he was working waving signs: Go Home Nigger.

An avalanche of hate mail hit them from all sides. Death threats at his shows in Reno, San Francisco, Chicago . . . At the Lotus Club in Washington the American Nazi Party picketed outside, Sammy nervously tugging at his glass eye.

Then came the public and private criticism from American

blacks, accusations of being an Uncle Tom, newspaper headlines asking, Is Sammy Ashamed He's a Negro?

Shit-scared Sammy hired twenty-four-hour armed guards. He and May stopped going out. And when they did, Sammy carried a gun or a cane with a knife concealed in the handle.

Man, Sammy was a *famous* black artist. What chance a poor no-count half-breed like Jimmy? Still, Jimmy had fucked plenty of white chicks before. But that had always been strictly undercover. This scene here with Kathy, with Linda, with these *English* white chicks, man, this was something else. Almost, you know . . . *free.*

CHAPTER FOUR

Little Frank

Mike was one of those guys that you just never knew what to believe. Soldier, spy, club owner and jazz lover; money-spinner, shadow gangster, ex-licensed killer. A man in a suit and tie and dark prescription glasses who said little and did much. Not a man you would necessarily trust but a man you would always keep faith with. A man with connections above and below ground. X-listed phone numbers, friends in low places. Favours. A southerner operating in the north, an Englishman who spoke fluent Russian. Heavy presence, light touch.

Everybody loved Mike. Everybody hated him. Mike didn't give a fuck which way. Mike had his head screwed on. Mike knew the score. Five foot six with thin side-parted hair and a cemetery smile, Mike was the kind of short, hard man that could fill a room with his intent. Always in a suit and tie, until he upped his game for Jimi and embarked on his first acid odysseys. Then Mike got hip. Coloured shirts. Kipper ties. Grass. Pills. Dom shampoo. Swapping expensive dolly birds for free-love hippy chicks. Hipster moustache. He still kept the camel-hair coat for cold nights, but his dark hair now touched the collar.

Mike *got* it. But he was good at throwing you off the scent. Reverse vibe-sender. Second-hand truth-seller. Professional sticky-finger. All the stuff he'd learned in the Circus as a warranted MI6 ghost, as an invisible CIA fink, borrowed aliases unknown.

Mike would tell you his story like it wasn't worth much. Then throw big, heavy stones into the pond, watch the ripples tsunami. See your face change. To wonder, *What if?*

Born Frank Michael Jeffery, 13 March 1933, Monday's child. Slippery Pisces. St Giles' Hospital, Peckham, south of the river. Only child of Frank senior and Alice: postal-employee plebs of Peckham Sorting Office. Old terraced housing. Cold water taps. Long washing lines. Nosy neighbours. Big Frank, Little Frank, it got too confusing, so Little Frank just became Mike.

By the time the war got really going the family had strayed to Catford, out on the London perimeter, its name dating back to the witch-hunts, when all the black cats were tossed shrieking into the river. Young Mike would walk past the Gothic-fronted Concert Hall and wonder what went on there. He preferred the cinema opposite. Tough-guy Saturday-night flicks, *The Third Man, Dead Reckoning, White Heat* . . .

He might have been better at school, but there was a war on and who cared? Good at sports, he liked rough-and-tumble boys' games. Hung on, bored, until he was sixteen, to please mum and dad, who pushed him to get 'a good job' – white-collar. An ad in the local paper led to a job clerking for Mobil Oil in Bishopsgate, a two-hour round trip every day on the number 47 bus. But he got to wear a smart jacket and tie, and the only time his hands got dirty was when his cheap fountain pen leaked.

London was a dump then. Hitler's bombs had fucked it all up good and proper. Travelling on the top deck of the bus each day, Mike looked down on the debris, took in the gradual rebuilding, and knew he was lucky. Frank and Alice shared the meat and sugar rations equally, but Mike always got an extra slice of National Loaf.

It was a relief when, in 1951, he was called up for National Service in the army, a statutory two years. Writing home every week. Getting to travel abroad. Meeting funny-speaking foreigners.

Losing his virginity. Learning things even his parents didn't know.

Starting as a private posted to the 17th Training Regiment of the Royal Artillery in Woolwich. Two months in he was transferred to the Royal Army Education Corps, now a ranking sergeant, at the regiment's depot. A couple of months after that he became an instructor at the Army Apprentice School in Harrogate.

Quick steps for a bright south London boy. But Britain was in trouble after the Egyptians stormed the army's Naafi storehouse in Ismailia. A young British soldier was stabbed and two Egyptians killed. Egyptian volunteers rushed to join the Liberation Battalions, as the Muslim Brotherhood in Ismailia declared a jihad against the British. More British soldiers died, nearly all conscripts. Something would have to be done.

Within months Mike became one of sixty thousand troops shipped out to defend the Suez Canal. He found himself in Fayid, where he became an active part of the BTE, MELF (British Troops Egypt, Middle East Land Force). And from there, just a few weeks later, attached to the 73rd Heavy Anti-Aircraft Regiment of the Royal Artillery.

It was the beginning of the end of Western control of the Suez Canal and the start of the three-year Suez Emergency, 'the forgotten war fought by a forgotten army' as historians would come to describe it. Taught to trust no one, to view the Egyptians as inferiors, to fear invisible snipers and well-disguised close-range assassins, few of the hastily conscripted, poorly trained British troops understood the danger.

Mike, however, with eyes in the back of his head, with his good head on his broad shoulders, thrived. Palling up with Nobby, Jock, Geordie, Taffy, Titch, Mac and Glen. Meeting up with some of the off-duty girls from the Women's Royal Army Corps, out at the Old Vic Lido by the Great Bitter Lake. Jumping off the long jetty that ran out into the lake, Mike learning to snorkel and dive. Then strolling down to the beach to get some grub and a cold beer or two. Lolling around in the sun, cooling off in the shade under the veranda. Having your picture taken next to the double-trunked palm tree at the water's edge.

Usually, though, Mike was working, scheming, looking for the chance to 'earn an extra bob or two'. When he discovered that in Cairo, off limits to British soldiers, you could buy British newspapers that were only a few days old, he arranged for military vehicles to fetch the papers from Cairo then sell them at a premium to his news-starved fellow recruits at the base. When a senior officer cottoned on to the scam, fast-thinking Mike escaped disciplinary action by agreeing to cut the SO in on the deal. The first of many rule-bending side deals Mike would make over the coming years.

Then, in March 1953, he was off again, after being vetted for intelligence work by the War Office and Scotland Yard. Two months later Mike left Egypt and returned to London, where his National Service officially ended in June 1953.

The day after it ended he re-enlisted and resumed serving with the Royal Army Education Corps, with the rank of acting sergeant. He immediately began an other-ranks security course at the Intelligence Corps Depot at Maresfield Barracks, near Uckfield in Sussex, where he was graded as 'C' – code for the Secret Intelligence Service now known as MI6. Transferred to the Intelligence Corps Centre, in September 1953 he left for Trieste in Italy, where he joined Unit 2 in the Trieste Security Office, part of the 5,000-strong army unit BETFOR (British Element Trieste Force).

This was where the serious work began. Trieste was an important strategic seaport in the Adriatic Sea close to Italy's eastern border, the south-east border of Austria and the western border of the communist bloc, then still Yugoslavia. Trieste had been a centuries-long pillar of Austria's Habsburg Empire, but had been returned to Italian rule in the wake of the First World War, and it remained under Mussolini's fascist control throughout the Second World War. Since 1945, however, Trieste had belonged to communist Yugoslavia under General Tito.

By the time Mike reported for duty, Trieste had been declared a free independent state and divided into two zones: the Allied Zone A to the north, under the occupation of joint British and American forces, and a Yugoslav-run Zone B to the south. The Trieste Security Office was one of the busiest hotspots in the world. Mike was twenty, no longer the ruddy-faced conscript of two years before, but a highly trained intelligence officer operating at a juncture where communist agents and agitators mingled with spies of the Allies, crisscrossing in and out of the communist zone.

Mike's main job was vetting the swathes of would-be Zone B defectors. Potential informants had to be vigorously interrogated and their information properly assessed. Rooms set aside. Doors locked from the outside. Field interrogations. Threats. Beatings. Mind games. You didn't ask permission. You did your bloody job.

Mike also worked as an active member of the Chinese Laundry – code name for the unofficial SIS base in Trieste. Mike was never an official SIS agent. Nobody was ever an *official* agent for SIS, or MI6 as they later became known. He simply 'ran errands', helping track down spies and liaising with the Italian Intelligence Service. Small change. Then going off-book for the big stuff.

Like the story he told his girlfriend Jenny Clarke, after he'd left the army, about the time he took part in a covert operation smuggling a high-value commie target out of Yugoslavia to Allied-controlled Trieste. How in the course of the op he'd had to kill a Yugoslavian guard. That it was a classic him-or-me situ, and that he now regretted it. How he'd kept a photograph of the guard's family, lifted from the dead man's bleeding body, having searched his pockets for money and valuables.

Mike never missing a trick, never letting his feelings, however bothersome, run away and spoil things, ruin the taste of it.

As soon as it was announced that Zone A was being returned to the Italians, early in October 1954, and that British and US troops were being immediately withdrawn from Trieste, Mike was on the first plane home. But while the Trieste Security Office closed for good in November, Mike was already deep into a three-month stint at the Army's Joint Service School for Linguistics in Bodmin, Cornwall. His speciality: Russian-language training. As soon as he'd completed the course in February 1955 he was back to the Intelligence Corps Centre then assigned to Northern Command, Field Security Section (FSS), where he served as acting corporal.

The FSS was about sifting classified info gathered from multiple sources, not least the Secret Intelligence Service. Handling enemy intelligence operatives, public and private sympathisers, proven and closeted collaborators, secret arrests, top-level interrogations. Covert operations. Kidnapping. Executions. Bond's fictional licence to kill: recognised, in reality, at SIS as a 'supreme breach of law'.

Mike spent over a year getting his lily-whites dirty, building an impressive classified record of his own. By the time he officially left the FSS in May 1956 he'd been in uniform and out for over five years. Immediately placed on Section B of the Regular Army Reserve list in June that year, he attended regular training courses in order to renew what was known as his 'life certificate'.

Like all former members of the SIS, Mike never spoke of any of this to his family. In company, though, Mike could be a lively raconteur, brandy wit and small-hours bon viveur, openly boasting of his undercover army exploits. Most believed him. Some did not. No one doubted his shady past.

Years later, managing the Animals, Mike treated singer Eric Burdon, his guest at his home in Palma, Mallorca, to an extraordinary spectacle. Several battleships from the US Seventh Fleet were docked at the island's port, and American sailors filled the town's bars and clubs – many of them owned by Mike.

The reason, Mike explained, was that the US Navy were trying to recover a hydrogen bomb, which had been lost off the coast of Spain after two US planes collided in mid-air and crashed into the sea. How did Mike know this? Mike just knew things, he said, blowing smoke rings. Ah-ha.

To shove the point home, Mike climbed into a wetsuit, snorkel and breathing apparatus, swam out to the area where the US fleet was anchored and set up some explosive devices. Later that day, over drinks back at one of Mike's shoreline bars, Eric looked on awestruck as his manager began to 'have some fun', detonating the explosives using a radio-operated device and causing a series of preposterously loud explosions in the midst of more than thirty of the warships. American seamen were running scared all over shore.

Did this really happen? Certainly, more than one of Mike's 'friends' from those days would later recall the story. More than one even claimed to have been there. More than one lied.

Did anything Mike say ever really happen?

CHAPTER FIVE

Jimmy and Maurice

New York, 8 August 1965. Letter home to dad.

> *I just want to let you know I'm still here trying to make it. Although I don't eat every day everything's going alright for me. It could be worse than this but I'm going to keep hustling and scuffling until I get things to happening like their supposed to for me.*
>
> *Tell everyone I said hello. Leon, Grandma, Ben, Ernie, Frank, Mary, Barbara and so forth. Please write soon. It's pretty lonely out here by myself. Best luck and happiness in the future.*
>
> *Love, your son, Jimmy.*

Hoping for a return letter with a few dollars in it. But no money ever came. If Al joined the dots he never showed it, always too preoccupied with his own problems.

After losing the Little Richard gig, Jimmy hooked up with Fayne again. Back in New York, hopping from one shithole Harlem dosshouse to another, only ever a day's rent away from being locked out and losing his gear. Fayne losing her mind when one day he brings home *Highway 61 Revisited*. You spent our dollars on *what?*

'Come on, baby, you never heard *Bob Dylan*?'

'Bob *who*? No, I don't know who Bob Dylan is.'

Jimmy unable to believe it but digging on the chance to turn her on, Fayne who always knew more than he did about everything. This here is *Bob Dylan*, dig? Fayne looking at him like all the brothers did that time in the club when Jimmy made them play 'Don't Think Twice, It's All Right'. Like, this some cracker shit, man! Fayne indulging the boy, waiting for the goddamn record to end, lighting another cigarette, leg swishing like a cat's tail. Jimmy all bug-eyed, ignoring the blank he is drawing.

'I figured Jimmy was so heavy into what I was into that he would never like anything like that.' Fayne, barefoot outside in the garden shade, talking in 1973, in her red polo-neck sweater, big, heavy medallion and white jeans; Fayne, so beautiful to look at and funny crazy to know.

'But he just loved it to death. I wanted to get up and go to the bathroom; he would grab me by my arms and sit me down, you know, like I'm gonna miss this part.' Fayne smiling at the memory. 'I *couldn't* miss it.' Jimmy had the record player turned so loud 'you could hear it to 42nd Street, probably. We almost got put out of the building behind Bob Dylan . . .'

Late 1965. What did any brother need Bob Dylan for, man? You got James Brown – 'Papa's Got a Brand New Bag' (parts I and II). You got the Four Tops – 'I Can't Help Myself'. You got the Temptations – 'My Girl'. You got Junior Walker & the All Stars – 'Shotgun'. You got Joe Tex – 'I Want to (Do Everything to You)'. You got Wilson Pickett – 'In the Midnight Hour'. You got Marvin Gaye – 'Ain't That Peculiar'. You got the Supremes – 'Stop! In the Name of Love'.

You want me to go on, brother?

You got Solomon Burke ('Got To Get You Off My Mind'), Sam Cooke ('Shake'), Ramsey Lewis ('The "In" Crowd'), the Miracles ('The Tracks of My Tears'), Otis Redding ('I've Been Loving You Too Long'), the Impressions ('People Get Ready'), Martha and the Vandellas ('Nowhere to Run'), Don Covay ('Seesaw'), Johnny

Nash ('Let's Move and Groove (Together)'), Edwin Starr ('Agent Double-O-Soul').

You need more, motherfucker?

Fontella Bass ('Rescue Me'), Little Milton ('We're Gonna Make It'), Barbara Mason ('Yes, I'm Ready'), the Righteous Brothers ('You've Lost That Lovin' Feelin''), Gene Chandler ('Nothing Can Stop Me'), Bobby Bland ('These Hands'), Ben E. King ('Seven Letters'), Roy Head and the Traits ('Treat Her Right'), Alvin Cash & the Crawlers ('Twine Time'), Fred Hughes ('Oo Wee Baby, I Love You'), Billy Stewart ('I Do Love You'), Barbara Lewis ('Baby, I'm Yours'), Little Anthony and the Imperials ('Hurt So Bad'), the Marvelettes ('Too Many Fish in the Sea'), Joe Simon ('Let's Do It Over'), the Spinners ('I'll Always Love You') . . .

All huge soul hits in America in 1965 and Jimmy didn't give a shit.

Strutting down 110th Street in his black witch's hat and processed hair. Carrying his guitar to the pawnshop again. He'd catch the jive.

'Are you coloured, nigger?'

Jimmy back in his hotel room with Fayne, burning up the record player to Dylan, digging the poetry, the surrealism, tripping on John Hammond Jr.'s *So Many Roads*, blues with a white man's twisted edge; getting high to the Stones and the Beatles, grooving on British Invasion cats like the Animals, head-rushing on the Byrds, hip to the changes going down, desperately wanting in. No way of knowing how. No real friends in Harlem at all.

Fayne was *baad*. Jimmy was no-way never.

'He didn't like to stand out, kind of timid, you know?' remembered Albert Allen, who lived for a while with his twin brother Arthur in the same cheap rooming house as Jimmy and Fayne. 'Except Jimmy *always* stood out!'

Jimmy sitting around with his guitar, writing words of poesy on stray pages in the early hours while Fayne slept or was just out having a better time with someone else. Jimmy stoned, sitting around with his guitar, reading sci-fi and getting strange, cosmological thoughts. Then out hustling for work with hardened black club players who despised him for his youth, his daydreams, his flash-ass ways. Jimmy getting ready to cut out.

Fayne hating those motherfuckers for the way they treated Jimmy. Even when they let him on the stage to jam, show what he could do, maybe make a dollar, they would fuck him around, know-better, shitty old never-was nobodies.

'They'd get up and just mess up so bad behind him. It was incredible, you know? And he'd be looking all disgusted on the stage, and he'd keep looking back at 'em. The other guys come and tell him he's gotta turn it down. You know, taking him through all kind of changes.'

Jimmy back at the hotel room, sitting on the bed, holding the sleeve of *Highway 61* in his lap, rolling a joint, looking down at Dylan with his big piled-up hair, holding his sunglasses, in a motorcycle tee and Marlon Brando-coloured shirt and a face like James Dean. Flipping it over, digging on the far-out notes: '... *then Rome & John come out of the bar & they're going up to Harlem ... we are singing today of the WIPE-OUT GANG – the WIPE-OUT GANG buys, owns & operates the Insanity Factory – if you do not know where the Insanity Factory is located, you should hereby take two steps to the right, paint your teeth & go to sleep ...*'

'Can you *see*?' Jimmy says. 'Can you dig what it is he's *really* saying?'

'Sure, baby.' Fayne yawning. 'Come to bed, baby.'

Jimmy not yet initiated into the mind's eye hurricane of LSD but wide open to the sea of possibilities he hears in Dylan's lyrics, his poetry, his defiant self-actualisation. No one *really* knowing what Dylan's *really* saying, just intuiting a whole new level of insight through modern rock 'n' roll. Jimmy reading about the electric show at the Newport Folk Festival just weeks before, where Dylan got booed, man, fucking booed, you believe that? Newspapers jumping right on it: 'He electrified one half of his audience and electrocuted the other.' Jimmy just *loving* that idea, seeing himself doing the same; if he only could he only would.

'Baby, come to bed.'

Jimmy sleeping in bed with his guitar on his chest. Fayne would go to move it, but he would open one eye: 'No, no, no, leave my guitar alone . . .'

Jimmy loved Fayne. Loved her so much it made him cry and made Fayne laugh. Every time Fayne stepped out on him Jimmy vowed he would never let another woman make him feel that way, begging her back for more. Drifting from one crap-hole rooming house to the next, trash piling up around them till it touched the sky, Jimmy still clinging to his Dylan and his poesy and his little science-fiction books. Jimmy still just a kid in Fayne's hot brown eyes, and what good's a kid when you got to live?

Jimmy laughed and looked away as he signed a piece of paper he already knew wasn't worth shit, giving over his management and contract recordings to Henry 'Juggy' Murray, mover and shaker at something called Sue Records. Sue had a stable of black acts, mainly early stuff by Don Covay, Ike and Tina, here today, gone later today dance shit. Juggy knew Jimmy didn't have any songs he could use, but he knew the boy could play, so signed him, put a few dollars in his pocket and told him to come back later.

Jimmy cashed the cheque and forgot about it. Two-year deal. Option for a further three. Those motherfuckers were *craazy*. Jimmy didn't have shit needed managing, didn't have any real songs to record yet, just long poems, half Oldie English and half Harlem street hustler. Just took the magic beans and ran home to mama. The next week it was straight back to zero. Jimmy and Fayne constantly fighting. Constantly down. Growing sicker of each other even as they fucked each other's brains out on the floor.

'He was very well endowed, you see,' Fayne would curl up and tell you. 'He was creative in bed too. There would be encore after encore . . . hard-driving and steamy like his music. There were times he almost busted me in two the way he did a guitar onstage.'

When they fought Jimmy always lost the war of words. He knew he had to get away but didn't know how. In the end he wrote Fayne a letter. 'It seems that this is the only way I can express myself and say what I want to say without being interrupted and without starting an argument.'

It only made things worse, Fayne tearing up the letters and tossing them. Jimmy so worn down when Fayne told him she had gone and married Arthur Allen behind his back. Arthur was cool, still let Jimmy stay in his place. But Fayne wanted Jimmy gone now, and after he overheard her arguing with Arthur about it Jimmy just split. Took the subway from 125th Street to West 4th Street – Harlem to Greenwich Village – carrying everything he wanted to take with him in his guitar case.

Recalling those days not much later, Jimi said, 'I used to go to the [Harlem] clubs, and my hair was really long then. Sometimes I'd tie it up or do something with it and the cats would say, "Ah, look at that: Black Jesus." Even in your own section [of town]. I had friends with me in Harlem, 125th Street, and all of a sudden cats, old ladies, girls, anybody would say, "Ooh, look at that. What is this, a circus or something?"'

The Village was where Dylan and all those hip white folk cats hung out, the poetry crowd. Jimmy had his ticket to ride, looking for a new place to fit in, just to be. Jimmy looking for his kinda people. But the Village had its own closed scene. Few blacks. That cafe society scene that Miles and Trane and Billie and the Bird and the Count and Lena and Nat King and all those kinda cats had once made home from home . . . that was another lifetime.

The Village was *white* now. Black tolerant, sure, but not for music, shimmy-shine dooby-wooby. All that dancing in unison, man, come on, singing 'bout love-love-love, finger-poppin' good darkie shit, that stuff's for *squares*.

Beatniks didn't dance. They liked *think* music. Hanging out drinking coffee and smoking reefer at Gerde's Folk City on West 4th or the Bitter End on Bleecker Street, or four doors down at the Cafe Au Go Go or the Cafe Wha? on the corner of MacDougal, or up the street from that, the Gaslight Cafe. These were arty hangs, painters, actors, models, writers, Ginsberg-Burroughs-Capote-McKuen-type places, queer factories, heroin brotherhoods, the music all acoustic and rustic and full of bile and beer and green tobacco. Dave Van Ronk. Tom Paxton. Phil Ochs. John Sebastian. Maria Muldaur. Good people but *serious*. Educated. Moneyed. Indoor sunglasses. Cravats. Pipes. Can anybody here say Tom Rush?

Jimmy dug it, saw the bigger picture, just couldn't see where his pretty black ass fitted in to that. Oh sure, you could catch Mississippi John Hurt at the Gaslight once in a blue moon, maybe Sonny Terry and Brownie McGhee giving it up for the white folks once in a while, but these were history acts. Museum pieces. Not hot-shit young blacks. Not like dangerman Jimmy.

In October Jimmy was back on the road, this time with the Mob-owned Joey Dee and the Starliters, ten shows in Massachusetts. Joey, who'd had the number 1 hit of 1961 with 'Peppermint Twist', sold a mil then got his first royalty cheque and found out he somehow 'owed' the label $8,000. When Joey asked where his bread was, the boys told him, 'Joey, you're gonna get hurt. Keep your fuckin' mouth shut.'

Back in New York, hanging on to himself outside his new digs, a West 47th Street dump called the American Hotel, Jimmy got yapping to another starry-assed Harlem refugee named Curtis Knight.

Now going by the name Maurice James – *Mo-Reece* sounding more *so-phis-ti-ca-ted*, more Bleecker Street, can you dig it, but mainly to try to shake off any heat from unpaid hotel bills and, uh, 'out of date' contracts – Jimmy listened good as dead-eyed Curtis laid down his rap. Knight was thirty-six, a singer and guitarist who'd released a number of no-go singles over the past four years and now fronted his own blues and soul group, the Squires. That was his story. In reality, he was a pimp from Kansas with a stable of whores operating out of west Manhattan. Hey, baby, a man's gotta do!

Curtis had recently lucked into a scene with an old-timey record hustler named Ed Chalpin. Ed had made his bones selling 'exploito' shit overseas. You know, do a cheaply made cover of an original hit so exact that the dumb ass in the street don't know it's a fake. Named his label Twin Hits – a gasser title under the umbrella of his real outfit, PPX Enterprises – and struck gold with make-you-shudder crap like 'Memphis Tennessee' by Bernd Spier, which hit number 1 in West Germany in 1964.

Ed saw the whole soul-singer thing as a comer, put a few bucks Curtis's way and booked him into the el cheapo basement studio at the American. Jimmy – Maurice – had pawned his guitar again, but Curtis offered to loan him his spare if he would join him with Ed in the studio and cut a couple of tracks as a favour, no biggie, dig, get you something to eat, nigger. Jimmy – Maurice – looking ahead to another night sitting alone and hungry in his seventh-floor roach palace, jumped at the chance.

As soon as Jimmy – Maurice – plugged in and began making the strings purr, both Curtis and Ed knew they had something here they could really use. Curtis, the protective big bro Jimmy never had, gave the kid a job in the Squires, gigging in bars and clubs around New York three nights a week, regular money, honey. And Ed came on all godfatherly and offered the boy a one-page contract to sign, another of those three-year bullshit promises.

Jimmy happy to sign any old thing just to get his guitar out of hock. Ed laying down coin to make the deal legal: exactly one dollar. Plus a line in the contract: 'and other good and valuable consideration'.

Why not? Jimmy saw this bullshit for what it was. When Curtis gave him the chords to 'Like a Rolling Stone' to play then began making up his own bullshit lyrics on top, renaming it 'How Would You Feel', like no one might notice the difference, ha, yeah. Jimmy didn't care. It was none of his business. He just played, got paid and went back to balling chicks and dreaming his own all-night-long dreams. Just another one-night stand, dig?

Curtis on the horn the next day telling him where to be for the next studio session, cutting the Wolf's 'Killing Floor', Brother Ray's 'What I'd Say', encouraging Jimmy to really stretch and moan on 'California Night', a sepulchral blues remodel of Albert King's 'Travelin' to California', Curtis's so-so vocal easily ignored, Jimmy's guitar reshaping the King's sun-worn notes into a jewel-edged lash, dice your sweet black ass.

Jimmy never paid outright for any of these sessions, all part of the deal that kept him off the streets. Jimmy in bed reading *Spiderman* comics, using his Spidey sense to feel his way round this latest scene.

CHAPTER SIX

Noel and Mitch

Eric Burdon was determined to hang onto the Animals. Alan Price had been the first to bail out, the summer before. John Steel had split nine months after that. Now Chas had gone. Eric was making a solo album in London, but Eric was no fool and wasn't about to lose his commercial lifeline if the great scheme to become a solo star didn't pan out. He still had drummer Barry Jenkins. But he didn't know who else to get, didn't know if it was going to be Eric Burdon's New Animals or Eric Burdon and the New Animals. So he placed an ad in the musicians-wanted section of the *Melody Maker*. Eric was looking for fresh faces that could play but wouldn't give him any trouble. What he didn't want was the little old man that walked in one afternoon in October 1966 carrying a guitar case and a long, thin face, mouth turned down at the sides.

His name was Noel Redding, he was twenty and the world owed him a big favour. He plugged in, played a couple of songs with Eric scatting along, then was told to go outside and wait. Eric had no intention of inviting the young sourpuss back in. The boy could play but what a downer to have around. Lip-purser. Vibe-killer. Going on about how this was his last go at making it. That if he didn't get the gig he was going to sell his guitar and amp and try his luck as a drummer. Or become a milkman.

Chas was roaming. Spotted the drink of water with the big hair sitting disconsolately in reception, and out of nothing asked him if he could play bass. 'No,' came the dispiriting answer. Chas, big Geordie, full of can-do attitude, tried again: 'Would ya give it a go?'

Noel said yes, adding that he had nothing better to do. Followed Chas into a small rehearsal room and was handed one of Chas's old basses. Also in the room was this coloured guy in a Burberry raincoat, holding a guitar. He also had big hair. Noel was vaguely intrigued.

His name was Jimmy. No drummer, just Jimmy and Noel jazzing away on a couple of low-slung songs from Jimmy's New York club act: the Tim Rose take on 'Hey Joe', and 'Mercy, Mercy', the old Don Covay number Jimmy had played on back in '64.

It was clear Noel couldn't really play bass – not as good as Jimmy could, that was for sure. But Jimmy liked the young English cat's hair – a big Dylan-esque do like his own – and his accent and what he mistook as his laid-back manner.

Afterwards, Noel and Jimmy went to the pub, where Jimmy drank a pint of bitter, following Noel's example. Jimmy's first taste of British beer – it made his head spin. They talked about this and that – the English scene versus the American scene, zzzzz – and Jimmy, light-headed, asked the kid, 'Would you like to join my group?'

Noel looked at him, owl eyes and worm mouth. 'What group?' he said. Jimmy laughed at that one. This crazy white English cat and his fucked-up sense of humour. Maybe it was the strong beer, or just the cultural jet lag, but Jimmy saw Noel as somehow fun, freaky, different.

Used to playing with pick-up cats on the lam, Jimmy just blurted it all out. Noel finished his pint, thought about it, and said he would be prepared to come back the next day – on condition that they gave him the ten shillings he would need to pay for his train fare up from Folkestone, where he lived with his mum and dad.

Jimmy laughed at that one too. Chas less so when they returned to his office, beer-sour breath, to ask for the money.

Born in 1945 on Christmas Day, like baby Jesus, Noel grew up in his Swedish mother's B&B in the tiny coastal village of Seabrook, along with his father, grandmother, and brother and sister. A grammar-school boy, he began learning the violin at nine, and then later the mandolin. He made his first public appearance at nearby Hythe Youth Club 'playing a couple of Eddie Cochran songs'.

Talented for his age but irascible, he graduated to electric guitar at fourteen, when he joined his first schoolboy group, the Strangers. Sacked 'for being too small', he was back in time for their equally unsuccessful evolution into the Lonely Ones when he was sixteen, unaware of the American doo-wop group of the same name.

A typical short-sighted English schoolboy listening under the bedclothes, the transistor radio against his ear, Radio Luxembourg the destination, dreaming of being Lonnie Donegan, Elvis Presley, Gene Vincent, Eddie Cochran, Cliff Richard . . . There was a privately pressed vanity EP, paid for by the family and recorded in 1963, by which time Noel was recognised locally – as he was bizarrely fond of telling people even after he'd joined the Hendrix Experience – 'as the best guitarist in Folkestone'.

His real claim to fame was that he had toured clubs in Scotland and Germany with Neil Landon and the Burnettes. Landon got a two-disc deal with Decca while Noel was still in the group, but neither 'Waiting Here for Someone' nor 'I'm Your Puppet' did doodly-squat in terms of the charts, despite a couple of look-mum telly appearances.

Meanwhile, Noel's previous unsuccessful group the Lonely Ones had turned into the equally unsuccessful the Loving Kind, which he also joined. It just wasn't fair, for fuck's sake. Noel was such a great player. Much better than most of the ones you saw on *Ready Steady Go!* or *Juke Box Jury*, ask anyone in Folkestone.

John Mitchell was one of those kids who acted all shy until you got him out of his shell – then watch out, mate! A skinny little short-arse who always had scabs on his knees from playing football in the streets or just rough and tumbling with the other neighbour-hoods scruffs, trouble if you wanted it, no backing down. Especially good with his mouth, he'd rather tell you to fuck off than actually fight you. A show-off whose parents had the inspired idea of enrolling him at the Corona Academy of Stage Training, in Chiswick, a number 65 bus ride from where the family lived in Ealing in the coal-dust fifties. Suddenly, saucy young John was using all that nervous energy to learn tap dancing, singing, acting, musical instruments – and how to play nicely with girls.

He was cheeky. Artful Dodger face and mean little jailbird eyes, perfect for his first ensemble role in the kids' TV show *Jennings at School*, which led to a similar naughty-but-nice supporting role in the 1960 comedy film *Bottoms Up*, starring Jimmy Edwards. Other quick-fit roles followed, along with radio jingles, TV ads, stage stuff.

'I worked with all these precocious brat kid actors,' John re-called later in life, 'doing jingles, singing boy soprano, and I met all the studio players through that. I was around a lot of drummers.'

A teenage jazz cat, he dug drummers like Ronnie Stephenson who crashed around on the cymbals while sitting there hunch-backed, looking like a hood. He'd been hooked on the notion, he said, after 'seeing Fred Astaire playing drums in a film. I was about eight or nine and I was tap dancing, and I thought, Wait a minute!'

He picked up tricks from Joe Morello, who knew how to bring

things to the boil even when the rest of the band was gliding, ultra per-*cuss*-ive, geddit? Joe played like ice cubes tumbling around the bottom of a frosted glass. Max Roach too, except Max liked to run wild, hard-bop, crazy waltzes in 3/4 time, getting into *mo*-dal-ity, dig? Then later, after John became 'Mitch' and started playing pro, there was the God-almighty Elvin Jones. Who *didn't* Elvin influence, then in the perceptual sixties, as now and tomorrow? Elvin and the classic Coltrane Quartet . . . You couldn't call your-self a drummer in any meaningful way to other modern drum-mers if you weren't hypnotised and dishevelled by that shit, man – didn't even deserve to be in the same room.

Teenage jazz cat, actor, voiceover artist and budding tap dancer, Mitch starts hanging out at the Ealing Jazz Club, in the basement opposite Ealing Broadway tube station and down the alley between the old ladies' teashop and the musty jeweller's. It is the early sixties and there is no hipper suburban club in London. Cyril Davies, Alexis Korner, Charlie Watts, Dick Taylor, Brian Jones, Rod Stewart, Long John Baldry, Dick Heckstall-Smith, all those cats, Manfred Mann, Pete Townshend, Eric Clap-ton, Paul Jones . . . all of 'em one-of-these-days. All here. Hoping and joking and good-bloking, trying to get by for the night on five bob and a packet of Player's No. 6 tipped.

Mitch's first Ealing Club outfit is the Soul Messengers, with sax player Terry Marshall, son of Jim Marshall, whose musical-instrument shop in nearby Hanwell will later become the place where Jimi Hendrix will order up his own custom-made-by-Jim 'Marshall amps' – soon to be followed by every wannabe loud band in the world. Through Tim, Mitch picks up a Saturday job working at the shop. Jim also runs a weekly drum school across the street, but Mitch refuses to attend. Mitch is already on the scene. He doesn't need to *read* music.

Mitch is a pig in shit, picking up occasional big-time 'dep gigs' – when the regular drummer is ill – with Screaming Lord Sutch and Johnny Kidd and the Pirates, lying about his age in order to get into over-twenty-one venues. 'Being smuggled on band buses to Hamburg and Frankfurt when I was on school holidays.'

Mitch leaving school to become a touring and session musician, working with Pete Nelson and the Travellers, Frankie Reid and the Casuals, Johnny Harris and the Shades, Billy Knight and the Sceptres, then, as the gigs got juicier, the Pretty Things, sitting in temporarily for Viv Prince, and one of rebel producer Joe Meek's goon gangs, the Riot Squad – where Joe, out of his mind after weeks hopped up on high-strength 'diet pills', held a loaded gun to Mitch's head to 'inspire' him while he was playing.

Some of the outfits had records out, some didn't. Only the Pretty Things had ever had a Top 10 hit – 'Don't Bring Me Down', in 1964 – which Mitch didn't play on.

There were close shaves. Drumming on a let's see basis for the Who after Doug Sandom got the boot – but Big Nose and the Dodger picked another nutcase named Moon ahead of Mitch to become full-time replacement, so that was bloody well that.

Hanging out in Denmark Street – London's own greasy-spoon version of Tin Pan Alley – he got to know a professional session drummer, name of Bobby Graham. Bobby was six years older than Mitch and several light years ahead in terms of his career, having already played on number 1 singles for the Dave Clark Five ('Glad All Over'), Dusty Springfield ('I Only Want to Be with You'), the Kinks ('You Really Got Me'), Petula Clark ('Downtown') and dozens more.

It was Bobby who tuned Mitch into the occult world of London recording sessions. Mainly these involved various BBC orchestras, guys in jackets and ties in their fifties and sixties who stopped for tea breaks and left promptly at 5 p.m. The only younger faces were hotshots like Little Jimmy Page – so named to differentiate him from that other guitar colossus of the session scene, Big Jim Sullivan – and John Baldwin, aka John Paul Jones. Clem Cattini was the other big drummer on the session scene, but even Clem, who would eventually play on forty-two number 1 singles, couldn't cover every session when Bobby decided he'd enough of the grind and lack of recognition.

Teen jazz cat suddenly became teen session rat, working a lot for songwriter-producer and orchestra leader Les Reed. 'It was quite lucrative,' said happy Mitch. 'But then it got very boring.' When he'd done three days on the road with the Pretty Things after Viv had gone on 'sit-down strike' over money, Mitch came back to London determined to get out of the session scene. He was working for producer Denny Cordell when he got his chance.

One of the acts Cordell regularly recorded with was Georgie Fame and the Blue Flames, who had hit it big in 1965 with their number 1 single 'Yeh, Yeh' and were about to have their second number 1 in the summer of 1966 with the Cordell-produced 'Get Away'. Mitch just happened to be in the studio with Denny, working on another session, when Fame asked him casually if he fancied coming to Brighton that night and sitting in as drummer. No explanation of what had happened to his regular guy Bill Eyden – just a casual come on down. That was in January. Nine months later Mitch was still in the group, picking up his weekly wage from their Soho office every Monday. Until one cold morning in October 1966, when he was casually informed that Georgie Fame no longer needed the Blues Flames, and that Mitch needn't come back the following week.

'My face sort of hit the floor, it was so unexpected,' he remembered later. 'I walked down Charing Cross Road past all the music stores, back to Denmark Street – and went to a coffee bar just to think things over.'

He was still sitting around at home, thinking it over, when the phone rang – it was Chas Chandler.

Jimmy had the notion of a nine-piece outfit, along the lines of the big soul revues he had appeared in. Before getting on the plane for New York, he spoke on the phone to his old army pal Billy Cox. But Billy was so poor he couldn't afford to even buy strings for his bass. Plus, he told this author, 'I knew the situation – that two black guys were not going to make it together. One black guy, maybe, but two . . . no chance.'

In London, Jimmy used Chas's phone to call his pal Terry Johnson, an adept organ player but one who was still in the service back home in the States. When Terry confounded him by telling him he had just re-enlisted in the air force for four more years, a nonplussed Jimmy told him, 'Just tell them you're queer.' Terry was like, 'Uh-uh, you trying to get my ass shot off? Or knifed in the shower?' Jimmy, so used to saying anything that might help him get out of a tight spot, truth be damned, put down the phone, angry and disappointed.

Chas thought anything but a power trio was madness. Big revue-style shows with horns and shit cost real money. They also took away from the spectacle of a crazy young black guitarist eating his guitar. Worried he was going to lose the boy's trust, Chas phoned Brian Auger, told him Jimi was the man to front Brian's band, an out-there rock-jazz-blues hybrid called Brian Auger and the Trinity. Again, Jimmy hit a wall. 'Are you taking the piss?' railed Auger. Then could Jimmy at least come down and jam at Brian's gig that night? Yeah, okay, whatever you say, Chas, but for fuck's sake he'd better be as good as you're saying . . .

That night, Trinity guitarist Vic Briggs kindly allowed Jimmy to set up using Vic's gear. Vic was plugged into one of the prototype Marshall amps – four six-inch speakers. Jimmy plugged in and turned the volume to the max – ten. Briggs nearly fell off the stage. 'I had never had the controls up past five.' Jimi counted the band in . . . two, three, four . . . and a wall of feedback and strafing distortion ravaged the room, turning every head towards the stage.

When he started playing the guitar with one hand, playing it with his teeth, soloing with it behind his back, grinning like it was a magic trick, Brian was awestruck. Brian was pure muso – unimpressed by pop-star gimmicks. It was the sheer musicality emanating from the kid that stayed with him the next morning. You could tell the influences in the playing of Clapton and Beck – principally that of the Three Kings, BB, Albert and Freddie – but this Jimmy Something cat, who knew where the hell he got his thing from. Mars?

Noel came back. Got another ten-bob note and came back again. Noel would do what Jimmy showed him to do, follow his lead, do what he was told. a previously unknown luxury for Jimmy, the till then gun for hire.

Chas started rolling in the drummers. Brian Auger's drummer, Micky Waller, was invited over to 'have a blow.' Micky was a very good drummer. But he was twenty-five – old in musician years – and would want a decent weekly 'screw' – at least twice the £20 a week on offer from Chas and Jimmy.

Next up was a twenty-year-old tearaway from Liverpool named Aynsley Dunbar. Aynsley was super-flash, had been a pro since he was seventeen. Had just come out of a stint with the Mojos, who'd had a hit with 'Everything's Alright' – which Aynsley didn't play on but would later bash the hell out of for David Bowie when he covered it on his *Pin Ups* album.

But that was the future, a concept that didn't exist in the pop world of 1966.

Aynsley was the guy Chas had been praying for. His drumming style was fast, heavy, flash, but at the same time fabulously agile. Aynsley had energy to burn, could meet Jimmy's guitar fire with flames of his own. Chas got it immediately, how that unlikely combo would redirect attention away from the bass player's beginner-by-numbers approach. How it would drive Jimmy to take his guitar out further than before, get him away from this old-fashioned revue cobblers and point his head in the right direction for the new, tight-ass rock market Chas saw the scene moving into. The Small Faces had just proved it by going to number 1 with 'All or Nothing'. Or 'Paint It Black', the most rocking Stones single since 'Satisfaction', riding the charts all the way to number 1 that summer, in Britain *and* America. Even the Beatles had taken the hint, going to number 1 that summer with 'Paperback Writer', their most rock-steady single since 'Help'.

Now just around the corner was Cream – Clapton's new band. The album wouldn't be out until Christmas, but everyone had already seen Cream destroy stages in London. They were now the ones to beat. Aynsley would help Jimmy do that.

Only Aynsley wasn't so easily persuaded. Like Micky Waller he would need paying. Thirty quid was his price. A week. Chas blanched. Mike Jeffery had made it clear he wasn't putting his hand in his pocket until this funny-looking coloured bloke Chas had lost his marbles over looked like a sure thing. Chas was down to selling basses to keep things together.

Chas offered Aynsley £20 a week. The tough Scouser just looked at him. 'Naw.'

Chas roped Mitch Mitchell into coming to the same basement strip club in Soho the next day. Jimmy, standing there waiting in his raincoat, a Fender Stratocaster turned upside down in his hands, got the surprise of his life when Mitch began blasting away, scattergun style, looking to Jimmy's guitar for its lead, then challenging it, furthering it, bringing real bubble to the stew while Noel stood there concentrating hard, trying to keep up.

Wow. This kid was as good as Aynsley. Maybe. Aynsley's playing had more fight. But Mitch had speed and lightness. Six of one, half a dozen of the other, Jimmy left it to Chas to figure out. He was the manager.

Chas invited Mitch back. The second time there was also a keyboard player in the room, an older white bloke, late twenties. It was Mike O'Neill, once of novelty act Nero and the Gladiators.

The third time Chas asked Mitch to come back the keyboard player was gone.

Afterwards, Chas took Mitch to one side. Gave him the spiel. Might only last two weeks, can't offer you nothing permanent, like, how does £20 a week – for two weeks – sound? See how it goes after that?

Mitch the not-so tough Londoner just looked at him. 'Alright.'

Later, Chas would spin a yarn about tossing a coin to choose between Aynsley and Mitch. You still hear that today whenever the Jimi Hendrix story is told.

It was also Chas who came up with the idea of Jimmy changing his name to 'Jimi' – much sexier. More now. It was Mike Jeffery who came up with the name the Jimi Hendrix Experience. Jimi and Noel and Mitch were still basking in that as Mike shoved their contracts under their noses and showed them where to put their marks.

Mike sitting in his sweet-as-fuck leather chair behind his cigar-shaped desk at the newly named Jeffery-Chandler offices – no cut yet for Chas, but it kept him happy – up some stairs in a small office in Gerrard Street – artist ghetto, porn hub, before the Chinese took it over and renamed it 爵祿街.

Mike keeping the books in Russian so those tax bastards couldn't read them – or any of his clients. Or Chas.

CHAPTER SEVEN

Al and Lucille

Al and Lucille. It was never gonna work out.

Lucille so sweet and pretty, always surrounded by friends. Al, gruff, muscular, short-tempered, ready to kill anybody who came near his gal. Both of them left feeling alienated and alone.

While Al had been in the army, Lucille had managed with the baby as best she could. Big sister Delores was there, and Lucille worked wherever she could – singing at the Bucket of Blood on Jackson Street. Working as a waitress at clubs like the Black and Tan, being felt up in the smoky dark for tips.

When the baby was born she was living at the apartment of her friend Dorothy Harding. Dorothy was seven years older, seven years stronger. Lucille called her 'aunty'. It was at Dorothy's that the baby was born. Lucille called him Johnny – Johnny Allen Hendrix. But Dorothy nicknamed him Buster – after the comic-strip character Buster Brown – and it stuck. Later Jimmy would claim he was called Buster after Larry 'Buster' Crabbe, the dude who played Flash Gordon in the movies he went to see as a kid. Jimmy loved Flash Gordon – and didn't want it known that he was named after a rich, sissy-looking white cartoon with blond hair.

Baby Hendrix, as he was also called early on, was three months old before his father saw a photograph of him, Lucille not being much of a letter writer.

Then her father, Preston, died and her mother, Clarice, had a breakdown. She had to be moved out of the house and looked after. While she was away the house burned down in a fire. Everything they had, even family photographs, was destroyed.

Lucille and Buster lived part-time with Dorothy, part-time with Delores. Buster would be left in their care at night while Lucille went back to work in bars and after-dark eateries. Clarice would also have the baby sometimes. Neighbours would sometimes help out when it became obvious Clarice was neglecting the child. Nappies frozen in winter with piss and shit, the baby screaming hungry. One of the ladies Lucille did cleaning for, Minnie Mae, appalled at the state of the baby, took him in for several weeks.

Lucille did the next best thing, took up with whatever man would tolerate a pretty black girl with a baby and no money to feed him, even for just a little while, holed up in some rat-infested shithole rooming house.

The worst was John Page, a dark-town chancer from Kansas who was 'a slime', according to Dorothy. John Page was different, Lucille told them. Sure, honey. John dragged Lucille and her child all over the place, a slum housing project in Vancouver; other short-stop dumps they would leave behind as soon as the rent was due. When she left with him for Portland, Delores and friends flipped out and set off by train to find them. They tracked her down to a hospital at the edge of town, where she'd been taken after being found beaten and bloody, still holding tight to her crying baby.

Page was arrested under provision of the Mann Act – which made it a felony to 'engage in interstate transport of any woman or girl for the purpose of prostitution or debauchery, or for any other immoral purpose'. As Lucille was still just seventeen they threw the book at Page, eventually sending him to jail for five years.

Back home in Seattle, things didn't improve. Lucille going off doing her thing, leaving the baby to Dolores, Dorothy, Clarice and another sister, Nora. Little Johnny got pneumonia, and, later, one of his earliest memories was being in hospital screaming and howling as he was injected with penicillin: 'I can remember when the nurse put on the diaper . . . She took me out of this crib . . . and then she held me up to the window.' The kindly nurse wanted the baby to see the Fourth of July fireworks. 'I remember I didn't feel so good . . . then she held me up to the window and the sky was all just woo-woo-woo.'

When mother and grandmother took the baby to a Pentecostal church convention in California, they left him there under the care of one of Clarice's church friends, Mrs Champ. It was meant to be temporary, but they never went back for him.

That's the way things were when Al finally got home from the army in 1945. Mrs Champ had decided to adopt the boy. She loved little Johnny as she would one of her own, and her daughter Celestine treated him like a proper little brother. Al could see it as he sat there drinking coffee. But he was the boy's father and he wasn't leaving without him, and that was final.

The three-year-old burst into tears, crying out for Celestine, as his father put him on the train for the journey back up the coast. Al was forced to discipline the boy, administering a good spanking. It would not be the last time.

With Lucille running around again with John Page while he awaited trial, Al and his son lodged at Dolores's apartment for several months. Hearing all about Page, Al put two and two together and changed his son's name from 'Johnny Allen' to James Marshall – Marshall after his dead brother, Leon Marshall. Though she would always spit and scratch at any suggestion Al made that the boy had actually been named after John Page, Lucille would later tell the boy that Al was not his real father.

Fact is, Jimmy, Johnny, Buster, Baby Hendrix grew up not knowing much at all of his true beginnings. Meanwhile, with

John Page on his way to the can, Lucille came back to Al like, I love you – you love me – oh, how happy we will be!

Al seeing it and putting up with it anyway, there was the boy to bring up. With his army pension, what he called his 'rocking-chair money', Al and Lucille lived it up at last, going out dancing again while Delores or Nora played babysitter. When Lucille became pregnant again it seemed like this time they'd do things right. Al pushing broom at a pool hall while he took advantage of the GI Bill, going to night-school training to be an electrician.

Everything was swell until their second boy, Leon, was born, then Lucille couldn't stand it no more and began moonlighting on Al again. Al coming home beat after work to be told Lucille was out hitting the bars, coming home juiced and loaded. Other nights, not coming home at all. Al rearing up, threatening to bust her chops; Lucille screaming at him do it, do it, do it.

Lucille got pregnant again but this time neither she nor Al could be sure who the daddy was, though Al allowed her to claim the boy as their own. But when Joe was born with a cleft palate, club foot and one leg longer than the other, ma and pa would fight over which of them was to blame. She said he pushed her over when she was heavily pregnant. He said she should have stopped drinking and smoking.

Summer of '49, she left. He threw her out. Depending on which of them you listened to. Jimmy, Leon and Joe were sent to stay with Al's mother, Nora, in Vancouver, Jimmy going to the same school his daddy once went to. The kids taunting him for the 'little Mexican jacket with tassels' that Nora made for him to wear. Grandma could be fierce too. When baby Joe wet the bed she beat hell out of him. Jimmy loved to sit and hear her tell mothball tales of Cherokee ancestors and adventures.

When Al's sister Pat's husband died that winter, Nora was needed there, and Jimmy and his brothers had to return home to Al in Seattle. But he had a surprise for them. Their mama was home. Christmas '49 the Hendrix family spent together. By New Year Lucille was out on the razz again, though. Al took the boys in the car with him, driving around looking for her in every dive bar in town. They found her drunk, holding on tight to another guy. Bad scene. Big fight. Lucille dragged to the car, the boys watching crying, broken up.

The car nearly crashed on the way home, the fight carrying on all night and into the next days and nights. When, not long after, Lucille found out she was pregnant again, that was the finish for Al – again. A little girl, Kathy Ira, was born late 1950, sixteen weeks premature, weighing one pound, ten ounces – and blind. Al swore the child was nothing to do with him, and a year after she was put into foster care.

Al would still see Lucille those days she would come crawling home, mournful and looking for a place to crash. Then goddamn if she didn't get pregnant a-fucking-gain!

Another girl, Pamela, another child soon put into foster care.

Somehow nine-year-old Jimmy endured all this the way kids do, closing down their emotions to avoid pain, filling their minds with other things to do and think about. In Jimmy's case, comic books, movies, TV, drawing, which he was good at. Though he felt it when he played cowboys and Indians with the other kids in the street, how he would always be one of the Indians, getting shot and falling off his horse, dancing round the totem pole, whooping. Being taunted as a 'dirty redskin'. Pretending to scalp them.

Finally, Lucille left for good. The couple officially divorced a week before Christmas 1951, with Al getting custody of the three boys. He soon had Joe fostered, though, unwilling to pay the hospital fees needed to deal with the boy's chronic birth defects. As time went by, Joe would see Jimmy and Leon in the street, sometimes even see his father. But he never saw his mother again. Lucille was gone, baby – had been a long time.

The next couple of years tumbled by, things getting worse, never better. Al was drinking all the time now too. Lucille had to go, she'd been making a fucking fool of him long enough, but God O'mighty, he missed her. Although they were now divorced they still got back together. Lucille coming and going, sometimes only staying for a day or two, sometimes dragging it out a little longer. When she told Al she was pregnant again, he threatened to kill her. You're too late, she sneered. She'd already done killed herself.

Their fourth boy, whom they named Alfred Hendrix, was born on Valentine's Day, 1953. When it became immediately clear that it was yet another baby with serious developmental problems, Lucille didn't fight it this time and the baby was put up for immediate adoption.

Lucille wasn't living with Al at the time so what the hell, right?

Al struggled bad to manage alone with the boys. Delores and Dorothy still came around, but only when Al was out on another three-day drunk. The two-bed pad was filthy, crumbling. Jimmy and Leon left to run wild. Jimmy was twelve, frying eggs for his little brother and him to eat dinner. Bills left unpaid, sink piled high with dead dishes and spiders' legs, carpet sticking and rotten, curtains filthy and torn, furniture broken and burn-holed. Living off welfare cheques that kept Al in booze and cigarettes and left the kids hungry and hopeless, the school's saddest freaks.

God forbid they should backchat him. Al would take them inside and give them a beating like they would never forget. Bring hell to one, make the other watch and wait for his. Send them scattering. Al pulling on his thin dime-store jacket, slamming the door closed behind him.

Government welfare workers finally came after being tipped off by troubled neighbours. Appalled by the levels of deprivation, they came down hard: Al could either have the boys adopted or put them up for foster care like all his other kids.

All Jimmy and Leon cared about was sticking together, who-ever their parents were, begging Al not to let them be split up. Al not listening, trying to save face by telling the welfare that Jimmy was nearly old enough to look after himself, that if they took anyone it should be just Leon.

Al drove Leon away the very next morning – both boys howling for him not to – the boy eventually fostered by a family just a few blocks away. This now a special kind of hell Jimmy and his family were living in. Jimmy becoming more and more withdrawn, be-ginnings of a bad stutter, unable to look anyone in the eye. The discovery that Jimmy had bad eyesight and needed glasses, Al's indifference and Jimmy's refusal even to try a pair on. Jimmy didn't need one more reason to be picked on at school.

Little Leon seeing Jimmy as his real dad, his only protector: 'We couldn't play with the black kids, we couldn't play with the white kids, we were kind of in the middle . . . look at me and Jimi, we look different.'

Jimmy with a crew cut, thin but getting taller. Freakishly big hands, bony face, huge eyes, like his mama. His mama so pretty, Jimmy missing her so much. Dreaming of her sweet face, her soft hands, the smell of her perfume.

More years. More tears, more of everything less even than before. Jimmy, alone, making what friends he can wherever he can. Turning up at friends' places, hanging around until after dark, hoping for a couch or floor to sleep on. Turning up at friends' places at breakfast time, smiling hopefully.

Anything to avoid Al, to avoid all that . . .

Lifetimes later, Jimmy would make a dream of his dysfunc-tional childhood. 'Before I can remember anything, I can remem-ber music, stars and planets,' he once said. 'I could go to sleep and write fifteen symphonies. I had very strange feelings that I was here for something and I was going to get a chance to be heard.'

But that was Jimmy, his whole life trippy fantasy replacing horror-show reality.

Other times, hanging round the market, stealing cheese and eggs. Getting caught, cops called, dragged home by Al, given another whipping.

Alarm tripped again. Al received another visit from the welfare, threatening to take Jimmy away. Al, desperate, but constantly on the juice and incapable of doing anything about it himself, arranged for Jimmy to go and stay with Al's brother Frank.

Suddenly luck took a hand in things. Al had brought in lodgers to help with the rent: Cornell and Ernestine Benson. They had Jimmy's old room. Ernestine had a big-ass collection of 78 rpm blues records: Bessie Smith, Howlin' Wolf, B.B. King, Muddy Waters, Lightnin' Hopkins, Big Bill Broonzy, Robert Johnson ... elemental blues. Devil magic. Crossroads soul-stealers. They would play them all whenever Jimmy came to visit. He instantly became hypnotised. Enchanted. Bewitched.

He would take the broom from the kitchen and hold it aloft like a wand, left-handed, playing along like a spirit haunting a castle. When Frank broke up with his wife in 1956, Al had the Bensons move on and brought Jimmy home again. But the bank repossessed the house after Al defaulted on payments one too many times, and Jimmy and Al were temporarily moved into a cheap rooming house.

Where Jimmy found an old acoustic guitar with one string.

Where fourteen-year-old Jimmy found something he could use, that would be good to him, that spoke of possible futures previously out of sight.

Where Jimmy, the boy who'd grown up at the bottom of the well the devil had thrown him down, finally found God.

CHAPTER EIGHT

Jimmy Hendricks

They put the boys to work. Shows, TV, radio, studio dates, photo sessions, interviews, glad-handing.

January: twenty-five gigs, four recording dates. Two days off. February: twenty-two gigs, five recording dates. One day off. March: eighteen gigs, twelve recording dates. One day off. April: fifty gigs (two sets a night), six recording dates. No day off. May: more of the same.

Spotlight: Thursday, 12 January, the 1967 International Racing Car Show. The Jimi Hendrix Experience make a special live appearance at the National Hall, Olympia. Miming to their smash hit 'Hey Joe' from the balcony, where Radio London have set up their display. The performance is not transmitted. Bummer.

Spotlight: Saturday, 14 January, Beachcomber Club, Nottingham. You bought your Scotch and Coke, lit your cigarette and went through the archway to the room with the tiny stage. Support that night came from Jimmy Cliff. Jimmy was a 'blue beat' artist, whatever that meant. Had a couple of catchy tunes and a dreamy one you could slow dance to.

Then, about half-eight, the headliner: Jimmy Hendricks. 'Jimmy' in a Charge of the Light Brigade jacket, making waves of sound in three dimensions.

Cream had played one of their first shows at the same venue six months before, but that had just sounded like the same old blues with a dash of rock thrown in. Truly nothing like the 'sweet and sour rock 'n' roll' Eric Clapton had promised readers of the *Melody Maker* when the new group had been announced.

This young coloured American bloke, though – boy oh boy – he was another thing entirely. There were similar clubs dotted all over the UK, with crowds used to visiting black American singers and guitarists. Martha and the Vandellas, Edwin Starr, Ike and Tina Turner, even Little Stevie Wonder, all dressed in their narrow-lapelled mohair suits or pastel satin shirts, hair processed into high pompadours. But there was nothing – *nothing* – like this Jimmy Hendricks fella.

He had a big city bluesman's voice, but his guitar came from . . . the sky. And the way he moved . . . Good God! The older order of American blues players who routinely visited Britain stood like brooding statues or sat down, tapping their feet. The wilder young soul singers did pretty little dance steps, acting out the sweet emotions of the songs with their hands clutching their hearts or fanned out in surprise across their faces, their eyes melodramatically sad one minute, overjoyed with happiness the next. Pure vanilla, old-school vaudeville.

This Jimmy Hendricks character, he was different alright, quite ghastly in some ways, intimidating, but strangely compelling. He thrust his groin out, feigned cunnilingus, played the guitar behind his back, all the while summoning blood thunder from the gods. Sexual intercourse in Britain might have begun in 1963, as Philip Larkin suggested, but this kind of leeringly explicit sexual invocation – and coming from a blackie – had simply never been seen before. It was as if both he and his big-prick guitar were having multiple orgasms, right there in front of everybody. Disgusting. Not that anyone looked away. They couldn't. They were too shocked. Too nervously turned on.

That there were two white blokes up there with the coloured bloke only made things . . . odder, harder to take in. Apart from his hair, which was a bit like the coloured bloke's, the beanpole on the bass wasn't really anything to write home about. Bass players never were though, were they? Look at the bloke in the Rolling Stones, or the one in the Who. Paul McCartney played bass, but he was the only one anyone cared about. And that was because he was a singer too. This bloke had nothing apart from the look.

The drummer was different. He was more like the guitar player, a really loud, big sound. Complicated but done in a way that you really felt it. Not like Ginger Baker in Cream, who just played really fast and loud, hit you over the head with it; this bloke was much more full of tricks. Drum rolls and . . . *fills* and . . . stuff like that. Drumming that really announced it.

You couldn't keep your eyes off the Jimmy bloke, though. Nobody could, even the ones jeering. He started with 'Wild Thing', the Troggs song, which was really strange. It was so ugly the way he did it, so twisted and upside down. Slower. Bigger. The girls in their poor-boy sweaters and plimsolls really liked it, though, when he went wild. Like Tom Jones when he started going crazy dancing; you expected them to start throwing their knickers onstage. The longer it went on the more the rest of the crowd got going too.

It was the same the next night at The Kirk – the Kirk Levington Country Club in Yarm, North Yorkshire – old screwy England. Billed as 'The Weird New Trio Jimmy Hendrick's Experience' – 'Wild Thing', people putting fingers in their ears, not having it at all. Like he didn't really know how it went. Then hotting up as the mental American boy kept going, the girls dancing, the boys trying to keep up, those not sneering at the darkie: who did he bloody well think he was?

There was nearly a riot afterwards when one of the sausage-faced bouncers in a Burton World Cup winners' suit called this Jimmy a nigger. His manager, big fella, hit the bouncer in the face so hard he knocked him clean over the bannister onto the floor below. Thought the fucking bouncer was dead.

The Kirk had seen them all – Cream, the Spencer Davis Group, John Mayall's Bluesbreakers, Brian Auger and the Trinity, the Animals, Graham Bond Organisation, Alexis Korner, P.P. Arnold, Geno Washington and the Ram Jam Band, the Moody Blues, Zoot Money and his Big Roll Band . . .

Now they had seen Jimi Hendrick's, they had bloody seen it all.

Spotlight: 18 January, second-ever appearance on *Top of the Pops* doing 'Hey Joe', now on its way to number 6. A groovy all-live performance, yeah, baby, but not so spirited as his first appearance on the show three weeks earlier. This one slower, snakier, more road worn: Mitch killing it anyway, Jimi still cruising at high altitude. Broadcast on BBC1 the following evening, Jimi watching back at the pad in Montagu Square with Kathy and Chas and Lotte, shrugging it off, rolling another joint then later going off to the Speakeasy to bask in a little backslapping Jimi love.

Spotlight: 28 January, the Upper Cut, London E7. Billed as 'The American Top Soul Singer and Guitarist Extraordinary'.

Spotlight: 29 January, support act for the Who at the Saville Theatre. A prestige spot. Jimi oblivious, though. All the licks and tricks that barely got him noticed in New York going down so easy and nice in old London.

In the audience, Jeff Beck, newly sprung from the Yardbirds, where he was England's moodiest guitarist, about to have his first solo number 1 with 'Hi Ho Silver Lining', a song he hates so much he will never play it live. Not after seeing Jimi do his thing, destroying Townshend on Pete's own turf.

Later, Jeff, shaking his head, blown the fuck away: 'I'd put a lot of work into playing guitar and was thinking I was pretty damn good. But Hendrix came along and destroyed everyone. I was deeply jealous, that was the first emotion I felt. A friend played the B-side of "Hey Joe", "Stone Free", and Hendrix was playing scat and singing along with it, and I thought it had to be a trick that he'd cooked up in the studio. When I saw him at the Saville Theatre, supporting the Who, I couldn't believe it. I felt excited, overwhelmed and also completely deflated. He changed all of our lives in an instant.'

Spotlight: 2 February, Imperial Hotel, Darlington, County Durham. Local advert: 'Don't miss this man who is Dylan, Clapton and James Brown all in one'. 'Wild Thing' now ending the show. Figuring that worked better. 'Killing Floor' the new opener, figuring if it blew Eric away it would everybody. Couple of originals: the hundred-mile-an-hour 'Can You See Me', and 'Stone Free', the B-side of 'Hey Joe' and the first song Jimi had written with his new white band in mind. Both songs spelt out the same story, the same story Jimi would repeat throughout his life onstage and off. Freedom. Don't slow me down. Angels and Devils. Jimi almost mumbling the words: *'They talk about me like a dog, talkin' about the clothes I wear / They don't realise they're the ones who's square . . .'* Jimi burning through the belt-whipping guitar solo like some kind of dust devil.

Spotlight: 30 March. Back on *Top of the Pops* for second single 'Purple Haze', released on Paddy's Day, now on its way to number 3 in the charts. Pre-recorded backing track this time, heavy duty, and faithful live vocals, two hot takes, Jimi hamming up the mimed guitar solo. Mitch still in overgrown mod haircut, Noel in stripy three-quarter length Captain Trip coat, Jimi swapping the ancient army jacket for black waistcoat, white high-collared calypso shirt with ruffs and frock-coat sleeves, and a white silk scarf tied into a tight knot round his throat.

Spotlight: 31 March, the Astoria Theatre, London. Opening night of Jimi's first British tour: a package job, opening for the Walker Brothers on their farewell tour. Two shows a night for thirty-one days straight, zero time off. Sharing the bill with Engelbert Humperdinck and Cat Stevens. Jimi putting together a special new set with *five* originals: 'Hey Joe' and 'Purple Haze', plus 'Can You See Me' and a couple of new ones never played before – the funky, far out 'Foxey Lady' and, to close the show, the baby-drives-me-crazy 'Fire'. All from the as yet unreleased album, performed in front of an audience lulled into peaceful submissiveness by Engelbert's fully ripened cheese and now waiting expectantly for the breathy, unruffled cool of the tenderly troubled, deeply voiced Walker Brothers.

Are you fucking kidding me, man?

But wait. Jimi's got more. Before the show, still plotting, Chas and Jimi joke with Keith Altham, nice-guy journo from the *New Musical Express*, about setting fire to Jimi's guitar – while he's playing 'Fire', geddit? Sniggering about what a showstopper it would be. You couldn't do it anyway, Chas points out. The solid-bodied guitar would never catch light so easily.

'What about if you squirted it with lighter fuel first?' jokes Keith.

Chas's eyes light up. Turns to Jimi. 'If we use lighter fuel it will just burn the lighter fuel and won't burn the actual guitar.'

Jimi laughs, says he'll do it. Ha-ha-ha! Jimi's joking. He must be. Everyone is still laughing as Jimi and the band hit the stage – pow!

The set goes by in a flash. About half the audience get into it. The other half don't know where to look or how to sit or what's supposed to happen. Then Jimi sidles to the side of the stage before the last number of the night, 'Fire', and puts on a fuel-soaked Strat, touches it with his lighter and – nothing. He tries again – nothing. Tries again – nothing.

Forget it, Jimi.

Quickly tries one last time – and big green flames shoot up in the air.

Jimi swings it out at the lip of the stage, starts yelling.

'Alright!'

People are horrified!

'*Now dig this, baby!*'

People are afraid!

Jimi laughing as he nonchalantly leans into the howling solo, teasing: '*Oh! Move over, Rover, and let Jimi take over . . .*'

The crowd, finally seeing it for what it is, enthralled – at a distance. Like playing it with his teeth. Like playing it behind his back. Like something only *he* would do, the coloured boy with the circus clothes and bad-wolf smile.

Jimi teasing, crooning: '*Do you like it like that, baby?*'

Yes, we see. (Sipping sweet milky tea, little finger crooked.)

Afterwards, pandemonium in the dressing room as fat, red-faced security men go searching for the charred guitar to show the police. Shouldn't be allowed! Ought to be locked up! Could have burned the whole bloody place down! Killed everybody!

Walker Brothers main man Scott Walker seething in his dressing room at this crude attempt to upstage him. *He fucking set fire to WHAT?*

Things settle, though, once the tour hits Ipswich, Worcester, Leeds, Glasgow, Carlisle, on and on, a new town each night . . . Jimi digging being the scene-stealer, digging the ride, Kathy playing it *coool*, letting Jimi do his thing, turning the other cheek. Waiting for him to come back down, finish fucking with the quickies, the no names, the ones waiting in the toilets then thank you, baby, bye-bye.

Scott and Engelbert also looking the other way, knowing Jimi is the one selling the tickets. Jimi now calling the tune: '*Purple haze, all in my brain / Lately things, they don't seem the same . . .*'

CHAPTER NINE

Kathy and Jimi

Kathleen Mary Etchingham lives in Australia these days. Has done for years. Because of the time difference between Oz and the UK, I am phoning her at what is almost midnight for me but nearly 9 a.m. for her. I am concerned I might have woken her, but the brightness in her voice, the energy and warmth, is reassuring.

'Hello, Mick!' she almost shouts, full of morning good cheer. 'No, you didn't wake me. I woke up at six o'clock this morning. It's so bloody hot!' She laughs in that wonderfully welcoming and friendly voice that speaks of her no-nonsense, come-on-in Derbyshire background. Earthy. Girlish. Unstoppable. Kathy will be seventy-three by the time this book comes out, but you would never know it from speaking to her on the phone. She sounds *young* and *fun*. But absolutely not someone you would even think about trying to mess with.

She has lived in Melbourne – 'by the Bay!' – since the mid-00s. 'It's all trails and bike tracks. It's very laid-back here.'

I remark on how much I enjoyed reading Kathy's book, *Through Gypsy Eyes*, first published in 1998. The story of her early years is particularly moving. The daughter of Charles Etchingham, a good-natured, zero-ambition Irishman from Dublin over-fond of a drink, and English-born mother Lil, who fled the family home – a small terraced house in the centre of Derby, with an outside toilet and a tin bath – when Kathy was just ten years old. She returned three weeks later – then abruptly left again, this time for good, taking the lodger, Tom, with her. Tom was twenty. Lil was fifty.

Consequently, Kathy and her younger brother John were sent to live with their father's sister Valerie in Dublin. Auntie Val had no kids of her own, fed Kathy and John a diet of porridge and boiled potatoes, and took them to church twice a day.

They escaped by hanging around the ferry port at Dún Laoghaire, where they pretended to be part of another large family's children and they somehow got onboard a ferry ticketless and made their back across to mainland England. Amazing scenes for 1957, but only the start of the adventures that later made hanging out with temperamental pop stars in London seem a piece of cake.

Her brother stayed with her alcoholic dad while Kathy got taken to live with a previously unknown half-sister, Jean, who despised her for her looks. 'Jean was plain-looking,' she writes in her book. And always referred to Kathy poisonously as 'the pretty one', turning Kathy's photo to the wall.

Kathy ran away again and ended up next with Aunt Lil, whose 'great passion was gambling and playing cards'. But her true love was reserved for two budgies. When one attacked Kathy she grabbed it and squeezed it to death. She was moved on to live with Aunt Kathleen, back in Dublin. Kathleen and her kindly husband Dermot meant well. It was Aunt Kathleen who then arranged for young Kathy to be sent to the Holy Faith convent boarding school in Skerries, a coastal town in Fingal – where the nuns did what they were famous for the world over and made her life a misery.

Kathy's story took another strange turn when her mother suddenly reappeared – snatching her daughter from the convent and spiriting her back to live with her (and Tom) in England.

It was now, in her teens, that Kathy decided, 'I did not need other people around me. They only let me down. I liked being part of a crowd, but I didn't want to have to rely on anyone else for anything in life. I intended to look after myself in every way, just as soon as I was able to.'

She took off on her own for London in 1964 – and never looked back. Lil would later visit her in London at the flat she shared with Jimi. She says that her mother and Jimi – 'two gypsies' – got along famously.

There is Romany blood on her mother's side, though Kathy was more likely to ridicule the whole cross-my-palm-with-silver stereotype than make any claims for how it might have affected her own sizzling personality. It was clear, though, that she was always going to be a match for any man who fell under her spell.

She's entirely correct, of course, when she points out that if you want the real detail of her life, with and without Jimi Hendrix, it is already written down in *Through Gypsy Eyes*. It is still good to talk to her, though. We laughingly discuss how writing one's life story often prompts deep-lying memories to suddenly spring forth, stuff you had forgotten you'd forgotten. Kathy mentions that she was staggered by how many people – old friends she hadn't heard from for years, others, not so close, who suddenly found a reason to make contact – were moved to get in touch after reading the original book.

Her main focus these days, when it comes to talking about her time with Hendrix, is to debunk the very many versions of a story she feels has been debased by people who have no clue as to what the real story is, but who have jumped on the bandwagon over the years with their books, films and theories, and now their blogs and social-media rants. Torn between not wishing to engage with the mixture of crazies, malcontents, dream-weavers, groupies (male and female), myth-makers and simple lie-tellers – so as to starve them of air – and a missionary zeal about trying to untangle the seemingly infinite layers of bullshit that now surround the story of Hendrix, Kathy strays off topic, gets confused at times, becomes obsessed, angry, then laughs, but her words are always real, always coming from the same good place. 'He was my friend,' she says. 'You look out for your friends.'

Your memory of first meeting Jimi – that still seems fresh in your mind, even after all this time?

Yes! Yes, I remember it absolutely. I mean, we were very young, so we weren't so worldly. But some parts of my personality are still the same now as they were then.

It was said that you were the only one who stood up to Jimi after he became famous.

That's right. I was always like that and I'm still like that. [Giggles.]

Was that one of the things Jimi found attractive about you, or did he find it very challenging, do you think?

Oh, no. I don't think he found it challenging at all. I think he quite liked it. I didn't boss him around, if that's what you mean. I didn't tell him what to do or anything. But at the same time I was pretty determined about what I wanted to do. In other words, I wasn't the little girl in tow, you know? And I didn't want to go to all of the gigs. So I'd rather go out with my friends. Because I was still very young, you see, and so girlfriends are very important and spending time with them was very important.

You could have just got swallowed up and left behind so easily.

I know. Could have ended up like a lot of rock chicks. Drug addicts and alcoholics or what have you. I didn't. I was too sensible. I have a letter from Angie Burdon. She got into drugs, but in the early seventies, not in the sixties. And she went to live with her family in Perth. And she wrote me a letter. This must have been in the eighties, the early eighties. When she'd been arrested for possession. And she said, 'Kathy, you were always more sensible than the rest of us.'

**Maybe because you were already a survivor of your own diffi-
cult upbringing?**

Yeah. And I wasn't prepared to get into all that drug nonsense.

You didn't want to end up in a worse place than you started.

No. I didn't. And I wasn't going to. There was never any
chance of me ever doing that. That's why the reason behind Jimi
and me splitting up was not because of his womanising or anything, because I didn't know the extent of it at that time. It's only
afterwards that you find these things out. I knew he was probably
up to no good. But they *all* were. Even Mitch and Noel, who was
married.

**You talk in your book about the turning point for you being
the trip to New York in '68, when you were both staying in the
Garden Suite at the Pierre Hotel – and Jimi being surrounded
by, in your words, 'whores . . . pimps . . . and drug dealers'. Chief
among them one shady-looking guy carrying a suitcase full of
cocaine and a gun . . .**

That was the absolute deciding factor. I looked at that and
thought, What kind of people are these? These people are dan-
gerous. Because, you know, as English people we're not used to
guns. And don't forget that New York at that time was very violent. It's been cleaned up a lot since then. It was like the murder
capital of the world.

New York – where everything is *all* night *every* night.

That's right. And everybody's armed. Well, not everybody, but
this guy was. I can remember that gun. I don't know what kind
of gun it was because I've never seen one since. But it was one
of those square-shaped ones. It didn't have a round barrel. It had
a sort of square. First thing I thought, within a nanosecond, I
looked at it and thought it was a toy. But within that nanosecond
I also thought, *It's real*. And I knew where I was. And I think that
was it.

This guy, whom you identify as Howard Krantz, you describe him in your book as putting you in mind of Columbo. A scruffy, middle-aged guy in a raincoat would have looked pretty odd in that company, though, wouldn't he?

He was!

He's dead now. But he was an attorney with Mob connections back then. Who did you think he was at the time?

I don't know because I never saw him again and I didn't know anything about him. All I knew was that he was very loud and he had a very strong New York accent. And he wasn't very tall. He was quite short. And it was all very furtive and there were all these people turning up at the door that I didn't know, that I hadn't met before. And they were all just sitting around, you know, enjoying themselves. What the hell's going on here?

I went into the bathroom. It was a suite. It had a bedroom, bathroom, then a separate living room with a little kitchenette affair, just to the left of the bathroom door. I went to the bathroom, and when I came out the bloody sitting room was full of people. There'd been nobody there when I went in.

We never had any hangers-on like that in England. Chas wouldn't allow it anyway. Until they fell out and we moved out to Brook Street, Chas was always there. And Chas was, you know, quite a tough bloke. He was an ex-Tyneside docker. He didn't allow any of that sort of stuff to go on. It just simply didn't happen. It was all in New York. It was *all* to do with, you know, New York. And all these hangers-on were trying to wheedle their way in with Jimi – because by then he was rich, you know – by supplying him with things.

That's the usual route they take. Because they're not musicians themselves, it's usually either sex or drugs.

Yes, exactly.

You talk about seeing hundreds of little bags of white powder in the case . . .

Well, I don't think there were hundreds and they weren't little bags. They were big bags! I think what was going on was that the big bags were then being separated into smaller ones – by order. Major dealer, yeah. That's why he had a gun on the top. It was like one of those holdall-type bags. And it just had great big packets – oh, I suppose, six inches by four inches. So there was a lot of money in there. Yeah.

By 1969 the acid and grass were being replaced with coke and heroin. Was that what you saw taking over with Jimi and his circle too?

Well, I think it was cocaine. But I don't . . . I don't think it was heroin. I think it was cocaine. And yes, I think that was the start of it. But it didn't really get to England until about 1972 or '73. So it was a typical American thing. There probably was cocaine around in England, it's just that I never encountered it. I never came across it, either heroin or cocaine. The first time I remember heroin being around was when Angie started taking it.

There's a scene in your book where you describe going over to the Londonderry Hotel, in Park Lane, to rescue Angie and another one of your friends. And you find Jimi in bed and he is shaky, feverish and grey. You suggest in the book that it may have been some kind of withdrawal he was going through. Do you think he was on heroin by then?

It's hard to know because there was nothing I could see, except for a bottle of Jack Daniel's, which had been mainly drunk. There were a couple of inches left in the bottom of it. And he had taken these tablets called Contac 400, which you take when you've got a cold [to 'relieve symptoms of body ache, chills and fever']. They've been banned now. It could have been the Contac tablets because the side effects were similar to withdrawal. So I don't really know [about heroin]. I mean, I didn't see anything like that. There was nothing there apart from the Jack Daniel's, no powder or anything like that.

I said to him, 'What's the matter?' He said, 'Ah, I've got this terrible cold. I've taken some Contacs.' I said, 'Well, it's very hot in here.' He had the heater on and the sun was shining through the curtains. I mean, the room wasn't cold and it wasn't a cold day. So I turned the heater down but he was cold. He could have had a fever, you see, that's the thing. It could have been that he had flu. So I think it's a step too far to suggest it had anything to do with drugs. Because don't forget, when they did the autopsy on him they found no trace of anything like that.

Where was he at by the end, when you saw him? Chas had gone. Mike Jeffery was all about the money. You're not with him anymore. He doesn't have any kind of steadying influence.

He was unhappy, yeah. Frustrated and he couldn't find his way out of it. He didn't have anybody close to him that could be relied on, that were looking out for him. He was surrounded by people that basically wanted a piece of him, you know? Not there to look after him but to . . . I don't know what it is. Be close to him so part of his fame and stardom would shine on them. None of them were there to look after his . . . issues. All combined with his childhood and everything . . .

Do you think he was lonely by the end?

Yes. Yes. He didn't have any real friends. None of these people could be called a *real* friend.

It seemed he had very few real friends in his life. How he'd moved around like you did as a child, going from place to place. Joining the army to get away from his father. Leading a pretty hard-knock life, playing in different bands, scrabbling around New York. You genuinely cared for him and he clearly responded to that?

Yes, absolutely. He had a home life. And it was fun! We had a comfortable place to live – *very* comfortable. Bit dated now if you saw the place, but it seemed to be a lot at the time. Food was cooked. Breakfasts were made. Cups of tea were made. We played games: Risk. We listened to music. Strategy was discussed, you know, with Chas and Jimi and how they were gonna move forward. And I was there watching the rush to put a band together. Working out whether it was going to be a five-piece band or whether it was going to be bigger or whatever.

On both the auditions they did with Mitch and Noel, and with Aynsley Dunbar, there was a pianist, because Chas was thinking a bigger band. I think it was only later that Chas realised he didn't need all of these people. All he needed was a steady bass line, a good drummer and Jimi. That Jimi would carry whatever. And so that's how it all came about. That's when they decided you only need three.

That was the first time in his life when there was a proper support system for him in place?

Yeah. There was. That's right. A home where he was comfortable and safe, he had everything he needed. I mean, to begin with we only had a stereogram, you know, in a sort of wooden case. [Laughs.] Once we'd moved to Upper Berkeley Street he put together a system, with a Leak amplifier, an awesome deck and two loud speakers. And they were *big* for those days. He had a 30-watt output on each one. We used to blow them regularly, because they had, like, paper cones inside. If you turned them up too loudly they used to blow the cones. I remember going down to Bromley in a taxi, with these speakers on the floor of a black taxi, *begging* them to do it straight away. They were like, 'Oh no, you'll have to come back next week.' The thought of having no music for a week in those days, now that was withdrawal! [Laughs.] I had to plead with them! It was expensive to get a taxi all the way down there and back. But it was essential. They got used to me in the end. I made about four trips down there. They were like, 'Oh, here she comes again . . .' Me with the speakers in the back of the taxi. 'Can you mend them?' And they would mend them while I waited. I think Jimi only went down there once. Mainly I was packed off to do that when he was rehearsing or doing other things. So it was quite an ordinary lifestyle in those first couple of years.

Do you think you were able to keep him grounded during those first couple of years?

Yes. That's right.

But you got very impatient once he started taking a lot of acid.

Yes. First of all, I didn't know that he was taking it. He was taking acid, but this is not in 1966. It was towards the end of '67. And I didn't know he was taking it. In fact, I'm not even sure that he was. But other people say that he was. Eric Burdon, for instance, says that he was. And I know that I drank Eric's drink down at the Speakeasy [which was spiked with acid]. And I had no idea because I couldn't taste it. It was just a Scotch and Coke. Mine was finished and instead of waiting – they were up onstage – I thought, I'll drink his then order some more. The next thing – I think it took about fifteen minutes to kick in – I didn't know what was the matter with me. Things were moving and I felt really ill. I remember going outside, past the entrance, sitting on the steps that lead to the club and saying to Angie, who'd come after me, 'I don't feel very well. I don't know what's the matter.'

Nobody suspected it was LSD until Eric owned up. So I went to St George's Hospital in Tooting, told them what had just happened. They basically said, 'Well, you've just got to bide your time. It will wear off.' [Laughs.] But in the meantime I had to stay there until it wore off. It took a few hours. I'll tell you, it was the most awful thing. I don't really remember much about it because I was so terrified. It actually frightened me. I was completely unaware of why things were moving and I felt so weird. I started getting panic attacks because I didn't know what it was.

I think I got blamed, for drinking Eric's drink. Jimi was wondering where I was, because Angela was with me, so nobody knew. There was a sort of all-out alert – where's Kathy gone? I finally made a phone call to the flat. It was about five in the morning. They were back by then, and I just said, 'I drank Eric's drink.' Jimi said, 'You shouldn't drink his drink! You never know what's in it!' I sheepishly went home about six or seven o'clock in the morning. That was a horrible, horrible night. Nobody ever offered it to me again. [Laughs.] And I never took anybody's drink ever again!

Can you tell me about that very poignant moment just before Jimi died, when you bumped into him at the Cumberland Hotel in London? Jimi saying, 'You should come over.' And you saying, 'Yes, I will,' knowing that you won't. We've all been there. Being polite even though we know that ship has sailed. Then you get a phone call telling you he's died. You rush out and buy the paper.

Yeah. Yeah. I couldn't believe it. I thought it was a mistake. You know, there he was alive and well, and the next thing I'm being told by Madeleine Bell, she'd just heard it on the radio. She'd stopped at a petrol station to phone me and tell me. It was a feeling of complete disbelief. I only really believed it when I went back to the newsagent. In those days the *Evening Standard* had three editions. There was the morning edition then what they called the 'stop press' edition some time after that. And the guy in the newsagent said, 'Come back in an hour when the next edition arrives.' So I went home and put the television on, and there was nothing on the television. I didn't have a radio, so I went back to the newsagent, it was just at the end of the street, and there it was: Jimi Hendrix dies. Age twenty-eight, it said. I remember thinking he wasn't twenty-eight yet.

You were only twenty-four at the time. Had you lost anybody else close at that point?

No. At that age you think you're immortal, don't you? You don't think people are going to *die* when they're perfectly alright. Yeah, it was a terrible, terrible shock. And then, you know, a drugs overdose.

How do you feel now about the whole thing with Monika Dannemann, claiming she was Jimi's fiancée and her version of what happened that night?

Well, it's all in the past now. She committed suicide, so . . . What we have found out is that early that morning [of Jimi's death] phone calls were being made, we do know that. And people were down there at six o'clock in the morning and the ambulance wasn't called until eighteen minutes past eleven. This we do know. And from the police investigation we found out that there was no telephone in the apartment. It was a payphone in the hallway. And you had to put four pennies in, didn't you? And press a button.

What did you conclude from the reopened investigation, which you instigated in the early nineties?

The police wanted to interview people like Eric Burdon. They all refused. [Eric Burdon's roadie] Terry Slater, he refused as well. But he's dead now so . . . all of the people that were down there. But recently a researcher interviewed Alvenia Bridges [Eric Burdon's girlfriend that night], who was the first one on the scene. And she confirmed that there was no traffic in London. It was just getting light. There were very few people. And he got her to go over that again, saying, 'Now, are you sure there was no traffic, no people and it was just getting light?' And she said, 'Yes, I'm absolutely sure.' Then he said to her, 'But the ambulance wasn't called until 11.18 a.m.' She went silent. Then she went, 'Why are you asking me these questions!' She got all uppity. In other words, she told the truth. Then when she was confronted with the timing of the ambulance being called she clammed up and started saying, you know, 'Why are you asking me these questions!'

So that confirms what Eric Burdon said in his book. That it was early in the morning. Now, [journalist] Harry Shapiro tried to get hold of Terry the Pill, as we called him [Terry Slater], and he ran off down the street. So none of them will speak, but they

were all down there that morning. Instead of calling an ambulance at the first sign of something being wrong, Monika panicked and started trying to phone friends to see what to do. And
probably that's what resulted in his death – and not only that, but
those tablets that he took, each one was a double dose. They were
prescribed to her in Germany. They would have been written in
German. She would have to have given them to him because he
wouldn't have known what they were – he wouldn't have been
able to read the pack. The Home Office pathologist who looked
at the very sparse autopsy report said that the toxicity level could
have been that of only five tablets. See? He wouldn't have known
that each one was a double dose.

**So what do you think happened that night, Kathy, in your heart
of hearts?**

I think she gave him the tablets and then he vomited and died
– and she panicked. Her father was an old Nazi, so being found in
a hotel room with a black guy wouldn't go down too well. That's
when she started saying, 'He was my fiancé! We were engaged!'
to cover up for the fact that it was a glorified one-night stand.

She took his guitar and kept it. Didn't hand it over to the family.
As for Eric, he was sort of . . . He won't talk about it anymore. All
the people who were down there won't speak of it anymore. We
know for a fact that they were all down there. And the police made
the mistake of sending the FBI to speak to Eric, because he lived
in California. And he just said, 'No. I've got nothing to say.' None
of them will talk to the police. The only reason that they wouldn't
talk to the police is because they knew they were all down there
and Jimi was lying on the bed, dead.

Terry Slater told me on the phone, this would have been in the
eighties, when I first started making a few enquiries, he said, 'Oh,
we got all the dope and we threw it down the lavatory.' Then the
police – the only thing that they actually told me – they wouldn't
say whether it was a man or a woman who made the emergency

call, but they still had it on record. Now, I assume that because they wouldn't tell me, it wasn't a woman. It was a man who made the emergency call. They said that they questioned Monika for four hours, and when they got to her house to question her she was lawyered up. She had two lawyers there from a powerful City firm who kept saying, 'You don't have to answer that.'

They asked her, 'What happened to the vomit-covered pillow-cases?' They did tell me that she'd admitted throwing them out the back, into the dustbin. Now, don't you think that's bizarre behaviour?

It's certainly suspicious behaviour. You'd imagine she'd be too busy calling an ambulance, trying to get help.

Yes. It's like Chas said to me. I met Chas in 1994 for drinks at the Dorchester Hotel and we chatted all about this. He said, 'Jimi basically died of negligence. He was with the wrong people at the wrong time.' In other words, had he not been with this particular set of people he probably wouldn't have died, you know? Vesparax are no longer available because of their dangers, and Jimi wouldn't have known what they were. He wouldn't have known that each one was a double dose. I mean, she went through life saying, 'Zee tablets were very weak.' Well, they weren't. They were very bloody strong.

She was the one that gave him those tablets, and she lived with that guilt until she committed suicide. And she was so fearful that she'd be cross-examined because she broke a court undertaking to stop calling me a liar, when she said that I lied to the attorney general. Because I didn't, and of course the judge was able to read what I'd written to the attorney general and decided that there was nothing in it that could possibly be construed as a lie. Just stating a fact of matter, you know, several facts. With the documents to back it up, and therefore she broke the order. And she was found guilty of contempt of court.

You're referencing the legal action you took against her after she broke an earlier court ruling to stop describing you in print and in public as a liar. She fought the case and lost.

What she expected next was that we'd start suing her for libel, because once you've overcome that hurdle – that it was all true – she was in trouble. Now, we weren't going to do that, but she didn't know that. And she went home and the neighbours said they saw her cut a piece of hosepipe and wondered why she was doing that. They didn't think anymore about it, and then her mother got up the next morning to find she wasn't in her bed, and her mother went into the garage to see if the car was there. And she'd threaded two pieces of hosepipe and used duct tape to seal it, and had a pipe going in through each window. Because the Mercedes-Benz coupe which she had has two exhaust pipes, one either side. She threaded them and then she taped up the inside of the window.

So there was no chance the fumes would escape. The scissors and the duct tape were on her knees. She was dressed in her nightdress. And her mother tried to say it was a cry for help. That she didn't mean . . . We don't want a suicide verdict. It was a cry for help. But the coroner said, 'No, this was a tragic attempt at suicide.' They argued she turned the engine off therefore she wanted to save herself. But the coroner said no, that a lot of people that gas themselves with carbon monoxide turn the engine off so that it doesn't draw attention. So nobody hears the car engine running in the garage.

She'd obviously studied how to do it. And that's what the coroner decided. The coroner said to everybody in the courtroom, including her mother and the people giving evidence, all the lawyers, that they were not to mention my name, and if they mentioned my name that she would hold them in contempt of court – to try to stop them from trying to blame me. So in court they referred to me as 'Monika's Adversary'. [Laughs]

It seems to me that Monika was responding to many years of living a lie, and now it was all unravelling.

Yes. Yes. And what's happened is, I've sent all her interviews to the coroner, saying, 'On this particular day she says this happened. But, then again, on *this* particular day she says *this* happened. This is not consistent.' And there were about a dozen examples of them. She changed her story like a lot of people do over the years, you know?

Especially if you're making up parts of your story, it changes.

That's what started me off, because when she was explaining Jimi's personality I realised that she didn't know him. She was giving him a personality that he didn't have.

You say in your book that she asked you lots of questions, like what his favourite food was.

Yep. Exactly. Exactly. Exactly. Exactly. And I knew there was something wrong. She said in one of her statements, 'Oh, I made him a tuna fish sandwich.' Jimi couldn't stand tuna fish. He wasn't very keen on salmon or fish at all. So I knew that was not true. Then, later on, she said it was spaghetti Bolognese. So I said to Terry Slater, 'Well, what was down there? Was the kitchen full of food?' 'No,' he said. 'There was no food in there at all. Not even a slice of dry bread.' *Nothing* in there. I said, 'Well, she said she cooked him a meal.' He said, 'Definitely not.'

I said to him, 'And what was Jimi doing at this time?' He said, 'He was on the bed knackered.' Now, I took that to mean dead. I should have got to him to clarify it because when you look up the word knackered it could also mean tired. But I took it to mean dead, because he's not going to say Jimi was on the bed tired. The tone of what he was saying was that he was on the bed dead. But he used the word knackered.

So I started getting very suspicious about all this and started looking further and further into it, and speaking to them without telling them that I was interested in it. Just wanted to know what had happened. And, of course, I started to realise that it was a completely different scenario to what had gone on [officially]. I then began to realise that all of these phone calls and what have you were being made early in the morning, at least four hours before an ambulance was called.

Now, if it's true, what she said, that he was still alive when the ambulance was called – which I don't think was true at all, I think he was well and truly dead – if it was true and they wasted four hours . . . See? But the coroner [at the time] believed every word she said, unfortunately, because she was [supposedly] the only witness. They asked her at the coroner's court, Was anybody else down there? And she said, 'Oh, well, we had some friends around but that was earlier.'

The whole story of her going out for cigarettes in the middle of the night sounded bogus too.

Rubbish! It's a long walk down the hill to Ladbroke Grove. That bridge that goes across the road [by Ladbroke Grove station], there was a shop there. And then back up again. I mean, you'd be gone for, what? Twenty-five minutes? I don't think that happened at all.

There have been plenty of commentators over the years who suggest that you are also not being honest about what happened. What do you say to them?

The suggestion is that I'm lying. Well, why would I need to lie? Why would I need to do that? What's the point? It is just wanting to know what happened to him. I mean, he was a friend of mine. I'd expect anybody to do something similar if they were friends. I just knew that they were all lying. And when I read Monika's account of Jimi's personality I thought, we've got a lunatic here. She said she saw the mark of Christ on his hands and feet. I thought, *Lunatic.* Isn't it bizarre? You're up against people like that.

Then you've got a situation where, in 1972 or something,

you've got this guy Curtis Knight giving me a credit in his book, like 'thanks for the interview' sort of thing then writes all this absolute crap. That I told him that Jimi broke my nose in three places. I mean, for crying out loud, you can't break a nose in three places. You can only break it in one. It's all an absolute load of old rubbish. And that I took an overdose of tablets and [Jimi's tour manager] Gerry Stickells took me to the hospital. None of this happened – it's completely made up!

So I took action against Knight, and in those days I didn't have that much money. The lawyer told me it would cost about fifty-thousand pounds. Well, that's like five hundred thousand now. So he said, 'What we'll do is for fifty pounds. I'll just send them a letter saying can you tell us the time and place these interviews occurred and any signed notes or recordings.'

So he didn't just lie about what you'd said, he lied about actually meeting and interviewing you?

Yes. I didn't even know him! I was living abroad during that time [when the book was written, circa 1973]. I'd been there since 1971. Didn't come back to England until 1974. I was with my boyfriend Kenneth, living in Hong Kong. Then we went to California, and from there I went to Hawaii. It was only when I came back that this book was handed to me by my flatmate, Scott. He said, 'You'd better read this.' I was like, what?

After about a week to ten days the publishers got back to my solicitor, saying they were going to pulp all the books. They'd only sold nine of them. They apologised and paid the fifty quid [for the lawyer's letter]. In other words, they'd gone to Curtis Knight, asking where did you interview her, when did you interview her and have you got any notes? And he must have had to say, 'Well, no, I didn't.'

Someone wrote on my website that Curtis Knight said in his book that John Coltrane and Eric Dolphy were really upset about Jimi's death, right, as if they were friends of his. Until somebody pointed out that one [Dolphy] died in 1964, and the other one [Coltrane] died in 1967. I mean, he's got Jimi seeing spaceships and phoning him and telling him, 'I know who was onboard.' All this stuff. So I think he interviewed Monika Dannemann because it's Monika Dannemann-type talk.

Curtis spent the rest of his career leaning on his brief relationship with Jimi, releasing albums with Jimi getting co-billing.

Yep. Yep. Yep. He was cashing in on Jimi's name all his life. If you read his book it's *turgid* and *awful*. When he gets to me, because he's put me in the acknowledgements it looks as if I'm actually saying these things.

A lot of other Hendrix biographies that followed over the years, and hundreds of articles, have used the 'facts' of Knight's book – that you told him Jimi had physically abused you – and repeated those stories. The most notable recent example being the 2013 movie biopic *Jimi: All Is by My Side*, written by Oscar-winning 12 Years a Slave screenwriter John Ridley.

Then what's happened since then – and is what John Ridley's talking about – is that other lazy biographers have copied it and repeated it. You can't sue in America because of their First Amendment rights, free speech. Then in 2010 Obama passed a new law saying any awards for libel or defamation awarded anywhere outside America are not collectible in the US. So even if I tried to sue over there I wouldn't be able to collect any damages or, more importantly, my costs.

Henry Barnes, who had given the movie a good review in the *Guardian*, interviewed Ridley and hit him between the eyes when he asked him, 'Where did you get that information from? She denies it.' John Ridley said something like, 'Nobody's done more than Kathy to maintain Jimi's legacy.' In other words, she's just saying it. 'And she's got every right to dispute the facts of the film. But she has to take it up with the people that originated them.' But he wouldn't say where they were originated, because he's stolen somebody else's material.

You mean he's taken stories like the one of Jimi beating you over the head with a phone from the Knight book, without checking with you?

Yes, because it's made up. It's not fact. I didn't say it. So it's made up, therefore it's creative. So John Ridley cannot say where he's got the information from because he's taken it from other people's books. Because I don't read these books. Why should I? Other people – amateur biographers who have day jobs – they've just basically copied it. You know, 'Jimi kicked me in the face with his boot and broke my nose in three places.' Everybody knows you can only break your nose in one place. It's just stupid. And Jimi never did anything like that. So what's happened is that John Ridley's interpreted this as a terrible beating with a phone.

There is no justice. You can't do anything. I mean, I wrote to John Ridley, saying, 'Can we see what you've written about me?' I get a letter back threatening to sue me under their First Amendment right to free speech. [Laughs] In other words, what he's saying is your life history is ours. And you're interfering with your own life history, so we'll sue.

We wrote back a really nasty letter saying if this is defamatory we'll sue. And you saying that you did your research – that you thoroughly researched me – but you didn't speak to me. How can you thoroughly research somebody when you don't speak to them? And we never heard back.

What we think happened – and we're only speculating here – Hayley Atwell [who plays Kathy in Ridley's movie], a year after the film was wrapped, was in Los Angeles and she was being interviewed about her part in *Captain America*, and she said, 'I'm also here working on *All Is by My Side*.' So we think that they were frightened enough by our letters that they went and took the worst of it out. We think it was even more defamatory than what it is. And that's why the film is so choppy, because they've had to edit out great tracts of it. And that's why it's got no basic story-line. Because they had to go back and take big chunks out of it. And then they brought in new editors – so they must have had a chopped-up picture, which they'd had to cobble together because they'd spent five or six million dollars doing it.

And not only that, a friend of a friend of mine went to see it at the Toronto Film Festival, when it first came out in 2012. He's a retired reviewer and he managed to get a copy of the sales notes, the promotion notes that they give out to distributors. He's read-ing these and he gets to Ruth Negga, who is playing the part of Ida, somebody who never existed, and it says, 'When John inter-viewed Kathy . . .' Yeah. So he was giving the distributors the idea that he'd interviewed me. See? So they all do it. He's just done what these other biographers have done. Saying that he'd inter-viewed me for the film.

Fortunately, the film was delayed long enough for me to get a Facebook site going and spend a year getting lots of people reading it. I started off with something like 80 'likes'. I've now got 140,000 'likes'. And only 10 per cent of people [who see or read the page] press the 'like' button. A lot of people – especially older people – don't press the 'like' button. So we totted it up and reckon something like over a million people have seen my site. And it's had a profound effect on their sales! [Laughs.]

I'm not denying that Jimi and I used to argue. We did! We used to have big arguments. But not as portrayed in the film – domestic violence on a regular basis. It also gives the impression that the end of our relationship came when he left me for this Ida – this fictitious character. Now, Ridley must know from his research that that's not true. But that's the impression he gives the audience. And here I am in the movie, I'm sitting on a chair with what looks like a bottle of whisky or something and there's snot coming out of my nose, and I'm taking an overdose of sleep-ing pills, one after the other, swept down with this brown liquid.

The next shot is, I'm in hospital with my face all beaten up. And I'm begging them to take me to Monterey. I'm going, 'Please take me to Monterey . . . Please take me to Monterey . . .' And at the same time he's saying to Linda Keith, 'Why don't you come to Monterey with me?' The fact of the matter is he didn't want to talk to me. He went out of his way to avoid me, because he didn't really think it was true himself. But it's what he wanted for his film. And Hayley Atwell, whenever anyone mentions the film on her Twitter feed she deletes it. She must be very embarrassed about it.

Nobody's ever seen me with a battered face. Had that happened it would have been the talk of the town. Everybody would have known about it. And it's quite clear that I've never had a broken nose – and I've never had any surgery! [Laughs.]

By now we had been talking for over two hours, and the interview was beginning to spiral, slipping into conversation. Kathy suggested I try to get in touch with Madeline Bell, the brilliant singer and entertainer and former Blue Mink star. She also said she would help me get in touch with another close friend from those days, Debbie. But she didn't get back in touch. And I, because of personal commitments – health, money, family; the full catastrophe – was forced to delay work on this book for a couple of years. So we didn't speak again. While writing this chapter, though, I had another look at Kathy's Facebook page, and the most recent entry was from December 2017, wishing everyone a Merry Christmas. I hope she is doing okay. A wonderful woman, so full of life – please do read her book, *Through Gypsy Eyes*. It's her true story.

CHAPTER TEN

Mike A'Gogo

You can leave the army but you can never leave the job.

Three months after being back on Civvy Street, Mike Jeffery was in Newcastle of all places, studying languages and sociology at King's College. A cockney on the toon, except Mike had shed most of his cor blimey accent, discarded like worn-out old shoes. His voice now said officer class, and he wasn't afraid to use it whenever it suited him.

He was twenty-three, a mature student, and it was the first year full grants were available. Mike made the most of it, leapfrogging from the committee of the college's jazz club to opening his own club – the so-called University Jazz Club at the Cordwainers Hall on Nelson Street, above a pub called the Gardeners Arms.

It was like Fayid all over again, only selling tickets instead of newspapers to bored youngsters. And no real rules: whereas the college authorities had come down heavy on the stomps, as they called them, which Mike and chums had held in the college union refectory, he could now open up his doors to all ages – and keep all the profits.

Despite the name, the new club had fuck all to do with Newcastle College. Soon it wasn't just students paying to get in, it was anyone looking for a late-night joint in the centre of the city. Any trouble from the punters was met head on. Along with his many other skills learned but rarely discussed from his days in the 'army', Mike was now a black belt in judo, fronting his own judo team in a display at a Mr Gateshead contest at a local gym.

With his black D'Artagnan beard and well-cultivated sense of entitlement, Mike became a big figure around town. He met his new girlfriend – a pretty art student named Cathleen Long – at the Jazz Club. He also got to know and eventually trust brother and sister Chuck and Kath Ward – both of whom became heavily involved in the running of the club and in Mike's dreams of a swashbuckling lifestyle. Jazz and art and after-midnight friend-ships with some of the city's own freeform characters, ex-forces, small-time crims, off-book cops and their grasses, working girls, arse bandits, pill pushers, scrubbers and clowns.

By 1959, however, Mike had outgrown both the College and the Jazz Club. He foresaw a new kind of venture. Not just a col-lege haunt, but a professionally run venue. Mike even had the name – the Marimba Coffee House. Now he just needed a venue – and some get-going holding-folding. Finding new premises was easy enough. There was a shop with an upstairs storeroom for let on the south side of High Bridge. The money was trickier, but Mike didn't think twice about dropping out of college and negoti-ating a 'loan' from a local businessman with an eye for the main chance, named Mr Capstaff, who would also become the only other shareholder. He had a haulage company with a depot at the top of Byker Bank, and another smaller licensed café-and-digs called the Highwayman. 'Cappies' would bankroll the Marimba. Mike would front it.

A simple idea, futuristic for the time in Newcastle: frothy coffee and snacks all day, student prices, loose cigarettes, a juke-box. At night, upstairs, a jazz club, higher-priced food – posh for-eign grub like spaghetti – live music and an older, more moneyed clientele. Brylcreem boyos. Switchblade smiles. Clip-on bow ties. Whoopsie-daisy skirts, pearl-bib necklaces, red kiss-proof lipstick.

Local paper ads for the Marimba ran with 'a rendezvous

created for students by students' – a line Mike had come up with himself. Meaning coffee instead of tea. Records, books, beards. Rubber-johnny machines on the wall in the gents. While by night the upstairs would become like a private members' club: booze, live jazz, an after-hours crowd. The kind of swish gaff where you could tap your cigarette to Tommy Henderson's Latin American Group or the Bernie Thorpe Trio, or maybe Mike Carr's EmCee Four.

The upstairs club eventually had a name of its own – El Toro. Bullfighter vibe. Masked marauder. Spaniards in bollock-cutting tight pants, a rose between their teeth, twirling like nutty tops while pretty maids in hair-buns and Cupid's-bow red smiles kicked their legs and wriggled their bums. A really *canny good neet oot, leek*, everyone said so.

Mike now had a new partner in Ray Grehan, with whom he started a limited company called Espresso Maze Ltd. Five years older than Mike, Ray was a typewriter salesman who'd blagged his way into a sales job at a ticket-machine company called Automaticket, eventually running the show as sales manager.

When Mike met Ray he was looking for a fast money-fix. Cappies had gone soft, unwilling to pour more money into the coffee-house or the upstairs club.

Espresso Maze Ltd was formed primarily to keep the Marimba and El Toro open. The punters were still packing the places out most days and nights, but the money side was like a toilet seat, said Mike – up and down. Mike using the take as his own money and throwing it away on all the usual – bubbles, blondes, back-handers. What was the point in making it if you couldn't bloody well spend it?

His new live-in girlfriend, a pretty blonde named Jenny Clarke he'd met when she came to work at the Marimba, saw sides of Mike others rarely got a glimpse of. Living together in a smart house in upscale Jesmond, north of the city centre, Mike would entertain his newfound love by playing an acoustic guitar and an elderly harpsichord.

Jenny already had Mike pegged as a real go-getter. A man's man, but far removed from most of the former National Service types she had known. She'd seen him deal with so-called hard men at the club, putting them in their place, no trouble at all. She also saw him scheme his way through difficulties, unflappable on the outside, able to speak to bankers, government officials and lawyers as easily as he did the doormen and waitresses who worked such long hours for him. But the musical side of Mike's soul still came as a pleasant surprise to her. Mike loved jazz, anyone could see that. But he could play, really play, without making it a calling card. Mostly, he loved having money, real money, loved having stacks of it in the house and at the club, in every pocket of every jacket and coat, in the glove compartment of every car. And he had a lot of cars. Always prestige motors, bringing home at different times an Aston Martin DB4, a two-door Jensen Interceptor convertible, a Morgan Series IV, anything that took his fancy. Anything with hot wheels that said, I am not like the others. Not even fucking close.

Mike loved Jenny in a way he had never loved a woman before. Even after they ceased to be lovers Jenny remained one of the most fondly recalled people in Mike's life. When Jenny wanted to move to London in 1962, Mike arranged and paid for her to train as a beautician. 'She was so loyal,' he later told an American girlfriend. 'When I had nothing she used to sleep with me on the floor.'

With Ray to back him up, Mike opened a third venue, another licensed club he called the Downbeat. The Downbeat was much bigger than the Marimba, situated in an abandoned former school in Carliol Square.

Mike's public partner in the Downbeat, which opened in March 1960, was Malcolm Cecil. Bassist in local jazz heroes the EmCee

Four, Malcolm was a veteran of dozens of gigs at Mike's other gaffs, a talented, super-smart young head destined to become a force in the music business in his own right in the coming years.

Mike had more in common with Malcolm than just droopy-eyed shadow music and smoky small-hours gigs. Malcom was still a serving member of the RAF when they met, and Mike was inclined to share details of his own military career with the younger man. Half a century later, Cecil was clear in his own mind that, as he put it, 'Michael Jeffery was a high-ranking officer in the British Secret Service.' The first hint he got of Mike's behind-the-scenes connections was when he 'arranged for me to have a posting down to London because he knew I wanted to go down and play in the jazz clubs'. The favour was gladly received. But it was a devil's bargain. 'It was in exchange for me handing over to him my shares in the club . . .'

Then came Mike's real brainwave. On a trip back to London, he'd checked out the Flamingo on Wardour Street and was envious that the club stayed open at weekends until 6 a.m. Later, hitting the hip new brothels and bars of Gerrard Street – where red-lit doorbells and open doors with little postcards inside advertising 'Large Chest for Sale' or 'French Lessons Given' had now replaced the Piccadilly street walkers of his youth – he found himself in the recently opened Ronnie Scott's Jazz Club. Mike was deeply impressed. Ronnie's was a basement joint, really boppin', like something out of one of his favourite films as a kid, *D.O.A.*

Mike arrived back in Newcastle full of it. Couldn't wait to sit down with Ray and start planning it out. This would be Soho in the North. Unlike anything ever seen there before. Go Daddy-O! The kind of sophisticated late-night den Mike could really see himself at home in. Art on the walls, red leather banquettes, low lamp-lit tables, mirrored walls. Live action night *and* day.

They sniffed out a suitable place on Percy Street, an abandoned haunt above the Handyside Arcade. Got a nice discount for cash on the building. It had previously belonged to the Newcastle Labour Club and would need a ton of work. Mike and Ray decided to set up another limited company – Jazz Stands – to borrow the money they would need to do the place up legit from a bank. But no bank would lend them all the lolly they needed. Mike's good luck returned, though, when in November 1961 a freak fire destroyed both the Marimba Coffee House and El Toro, and the resulting £75,000 insurance pay-out allowed him and Ray to invest in their new club. It was doubly fortunate that both the Marimba and El Toro had been empty the night of the fire. Newcastle CID investigated the fire and concluded, said a spokesman, 'There is no question of criminal proceedings.'

Phew, what a relief. Someone could have died or been badly hurt.

Mike and Ray rubbing their hands with glee, canny lads, they had the new place on Percy Street – fabulously named the Club A'Gogo – open for business by the following July.

The big deal about Club A'Gogo was its deliberately broader appeal: not just pure jazz outfits on the podium but Latin American-themed music, blurring into the kind of Caribbean beat stuff Mike had witnessed at the Flamingo. The coloureds had money and women too; why not welcome them in as well?

The real hook, though, was Ray's roulette wheel – a French model he'd bought especially because it came without the zero pocket on the wheel. This amended form of roulette, called legalite, was taking off in London, and Ray thought it would be a great new thing – and hugely profitable – to introduce to the North East. The missing zero, which in conventional roulette belonged to the house, allowed for the gambler to have better odds – in theory.

Sure enough, Ray's new 'continental' roulette table was an instant hit with the regular faces at the Gogo. Only snag: it wasn't legal. Nor were the side tables in the room, offering poker and blackjack. That's why you had *private rooms* though, *am ah reet, pet?*

Mike's luck eventually began to run out after an undercover police operation that led to both Mike and Ray appearing in court in January 1963, charged with offences under the Betting and Gaming Act. Taking advantage of how little most club-goers actually knew about roulette or legalite, they'd been making up their own rules as well as adding a 'nominal charge' to gamblers each time they placed a bet. Mike and Ray pleaded ignorance, paid heavy fines and walked free – but the gaming room at the Gogo was shut for several weeks.

An even bigger kick in the head arrived in a separate prosecution that saw Mike lose his special late drinks licence after yet more undercover coppers testified that the Club A'Gogo did not always serve food, the major requirement for establishments with such a licence. The club was forced to revert to 'pub hours', and suddenly the place was empty after 10.30 every night. The late licence was eventually reinstated in July 1963, but by then Mike's lack of readies was growing chronic.

And the shit hit the fan when Ray cottoned on to the fact that Mike had secretly been helping himself to cash from the gaming-room takings. The two men had a big falling-out, and suddenly Mike was on his own again. A bad blow, as Ray had been the pragmatic money man whose creditworthiness had kept Mike's ambitious lifestyle afloat.

A soured Ray would later recall how, 'I ran the gaming side and emptied the cash box at night. One night there were no £5 notes in it at all. I said to the croupier, "I watched the game earlier and there should be at least £50 to £100 in £5 notes." She was very indignant and said that Mike had come around and taken the big notes the way he did every night.'

Ray puffed his cheeks and fanned out his hands. 'Mike didn't believe in paying for anything and was permanently on the run from the sheriff's officer wielding writs for debts.'

Ask Mike, he'd tell you the Geordie coppers had taken against him after they'd found an unregistered Colt 45 pistol in his jacket pocket. They had taken him to court for that one too, and he'd received yet another fine. Mike shrugged, spat in the kerb. He'd been using guns since he'd been in the army. In Trieste he'd become accustomed to handling firearms, with or without the 'proper authority'. Words on paper, fuck's sake, nothing to do with his real duties. Another time he'd had his wrist slapped for 'discharging a firearm illegally' – as a *soldier*. I mean, fuck off you pen-pushing cunts. It was guys with real guts like Mike who kept the flag flying. The real top people knew that and appreciated him for it.

They still did.

After the malarkey with Ray and the bizzies, Mike put the focus in the Gogo back on the music. Never mind the suit-and-tie crowd. Mike was now all about the youth. The ones who wanted to dance, not sit around moaning about losing at the tables. Suddenly jazz and lipstick cigarettes were out, and the Beatles were in.

Rhythm and blues. Rock and roll. Boys with hair down to their collars. Girls with skirts above their knees. New young groups Mike booked into the Gogo like hot local faves the Alan Price Rhythm and Blues Combo. Old coloured American blues singers like John Lee Hooker and Sonny Boy Williamson. Fuck Ray. Fuck the filth. Some nights the queue to get into the Gogo stretched from the doorway in Percy Street all the way around the corner to St James' Park.

Mike started making money again. Mike started blowing money again. 'There was always plenty of money, but the club was run very badly,' said Jenny Clarke. 'If it had been run as a business someone could have made a lot of money out of it. But it wasn't about money. That just didn't come into it. All the takings would be spent the next day. Mike liked his Morgans and Aston Martins.'

Mike liked being Mike.

Mike had lots of new ideas. The day after 'She Loves You' by the Beatles went to number 1 he paid for Gogo regulars the Alan Price Rhythm and Blues Combo to go into Graphic Sound, a small spit-and-sawdust recording facility in Wylam, Northumberland. At the end of the day Mike had a 12-inch disc with four tracks on one side, which he suggested they title *I Just Wanna Make Love to You* after the ancient Muddy Waters hit, but which quickly became known locally as the *Graphic Sound* EP. As well as smart-boy Price on organ, there was a coal-faced singer named Eric Burdon, good-looking Hilton Valentine on guitar, a human giraffe named Bryan 'Chas' Chandler on bass and a who-cares drummer named John Steel.

Mike played the EP at the Gogo – and to anyone he could trap into listening. No dice. Ah, well. Spark another gasper and count the night's take.

Then the Graham Bond Quartet arrived to do a gig at the Gogo and something unforeseen happened. Mike had booked Pricey to open the show. Bond sat in and listened. Bond played Hammond organ like Alan, only he could do it while simultaneously blowing an alto sax. His band was also virtuosic, real fire and guts geezers, onstage and off. When Bond said he wanted to jam with Alan's Combo it was taken as a badge of honour. But forgotten about the next morning after the Quartet had fled back to London.

When Bond, a very heavy cat, prone to acts of mental self-flagellation, a career self-harmer who would one day throw himself under a train, began talking up this far-out Geordie combo he'd dug up north, people in town listened, so rare was it to hear the big man rain good thunder on anything.

Paying special attention was Ronan O'Rahilly, a fast-moving young Irishman who owned the Scene Club in Soho. Like Mike,

Ronan was a club owner with one eye on what was coming down the pipe. He'd already made his move to wheedle Georgie Fame from the clutches of old showbizzy lag Larry Parnes. Like Mike, he'd paid to have his boy make a record – only to see it smothered at birth when no radio station would touch it. Ronan's solution: to talk his ship-owning father into gifting him 702-ton former Danish passenger ferry *Fredericia*, which he converted into a radio ship at the Irish port of Greenore. Ronan named his new station Caroline – after Caroline Kennedy, six-year-old daughter of JFK – and immediately began playing Georgie Fame's records and any others the grasping London record labels would pay him to.

When Ronan caught Graham Bond barking on about some shit-hot band he'd played with in Newcastle, he sent a minion up to check them out. His first port of call was the Café A'Gogo, where he was immediately directed to the man in the know: Mike Jeffery.

Mike spoke to Ronan's messenger boy. Promised to put on a special show so that he could see for himself just how wowie the Alan Price Rhythm and Blues Combo were. He also explained how he was, in fact, the Combo's manager. Then hurriedly had a contract drawn up that he pushed Price and the lads to sign, promising them prestigious shows in London as an immediate reward – because that was the kind of thing a powerful manager like Mike could do for you, boys.

CHAPTER ELEVEN

Linda and Keith

Jimmy banging white chicks, man. Right there in New York City. Like it's going out of style. There had been some pretty little bitty ones out on the road before, but you took them into the shitter at the show, locked the door, where no white man could see you know what's good for you, boy. You didn't – *never* – put 'em on the bus with you, or God forbid smuggle them back to the motel. Things were less uptight on the East Coast, especially after everyone started growing their hair, digging the Beatles and Dylan. The three Asian chicks who had balled him all together because they said he had the face of a Hindu god. The married chicks who begged him to slap them around.

After Fayne, the next chick Jimmy had a big-style, in-deep scene with that year was a sixteen-year-old runaway named Diana Carpenter. Diana was that chick you ran into everywhere around 42nd Street and Times Square: a victim of childhood sexual abuse who had fled her Midwest home and was now turning tricks in hourly rate rooming houses.

Who Jimmy met one night in a 52nd Street diner and fell for. She was with her pimp, but Jimmy didn't give a shit. Grinned at her, told her she was 'so cute', and had her pimp rear up on him, tell him to shut his motherfucking mouth or else. Diana was so impressed that when they ran into each other again – this time *sans* pimp – they hooked up the same night.

Diana said Jimmy was so broke he couldn't afford to eat, didn't have more than one thin shirt, and was very happy for her to pay for their meals. It didn't matter that Jimmy could never hold it down with just one chick at a time, he hated that Diana fucked other men, even though she was getting paid for it – and was using that money to help her new dream lover stay alive on the street.

Diana was another tea-coloured teenager Jimmy said reminded him of his mother. Diana only tricked in daylight hours – easier to avoid arrest – and would come to the shows at night. It didn't matter how many tricks she'd turned that day, she and Jimmy would fuck 'two or three times a night'.

Just as he did with his other chicks, Jimmy would regale Diana with stories of all the pretty things he was going to buy her when he got rich and famous, and like all the others she believed him. 'If I don't get rich and famous in a year, I'll go crazy,' he told her.

But Jimmy was getting more and more antsy about Diana whoring herself out. When he came back to the hotel one night and found her being strangled by one of her johns, he went fucking nuts and threw the guy out of the room. After that, he couldn't leave it alone. She should stop, he kept telling her. Then he'd gratefully accept the few dollars she laid on him.

A few days later Diana was arrested, thrown in police lockup overnight then put on a bus back to the Midwest, where her folks still lived. But she was too smart for that and was back in New York with Jimmy within forty-eight hours. Jimmy was having a breakdown; he thought a john had killed her – dropped her body in an alley.

When Diana found out she was pregnant, Jimmy went whole-hog folksy and insisted she stop turning tricks. Good on paper or in the movies, but no use in real life. Without Diana's street dollars they were forced to steal just to survive. But Jimmy was no pro, and these weren't heists or break-ins. This was petty thieving of food from the shelves of all-night stores, and they were nearly caught out more than once.

Chased for several blocks down a street by a maddened store owner wielding a baseball bat, Jimmy finally gave up. 'I gotta change this bullshit,' he told her. She knew he was right, and went back to turning tricks behind his back.

But then Jimmy found out – and went *insane*. He took off his leather belt and began flogging her with it, screaming, 'When I tell you to do something, you do it!' Terrified she might lose the baby, Diana retreated into a ball on the bed and let him get on with it. Suddenly it was Jimmy's father Al's voice booming around the room. 'I'll show you! I'll show you that fat meat is greasy!' Whatever the fuck *that* meant.

It was over, but they carried on for a while, not knowing what else to do, worrying about the baby, worrying about what Jimmy was turning into. When Diana was later arrested by an under-cover cop, posing as a john, who found out she was underage, she was given an ultimatum: up to three years in jail or another bus ticket home to her folks. Diana didn't have to think about it. She did the smart thing and got the hell out of Dodge.

Jimmy and Diana's baby daughter, Tamika, was born in February 1967. Because Jimmy was always flitting between crash pads they had lost touch almost immediately when she fled New York. It wasn't like Jimmy was in a hurry to stay involved. By then he was in London anyway, so what the hell, right? It would be years, in fact, before Jimmy – now Jimi – would even acknowledge he had a daughter. The kid was just as likely a john's, he reasoned when he could be bothered to think about it all. But Tamika was black – like her parents – and Diana had a rule about only ever tricking with white johns.

Hey, man – Jimmy had a lot of other shit to deal with, dig?

Like, his first real boyfriend-girlfriend thing with a white chick. Her name was Carol Shiroky – Kim to her friends.

It was while Jimmy was still hung up working for *bupkes* for the Squires, playing second fiddle to Curtis Knight with his cookie-cutter songs and half-assed vocals, knowing he was now the real attraction, ready to start his own thing, but unable to do so while he didn't have his own guitar, just the one Curtis had 'loaned' him. Going in ever-decreasing circles in clubs like the Purple Onion and Ondine on the Upper East Side, dancehall joints that only really jumped when they saw Jimmy biting his guitar and swinging it around his back like Fred doggy-fucking Ginger.

Even picking up another gig – second banana guitarist in sax player King Curtis's band the Kingpins – brought nothing but a few extra dollars. The Kingpins were one of the tightest bands on the circuit and Jimmy had to work his ass off to keep his spot. But he was back to wearing a band uniform and doing unison moves. Cheesy-as-fuck shit he thought he'd left behind. You couldn't even take your jacket off unless the King took his off first, and he almost never took his jacket off first. Jiving around, playing second lick to 'Stand by Me' and 'Yakety Yak'.

Bullshit gigs. Then crawling back to his cheap hotel and putting *Rubber Soul* on the portable record player, aching to the bitter truth of Lennon's 'In My Life' and seeing his own past and future shrinking to the head of a pin. Not a kingpin either, a tack. Worse, laying Coltrane's *Ascension* on the deck and feeling like no one told him when to run. That it was already all over for him.

He changed his name again – Jimmy James – and finally started his own group. Going for broke with the Village hipsters, he called it the Rainflowers. *The rain fucking what, Jim?* Quickly realised his mistake and renamed it the Blue Flames, after Little Junior Parker's band in the fifties – as in, 'Ladies and gentlemen, please welcome to the stage the one and only Jimmy James and the Blue Flames!'

Cue roof-raising applause.

That's how he sold himself to Carol/Kim anyway. But at first she wasn't buying it. 'I thought he was on an ego trip.' He was. But that had been offstage, at some friend of a friend's pad. When they met again, after a Curtis gig at a new club on Broadway and 53rd called Cheetah that opened in May, it was a different scene. The Cheetah was all sub-Warhol popping lights bouncing off shiny aluminium. Fake-cheetah print walls, a long bar down one side. A big deal for five minutes, Jimmy came offstage and made straight for the white chick that had blown him off before. Now she'd seen him play the new happening joint . . . right?

He swaggered over to her table, went down on one knee and began whispering in her ear, some bullshit about wanting to kiss her knee.

'So, of course, I laughed. I mean, how many people tell you they wanna kiss your knee? Three days later we moved in together. It was like an instant fire kind of thing.'

Living together at the Lenox Hotel, having a white chick support him gave Jimi a lift, helped him feel like he was still moving forward somehow. It didn't matter that Carol was another prostitute; she wasn't a street hooker like Diana, she was a high-class call girl, had taste and a way about her. Carol would cook Jimmy his favourite breakfast – spaghetti and garlic, fuck eggs – would help him put his curlers in at night and do his hair, wouldn't make a scene on those nights he didn't come back to the hotel. Carol was there those nights he returned from another gig with Curtis, ready to blow his top, moaning how Curtis had ripped him off again for the money he'd been promised, how Curtis played bullshit songs that embarrassed him.

Carol didn't get it: why didn't he just quit, then?

'Because it's *his* guitar.'

Carol got so tired of hearing about it she went out one day and bought him a white Fender Stratocaster. Jimmy nearly lost his mind! Now he had his own guitar he could do what he wanted. Two nights later, playing with Curtis again, Jimmy unplugged his guitar and announced, 'That's the last time I play this shit.'

Jimmy James and the Blue Flames couldn't get booked at the Gaslight, where all the real blues heavies played, so they did one-offs at the Kettle of Fish on MacDougal, the Night Owl Cafe on West 3rd Street. Most especially, when they could get it, the Cafe Wha? – the basement joint under the Players Theatre where the poetry and hopped-up beatnik cats held sway. You played for free in the afternoon, and if they liked you they invited you back in the evening.

Jimmy told Carol he was getting forty bucks a night to play there. He was getting seven dollars. He didn't care. The Cafe Wha? was the first place where he could finally start to extend his reach, doing his own versions of new-today stuff like 'Like a Rolling Stone' or 'Wild Thing', or re-jiving old shit like 'Hey Joe' and 'Shotgun'.

Jimmy didn't mind who joined him onstage. For a while he had a fifteen-year-old white runaway on guitar with him, name of Randy Wolfe. Because the bass player was also named Randy – Palmer – whom Jimmy had nicknamed Randy Texas, he called the young Wolfe, who'd been born in LA, Randy California. The white kid was so good Jimmy wanted to keep him on, but Randy's parents nixed that idea once they tracked him down, forcing their son to go back to school when summer was over. Randy did okay, though, when he later formed his own cool-dude outfit, Spirit.

Jimmy meanwhile was getting lost trying to be all things to all people. A black guy playing white rock music; a white girlfriend who supported him but whom he couldn't stop cheating on; a serious musician who spent his days reading Marvel comics and digging the new *Batman* show on ABC. A Dylan freak with pro-cessed hair and re-conned stage moves. He had worked his way up to six nights a week at the Café Wha?, splitting whatever he was paid each night evenly with the band. But the performances were becoming more wilfully erratic.

Carol, who'd hung on in there long past the call of duty, finally bailed out.

'He would go off. The last song would be forty-five minutes of feedback and freak everybody out . . . I saw him lie down on the stage and cry during a performance.'

Slowly, though, word was getting out about the crazy young black cat in the Village who played left-handed guitar upside down. Important people were starting to pay attention. John Hammond Jr., who'd introduced Dylan to the Band, said Jimmy was 'one of those things that just boggles your mind, I just could not believe it'.

Mike Bloomfield, the fieriest guitarist in New York, who'd also been store-bought by Dylan for *Highway 61 Revisited*. Before he'd seen Jimmy James at the Café Wha?, he said, 'I thought I was *it.*' Afterwards: 'H-bombs were going off, guided missiles were flying . . . I didn't even want to pick up a guitar for the next year.'

Away from the club, however, during those other twenty-forever hours of each day, life was still fucking impossible. He stayed friends with Carol, who introduced him to Mike Quashie, the big Trinidadian singer who brought limbo to America. Mike assumed Jimmy was a Harlem pimp the first time he saw him lounging round Carol's in his blue and yellow curlers. Mike used scarves in his act, long silk colours-of-the-rainbow air-ties that Jimi began to 'borrow' and bind around his arms and legs. Mike would lend Jimmy a few bucks here and there and never ask for them back. Tell stories of fire-walking and African voodoo, Jimmy agape, hugging his guitar. Jimmy was moved, man, and later, when everything in the world had changed, Jimmy picked up the tab when his old friend found himself in hospital.

Mainly, though, Jimmy still relied on his lovers to help him get by. Like beautiful sixteen-year-old Jeanette Jacobs. Soon to be a singer in an all-girl group called the Cake, Jeanette was a coffee-coloured innocent who would later marry Chris Wood of Traffic and die at thirty-two from an epileptic seizure. She and Jimmy would be in and out together until his death four years later.

'When I met Jimi all he had was two pairs of pants, two shirts and a guitar,' she recalled in 1972. 'That's all he owned. But he had a premonition about being a star. "I'm going to be very big," he once said, and that was before he met Chas. He said to me, "You're going to have all the clothes you want when I'm a big star." He'd take down the addresses of clothes shops, and say, "You can have this, and that . . ."'

Jimmy, living out the same old fantasies with different young ladies. 'He was a very sensitive person and that shyness was real. Lots of people say he put it on, but he didn't. And he wasn't at all stupid. He played stupid, but that was one of his games to see how far people would go in taking advantage of him.'

Jimmy was good at taking advantage too.

'I think because of his mother's death he didn't have a happy childhood. That really played in his head all the time. He used to grab drinks out of my hand and say, "You've had enough." His mother used to drink, and he'd say, "Please don't drink, you're the only girl who could make me cry, apart from my mother."'

It was through Jeanette that Jimmy met the more worldly Emeretta Marks, whom Jeanette knew a little from the scene, when they bumped into one another on a busy Manhattan street one afternoon. Emeretta was a singer, dancer, musician, actress; girlfriend to Eric Burdon, girlfriend to Bill Wyman. A year later she would achieve a measure of fame in the musical *Hair*. Emeretta was a stone-cold fox who would later nurse Brian Jones back to near-health after a particular nasty week-long drug trip. She had looks, talent, brains, all the stuff Jimmy looked up to.

Emeretta later recalled: 'Jeanette said, "We haven't eaten in three days. I didn't get paid, and we have a cat." I had three dollars in my pocket, and that's all I had. I gave it to them and told them to go buy three cans of tuna so the cat could eat too. This was even before I knew he was a guitar player. They were just hungry.'

Bowled over by such kindness, Jimmy started to get to know Emeretta better, shyly giving her pages of his lyrics so she could correct the grammar. 'He liked the way I spoke,' she said. Jimmy liked a lot of things about Emeretta. She was class and Jimmy knew that was something he could use.

It was the same the night in May when a white, super-cool, super-bombed twenty-year-old English chick named Linda Keith walked into the Cheetah and caught Jimmy doing his best to up-stage Curtis Knight. There were fewer than fifty people there, but the weird-looking young guitarist mesmerised Linda. As soon as the set fizzed to its end, she pushed her way backstage into the dressing room.

Now this was new. Chicks getting their rocks off watching Jimmy doing it to the guitar, black and white, that was expected. But this chick was white *and* English *and* already connected. This chick was with the Stones, man. This chick was Linda *Keith*, dig, girlfriend of Keith *Richards*.

And she was beautiful. *Vogue*-model beautiful. English upper-class beautiful. Like, Marianne Faithfull, Julie Christie, Jean Shrimpton beautiful – only younger. Way out of Jimmy's league. And there was more. Photographed by David Bailey, best friends with Sheila Klein – Stones manager Andrew Loog Old-ham's girlfriend – Linda was at the epicentre of London's new pop-meets-fash-meets-aristo-gangster-drug-film-beau-monde.

Linda Keith was the kind of impossible-to-impress, hot-blooded beauty that pop stars like Keith Richards begged to come on tour with them. Even Mick Jagger would put on his best lolli-pop accent for Linda.

And there was more. Linda knew music – really knew it. Au-thentic American blues, especially. Linda was a blues *purist*. Trav-elled with a suitcase full of records wherever she went. Could take on Keith on the subject. Could even surprise Brian Jones sometimes, and nothing could ever surprise Jonesy, not when it came to music.

Linda had seen Sonny Terry and Brownie McGhee when they played in London, and had made a point of getting to know Sonny Boy Williamson when he showed up. Linda was such a blues snob that the Stones barely registered on her radar.

'I'd seen them in clubs,' she barely recalled. 'They were interesting but it wasn't anything that really grabbed me.'

Linda was bohemian, educated, high-born Jewish, exquisitely on point. A teenager when she found herself at a party where the Stones were supposed to be the main attraction, she saw Richards, decided he would do, and went straight over and stole him away.

'It was love at first sight,' Keith was still telling people years and lifetimes later.

'He was a blues aficionado.' Linda shrugged. 'And that was why we got on so well. It completely counteracted his shyness and that's all I wanted to talk about anyway.'

She had zero interest in discussing the Stones and banned Keith from playing their music on her expensive new record player. 'He knew I was never a huge fan. I was hugely into black music, so they sounded a bit pale by comparison.'

In May of 1966, a month before the Stones took off for their fifth US tour in three years, Linda told Keith she was happy to come along – but that she would base herself in Los Angeles and New York. God forbid he try to drag her off to some dreary hole like . . . Cleveland, or Pittsburgh, or whatever those awful places were called. She would fly to New York alone, ahead of the tour, and check out the scene.

The first time she saw Jimmy play she hadn't gone out expecting anything particularly interesting to happen. But as soon as she saw Jimmy start to do his act, she said later, 'It was so clear to me. I couldn't believe nobody had picked up on him before because he'd obviously been around.'

Linda knew a used car when she saw one. She also knew what a Ferrari should sound like. 'He was astonishing – the moods he could bring to music, his charisma, his skill and stage presence. Yet nobody was leaping about with excitement. I couldn't believe it.'

After the show Linda and her friends dragged him back to the plush apartment on 63rd Street where she was staying. Linda told Jimmy the words he longed to hear. That she was from London, with the Stones, and that he was the new magic man and she was there to make his wicked dreams come true.

When he complained that he'd had to hock his guitar – the one Carol had given him – Linda offered to let him borrow one of her boyfriend's cherished white Fenders. She also promised to spread the word about her new find and bring friends from the biz to his shows. She was convinced that all it would take was one viewing for anybody to feel what she had felt, see what she had seen – and simply freak out.

'I was determined that he should be noticed, get a record deal and blow everybody's mind. I knew it was all there, so I went for it.'

The first one she thought of was Andrew Loog Oldham, due in town ahead of the Stones tour. By then Jimmy and his newly formed Blue Flames were holding down a regular slot at the Cafe Wha? Andrew was hip and shrewd; Linda was sure he'd get it straight away. But the evening was a disaster. The Loog only went because Keith's bird had pestered him to do so. She was raving about this guy. Maybe it was worth a punt – maybe not.

'It was a dreadful night,' Linda recalled. 'Jimi was dishevelled in his playing and in the way he looked. Andrew was weird as well. He didn't want to know. Maybe he'd heard the rumours that

I'd been hanging out with this guy. Maybe he'd been sent down by Keith. But it made me very anxious.'

Nevertheless, after the show she went back again, soothed Jimmy with her sexy English honeyed accent, her opulent charms and luggage full of records – and her promise to keep trying on his behalf.

A week later she brought the Stones to a show at Ondine's. But Jimmy was mediocre and the band ignored his set. Only Keith kept his eyes on the cat. Keith could see what he meant to Linda. But the Stones left the next day to resume their tour and all Keith could do was pine.

Next, Linda dragged Seymour Stein to a gig, the New York-based mogul who would one day sign Madonna. Then she sat there mortified while a fucked-up Jimmy petulantly smashed the beautiful guitar she had loaned him to smithereens.

Afterwards she flew into a rage and threatened to abandon him to the scrapheap. Maybe she'd been wrong. Maybe he was just another cheap hustler that didn't deserve her help. Jimmy was beside himself promising, apologising, vowing, swearing, pleading.

Linda is beginning to see everything now. The way Jimmy bullshits every woman he is involved with, making them believe they are the special one. Maybe even believing it, making himself believe it, while he is with them. Is that what he's doing to Linda too?

When she walks in on him one morning and finds him in bed with seven of these fucking chicks, she throws up her hands and walks out. Jimmy runs after her, complaining that he can't help it, it is just his nature.

Linda gives it one last shot. Persuades Chas Chandler, who happens to be in town on his last tour with the Animals, to come down to a show, see 'this incredible guy I've found'. Though by now even Linda is having her doubts.

'Some of his movements were great but he was also a trick-ster – playing the guitar over his head or with his teeth. He didn't really need any of that.' He also didn't know how to dress. One thing about hanging out with Keith and Mick, they really knew how to put on the style when they walked onstage. Knew it was 1966, not '56.

'Oh, Jimmy's fashion sense was absolutely dreadful. He wore dreadful clothes – big Copacabana shirts with too-short bell-bottoms and shoes with holes in them. He had processed hair that had spent the night in curlers, so when he took the curlers out it remained in exactly the same form. It wasn't a good look.'

It is now or never, both Linda and Jimmy sense it. Chas agrees to come to a Wednesday afternoon slot at the Cafe Wha? Linda no longer giving it the big sell, not really knowing what to expect now.

They stroll in from the bright sunny afternoon, down into the cave-like cellar of the Wha?, their eyes taking a moment to adjust. Then, with God-given timing, the lights burn up the stage and here comes Jimmy James strumming the moody opening chords to 'Hey Joe'.

And Chas Chandler's mind is blown. Instantly.

Chas, who has been looking for a way out of his own career graveyard, searching blindly for a way out of the darkness and up into light. Somehow, somewhere.

'It even blew my mind,' said Linda, still seeing it, all these years later. 'And I knew it was coming!'

Chas is so excited he spills a milkshake over himself. Taken by Linda afterwards to meet Jimmy, Chas knows in his bones that nothing comes to you this easy, feels sure there has to be a catch somewhere. But Jimmy is in full-on *shucks, what, me? I'm no trouble at all, boss* mode, and Chas is charmed into taking a chance.

Tells the kid he will come back to New York in September when the Animals tour is over – and will bring him to London. Jimmy nodding politely, smiling-smiling, holding Linda's hand tight.

Later that night Linda introduces Jimmy to a new experience. LSD. He'll really like it, she says.

Linda is right again. Linda sees. Linda knows.

Jimmy has never experienced anything so . . . so . . .

He catches a glimpse of his own face in a mirror – and sees Marilyn Monroe staring back at him.

Jimmy, on acid for the first time, catches a glimpse of his own face in a mirror – and sees the future. His future.

Jimmy, tripping, zooming past the moon, far out beyond the stars, merging into space-time with Linda the angel, Linda by his side, catches a glimpse of his own face in a mirror – and sees it all too.

CHAPTER TWELVE

Chas and Jimi

Chas had hustled. After Decca had turned him down he did a quick handshake deal with Chris and Kit, the Who's wide-boy managers who were starting their own label, Track. Paid brown-bag dosh to Harvey the chart rigger – the one all the big boys like Don Arden used – to get 'Hey Joe' into the right chart-return shops, so that it showed in the Top 30 that Christmas, encouraging all the other shops to order it in, enough to persuade radio to play it and get the telly interested. Jimi shimmying on *Top of the Pops* had done the rest.

Same with the next single, 'Purple Haze', only even better. Jimi, forced to come up with his own thing, overcompensating on the guitar, using a Fuzz Face distortion pedal, threading guitar parts through a mental new invention called the Octavia, bring-ing pages of lyrics to the session, stuff he'd written out of his head in the upstairs dressing room of the Upper Cut club on Boxing Day. Chas forcing him to rein it in, taking the lyrics from him and crossing everything but three verses out, telling Mitch and Noel, 'Keep it fuckin' steady, lads!', allowing Jimi to have his big Octavia freak-out on the outro, in the wake of his growled psychic warning: '*Is it tomorrow – or just the end of time?*'

When the single reached number 3 Chas felt vindicated. Chas was hip to what Jimi wanted. But the Animals had recorded 'The House of the Rising Sun' three years before in just two takes – one run-through, one as-live recording – in under fifteen minutes at a studio cost of less than a tenner. He didn't see why Jimi's recording sessions should be much different.

Jimi happy to go along with this, seeing his records go into the charts, selling thousands of copies a day. Jimi on TV, filling clubs, giving magazine interviews, doing photo sessions, getting on the guest list at all the clubs, not paying for anything anywhere he went, digging his new life with his groovy new white English chick and his cool new white English manager and his far-out white group.

But this was just the *surface world*, you dig? Jimi had been thinking about the world of the purple haze for a long time before anybody gave a shit about him. Jimi long ago head-tripping on Frank Waters's *Book of the Hopi*: long nights in cold temporary beds reading about the four worlds of the Hopi Indians, the time of the dark purple, before man. Jimi singing of kissing the sky, journeying to the end of time, referencing his obsession with science-fiction oracles like Robert A. Heinlein, whose latest, *The Moon Is a Harsh Mistress*, Jimi bought copies of for all his new friends.

Similarly, the next Jimi Hendrix Experience hit, 'The Wind Cries Mary', in May '67. Eager music-press hacks lapped up the story of it being about a fight Jimi had with Kathy, after which he ended up walking the London streets all night. Mary was Kathy's middle name, like, wow, right?

But Jimi had been working on those words a long time. The melody went all the way back to Jimmy James and the Blue Flames, the lisping high vocal borrowed from Curtis Mayfield, the lilting cry-baby guitar taken from Brother Bobby Womack. The lyrics: pure pre-motorcycle crash Dylan. '*After all the jacks are in their boxes / And the clowns have all gone to bed . . .*'

Jimi fought Chas hard in the studio on this one. Forcing the band to do take after take, looking to build, to embellish, to display. Before a worn-out Chas simply took him back to take one – and they wearily agreed to use that. Chas's faith in simplicity borne out again when the single became Jimi's third Top 10 hit in a row.

The real proof of validity, of artistic standing and, most crucially for both Jimi and Chas (and Mike and the rest of the group), commercially viable critical success, would be when the first Hendrix LP, *Are You Experienced*, was released, just a week after 'The Wind Cries Mary'.

Sales of singles were still larger in Britain and America than those of long-playing records, but the past twelve months had seen the rise of the critically anointed 'album-oriented' artists, led by the Beatles and Dylan, now rapidly expanded by the arrival of new avant-rock groups like the Doors, Jefferson Airplane and the Mothers of Invention, and the overlapping catch-up of previously considered inconsequential pop acts like the Beach Boys and even the Monkees, whose third album, *Headquarters*, also released that month, was their first with substantial songwriting and instrumental performances by members of the group itself, and – very far out – it didn't include a hit single.

Sessions for Jimi's debut album had been sporadic, in-out affairs: three different studios around town, in three-hour jolts between tour dates and promotional work and whenever. Chas led the way. Costs kept to a minimum. Focus entirely on Jimi. Mitch and Noel to do what they were told. Mitch especially good at this, his high-flying, ultra-smart percussion working thrillingly in tandem with Jimi's extravagant, different-every-take guitar rocket rides; Noel begrudging, disgruntled, still somehow deluded that the Experience was a real three-way-decision group. But keeping up, staying true. Not so easily ignored.

Chas worked them fast. 'Mary' had taken less than twenty minutes. Tracks like 'Fire', 'Can You See Me' and 'I Don't Live Today' a little longer, but no messin'. Everything live. Mitch and

Noel often hearing stuff for the first time in the studio before they did a take.

You could feel the crackle and burn as opening track 'Foxey Lady' came quivering on a wave of distortion out of the mono speaker. Here in one hot blast was Jimi in his absolute youthful essence. Feedback, distortion, bent notes, dirty sex (the only good sex there is), tail-swishing funk corporeal, night-ravaged rock elemental, Jimi bearing down on his target like a snake with its tongue out, sizzling.

There was a lot of knowing conversation over which foxy lady Jimi was actually singing about – it already being understood that everything that came out of Jimi's mouth came straight from his real-life head, his unmade bed. Some assumed it must be Kathy. Others from further back said it had to be about Fayne. Others, more knowing still, identified the fox as Heather Taylor, teenage dancer, model, born in Hammersmith but raised on the same New York dusk-till-dawn rock scene as her girlfriend Linda Eastman, in the days when the girls were gooood friends of the Stones. Jimi and Heather had maybe had scene not long before he left for London. It didn't matter. They were all foxy ladies to Jimi now.

The rest of the album was schizo Jimi. Monumental highs like 'Manic Depression', hypnotically up-tempo, Noel's bass star-tracing Jimi's guitar – for once beam for beam – Mitch drawing heavily on his Ronnie Stephenson obsession – in this case Johnny Dankworth's jazz-pop hit 'African Waltz'.

Jimi just liking the way the words rolled off his tongue – '*MAN-ick deeee-pression!*' like some space-age-sounding brain-thief deal gone sideways – rather than having anything to say about vicious mood swings or suicidal duck downs – heavy-metal teen fiction with extra groove.

Purple waterfall – 'May This Be Love', Mitch excelling himself, pitter-patter against the window, Jimi singing so sweet, canoodling, his Hawaiian guitar and rainbow melody like gentle rain, a goddess's oyster tears.

Straight psychedelic blues – 'Red House', Jim's acid reworking of 'California Night', one of his showcase crowd pleasers from the Curtis Knight days, itself thieved from Albert King's 1961 'Travellin' to California', old dark town lament, nobody loves me now I'm down and out, we all bin there, sugar.

None of the three hit singles were included, though they were later added for the US version released in August, post-Monterey. Instead, the original UK version put up with tracks like 'Can You See Me', 'Remember' and 'Love or Confusion', classic album-fillers. Striking at the time because of the polychromatic sound, the swashbuckling execution bathed in off-planet side effects. Overworked throwaway like 'I Don't Live Today', supposedly Jimi's personal dedication to the American Indians, referencing his Cherokee bloodlines. The dancing round the totem-pole riff cuts and bites, wreathed again in the dense smoke of feedback, distortion and other dope-filled studio tricks, but the words, man, all grim downer shit . . . 'I wish you'd hurry up and execute me / So I can be on my miserable way . . .'

The title track somewhere in between, all studio sleight of hand, new for its time, now stuck in its time; Jimi stoned immaculate, on a Dylan put-down trip, telling someone how it is, lording it, blowing know-better clouds in their eyes, clever minstrel clown from tomorrow. Far out then, not nearly convincing enough now.

Best of all, 'Third Stone from the Sun' – psychedelic jazz fortified with spoken-word sidebars, sonic messages from other worlds communicating at last, from the hipster shithouses of Harlem to the rogue rings of Saturn's ancient carnival.

Third stone, third rock, third planet, now spinning out of control; Jimi to Earth, come in, are you receiving me? Another one Jimi had been tooling around with back at the Cafe Wha? No place for it then, too introspective and spaced out. But Chas had got a buzz off it. Chas, whose sharp mind he liked to wrap around intelligent sci-fi too, both men surprisingly bonding over Philip José Farmer's World of Tiers series.

When Chas lent Jimi the George R. Stewart no-hope dystopian classic *Earth Abides*, it blew his mind, truly.

'That's where "Third Stone from the Sun" came from,' said Chas.

The interplanetary guitar solo, though, came straight from the cratered moon valleys of Jimi's own mind. Apocalyptic sound effects, horror-show screams and sirens, the band channelling an end-of-days auto-destruct stream of consciousness.

Jimi and Chas trying to outdo each other with their stoned, spatially distorted dialogue, slowed to half-speed.

Jimi: 'Star fleet to scout ship. Please give your position. Over.'

Chas: 'I am in orbit around the third planet of star called the Sun. Over.'

Jimi: 'You mean it's the Earth? Over.'

Chas: 'Positive. It is known to have some form of intelligent species. Over.'

Jimi: 'I think we should take a look.'

Later, Jimi cracking up, trying to explain it to someone with a tape recorder, taking notes, like everything is everything.

'These guys come from another planet, you know . . . they observe Earth for a while and they think the smartest animals on the whole Earth are chickens [and] there's nothing else there, so they just blow it up at the end.'

In the summer of 1967 this is the sort of shit that gets you noticed in the pop world. This is the sort of thing considered advanced, experimental, daring and – in this case – actually danceable. It is also, of course, exceptionally good to get stoned to, as it would remain.

Released on 12 May, *Are You Experienced* became the first LP of the summer everyone was expected to own or at least know.

It would get to number 2 in the chart, only kept from number 1 when, two weeks later, the Beatles released their even more advanced, experimental and daring new LP, *Sgt. Pepper's Lonely Hearts Club Band.*

But Jimi beats everyone for ultimate cool when, nine days after that, he plays the Saville Theatre and opens his show fucking unbelievably with a blazing version of the track 'Sgt. Pepper's Lonely Hearts Club Band'. Sitting in the audience, the Beatles. Paul, who wrote the song, who owns the theatre, who has his own plans for daring experimental advancement, sits there grinning, a look of devilish delight on his face.

Fuck the future.

CHAPTER THIRTEEN

Jimmy and Billy

Jimmy could play that one-stringed thing from the moment he rescued it from the dirt.

Jimmy sitting by the radio, digging Chuck Berry, digging Little Richard, imitating the lead line on that thin one-string, tightening it for high, loosening it for low. What he couldn't play he would make the sounds with his mouth.

Jimmy showing Leon later on, the boys laughing as Jimmy sits there showing off.

One string.

Playing it. Making sense of it. No chords, no nothing. Just his ears and his brain, twanging away to Mickey and Sylvia's 'Love Is Strange', Jimmy somehow managing to make that one-string beat-up wood sound almost as good as Mickey and Sylvia with their duelling guitars.

Leon like, 'Show Dad! Show Dad!'

Jimmy forcing Al to pay attention long enough to show him what he could do, Al frowning at the boy for playing it left-handed. The left-hand path was the road to hell, according to Al. Threatening Jimmy with a smack upside the head if he ever caught him doing it again. Jimmy smiling nervously, flipping the guitar upside down and carrying on, just as good.

'He played upside down, backwards, he was like a dyslexic genius,' said Leon.

The old axe belonged to the rooming-house landlady, who told Jimmy he could keep the thing for five dollars.

Five dollars? Shiiit . . .

Jimmy knowing he had no shot begging his father to buy him the guitar. 'Please, Daddy, I'll do anything, please, Daddy, please Daddy, I promise I'll be good, please, Daddy, please, Daddy, plea—'

Al standing firm. He don't got no money for no damn piece of shit geetar with but one string. Get the fuck outta here, boy!

Jimmy at the movies, seeing *Johnny Guitar*. Sterling Hayden as the gunslinger seducing Joan Crawford's sultry Vienna with his baad-ass Spanish guitar. Now this is who Jimmy wants to be. Cat in a hat holding a guitar, chicks falling over him . . .

Finally, Ernestine Benson took pity and gave Jimmy the five bucks to buy the guitar. He started wearing it across his back like Johnny Guitar, taking it to school for show and tell.

When Elvis came to Sick's Stadium in Seattle, Jimmy couldn't afford the buck-fifty ticket but looked on from a nearby hill. Elvis in a gold lamé suit, punching an acoustic guitar, girls going absolutely fucking craaazy!

A year later Little Richard hit town – not singing, but preaching. Jimmy and Leon sneaked into the church to see him. Could not take their eyes off him. Hung around after putting up with all the Bible fire and brimstone just to be near this guy who was *famous*. Imagine that, brother!

Things started to pick up speed. Jimmy finally got another five strings and really began to play seriously, still taking a beating anytime Al caught him playing left-handed, getting used to just flipping the thing over and playing it right-handed.

Lucille reappeared here and there, those nights she and Al would find each other in the same downtown barrelhouse. Stay a night or two then split again. Jimmy couldn't wait to show his mama how he could play that guitar. Mama delighting in his joy, getting up and dancing round the dusty little room in her bar-room finery. The boy's eyes shining like black diamonds.

Lucille now had the hellhound of her trial. Maybe he'd always been there. Bad blood and worse luck a heavy load to bear. She was thirty-one when the docs diagnosed cirrhosis of the liver. Admitted to Harborview hospital twice in 1957, Lucille was told she had to quit drinking immediately or else. She would be back on the bottle the day she was released.

Lucille had a new boyfriend and drinking partner in her life now, a retired longshoreman in his sixties named William Mitchell. They married first week of January 1958. Two weeks later she was rushed back into Harborview. Diagnosed this time with Hep C, she was given a month at best, even if she stopped drinking.

Al didn't want to know, let her new husband deal with it, but Delores took Jimmy and Leon to see their mother. Jaundiced and slumped in a wheelchair, Lucille was a harrowing figure for her boys to see. Holding them and kissing them while crying hysterically, she told Delores, 'I'm not gonna make it.'

Two weeks later she was dead. Found unconscious in an alley next to one of her regular haunts, she was taken to the emergency room at Harborview where she lay among the shooting and stabbing victims. She died that night from internal bleeding. An addict's death.

Al put his angry foot down and refused to let the boys go to the funeral. Made them sit down with him and drink whisky. Telling them that's how real men handled death. Jimmy and Leon crying pitifully into their glasses. Jimmy never got over it, vowed to get the hell away from the old man as soon as. Sooner. Fuck Seattle too.

It all went to shit after that. Jimmy not even trying anymore, except for the damned guitar, which he kept in bed with him, snuggling it like a teddy bear. Skipping school, stealing, running around all night. Met a girl, Carmen Goudy, poor as he but with two parents, and that worked out okay for a while – then back to po' boy square one.

Desperate for an electric guitar, he turned to Ernestine Benson for help. It was Ernestine who finally persuaded Al to do right by the boy, buying him a right-handed Supro Ozark on a payment plan from Myers Music in town. White with a black pinstripe and a big lap-steel pick-up, designed for bottleneck boogie and heart-shaped blues. Jimmy flipped it upside down, restrung it and decided he musta died and joined his mama in heaven.

Carmen's eyes nearly popped out of her head when Jimmy showed her. She would be his first fan, she said delightedly.

They began calling him the human jukebox. Duane Eddy was his ideal, flashing it up on 'Forty Miles of Bad Road', but Jimmy could turn his hand to anybody. Different songs every day – he'd hear it, think, then play it.

Kept behind a year at school cos of his shitty grades, Jimmy began looking for a band – any band. Auditioned for one but got told to split because he was too flash. *Too* flash? No such thing in Jimmy's mind.

Carmen got tired of Jimmy giving all his love to his guitar and not her, and faded into the background, dating older guys who had money and cars. Jimmy finally found a gig with a group of high-school dudes called the Velvetones. Doing covers at dances.

Al turned against the whole thing and Jimmy took to hiding his guitar at other people's places, scared his father would take it and destroy it. Then the guitar got stolen from a gig and Jimmy nearly died for real after Al got his hands on him that night.

He began something with a new girlfriend, Betty Jean Morgan, a pretty country girl from the South. He got a job as a newspaper delivery boy and Al would give him a dollar for mowing lawns. At seventeen Jimmy was still a virgin. Other kids he knew, younger than him, had already fathered children.

He joined the Rocking Kings, who pitched in when he lost his guitar to buy him a new one: a fifty-bucks Danelectro Silvertone. Jimi painted it red with 'Betty Jean' in big letters down the front. School was out permanently in Jimmy's mind, but he still had to put on a show for Al.

He began hanging out at the Spanish Castle, after the Rocking Kings opened for someone else there one time. The Castle was the hippest live-music venue in town. The crowd was mostly white. A coloured boy playing rocking guitar was a novelty. Jimmy was allowed to hang around, but his old, worn clothes and lack of any money to spend meant he was always hustled out the door sooner rather than later.

He was eighteen when he asked Betty Jean to marry him. She laughed. Her folks liked Jimmy but there was no way in hell they were letting their daughter, then still at school, marry a raggedy-ass cheese-eating nigger like Jimmy. He blew any chance he had when he and three buddies were arrested for riding in a stolen car. He spent the day in jail but got away pleading to the white cops that he didn't know the car was stolen, had only been sitting in it as it was parked.

Okaaay. But don't ever let us see your black ass in here again, *boy*.

Three days later he was arrested again – for riding around with the same buddies in a stolen car. He spent the next week and a day in juvie then went home to await trial. Al was told the boy was looking at five years.

A public defender was appointed: a half-hearted plea bargain offered. A two-year sentence, suspended on condition that the boy went into the services. Jimmy was told straight: jail or the military, what's it to be, *boy*?

Early the next morning Jimmy signed up for three years in the US Army's 101st Airborne Division. Jimmy had always liked the badge with the screaming eagle. Jimmy would be sent on the night train down to Fort Ord in California to train as a parachutist.

Jimmy had never even flown on an aeroplane. Never even left Seattle since he was an ankle-biter.

The train was leaving the station and Jimmy was shitting his pants.

Three months later he completed basic training and was given the rank and uniform of a private. Writing home every other day to his father, he asked for money, shoe polish, food – now signing his letters 'James'. He wrote to Betty Jean every day too, asking her to be his army bride.

Most of all he begged Al to send him his guitar, which Betty Jean was looking after. The guitar arrived and so did his assignment: supply clerk with the 101st Airborne Division in Fort Campbell, Kentucky. He also got to do his first training jumps. He hated every minute on the plane, being shoved out the open door. Then felt his blood shoot sky-high as he touched down. His head whooshing – it felt goood.

He was now private first class, told to prepare mentally for a stint in some South Asian conflict, or maybe Cuba, gunning for Castro, or maybe someplace close to Russia, fuck up some other Commies.

Jimmy consoled himself by practising on his guitar alone, usually in a corner of Fort Campbell's Service Club No. 1. It was here that he met another young black recruit who played guitar – Billy Cox.

Billy came from Wheeling, on the humid banks of the Ohio River, a town still suffering from the hangover of the Great Depression, and grew up in Pittsburgh. A young black boy in a big city where the population was over 90 per cent white, Billy learned quickly how to get along.

A year older than Jimmy, he was also feeling lost as a grunt in the 101st Airborne, playing his bass guitar to help him forget his lowdown blues. Hearing the sounds of a guitar being picked at one day, Billy invited himself to sit down. Like two flies meeting at the sugar bowl, neither boy could believe the luck in finding someone else who could play guitar. When Billy said he played bass, Jimmy nearly fell over with joy. Together they would jam on a couple of titchy amps, volume turned low, making up riffs and melodic doodles, the hours suddenly zooming, where before they'd dragged like an interrogation.

'We'd try and come up with the best riffs,' Billy would tell this author. 'He'd come up with something really great, then I'd top him with something I came up with, then he'd top me with something else.' Jimmy would get Billy to help him return to and figure out anew a lot of this stuff just a few years later, on another planet where they would meet.

Checking what was going on, other guys in the barracks started asking to join in. A couple of nights they got up and put on a little show for the guys in Service Clubs 1 and 2. Jimmy and Billy and three other bored uniforms. Then an outside gig was arranged at the – don't you fucking laugh! – Pink Poodle Club. It was hit and miss but big fun. Jimmy telling Billy about the groups he'd played in back home, the two of them deciding to take it the next step and form a legit band of their own, the King Kasuals: Jimmy and Billy and another private from Toledo on drums, Gary Ferguson. Occasionally a Major Charles Washington joined them on sax.

Suddenly the King Kasuals were a real thing, the line-up expanding to six, sometimes seven, including Jimmy. Doing regular spots at the Club Del Morocco in Nashville – a 200-mile drive away. Jimmy skipping duty to make the shows – sacking out on the job – hellfire officers constantly on his ass about it.

The Morocco was where it was at, though. Playing backup to a lot of very cool cats like Nappy Brown, Carla Thomas, Ironing Board Sam, School Boy. With Billy coming to the end of his three years, Jimmy was now scheming to get out of the army too: lying in his bunk smoking, thinking deep about it. The army 'wouldn't let me have anything to do with music', he would recall. That meant the army had to go.

Sleeping with the guitar in his bed, shunning the company of the gung-ho grunts who couldn't wait to get out there and start killing people, Jimmy seen as a loner. Crazy-ass nigger, rather cradle that damn guitar than shoot a weapon.

Jimmy came up with an escape plan. Thought about going AWOL, just splitting when Billy left, change his name – this was America, man, names didn't mean shit. Become a travelling guitar man, gun for hire, different towns every day. Then realised he was dreaming. The army would eventually find him, stick him behind a bars for a long, long time.

No, fuck that. He needed a better plan, something fool-proof.

He'd looked into it, discovered the army would throw you out if you were queer. They'd have to before one of the other guys put a bullet in you. The army didn't tolerate fags. Jimmy thought about it some more. He had two more years of the army ahead of him. He knew he'd never make it. That he'd eventually make a run for it. Wind up being fucked in the ass in jail. Might as well be queer . . .

He reported to the base hospital, said he needed to see the psychiatrist – it was an emergency. Then put on his act. Said he'd been having wet dreams about his bunkmates. Feared he was turning queer. The doc looked at him with distaste, reminded him that it was against federal law to be a fairy and told him to go get some rest.

Frustrated, Jimmy saw he'd have to up the stakes. Kept going back, week after week, demanding to see the army shrink, said he couldn't stop jerking off, thinking of his bunkmates. The doc looking at him funny, knowing a con when he saw one, sending him away again. Get some rest, soldier.

In for a penny, Jimmy allowed himself to get caught with his pecker in his hand, standing over one of the bunks. Reported back to the head doctor, he told him it was cos he was now in love with one of his squad mates. Said he couldn't eat, sleep, wakes up shouting and yelling with the night sweats. Pissing the bed, out of his mind in lust for this boy in the next bunk. Doc, you gotta help me, pleeease!

Six weeks solid of this shit before the squad captain ordered a complete medical. Aside from his past stutter, Jimmy had been passed with a clean bill of health when he'd had his entrance physical a year before. Filling in the same forms now he ticked everything from chest pains to insomnia, homosexuality, mastur-bation, dizziness, depression . . . Boy was fucked up!

The army finally caved and Jimmy was officially discharged from the 101st Airborne in May 1962 because of 'homosexual tendencies'. It said so right there on his medical records. Not that he ever *told* anybody that, not even Billy. He said it was cos he'd broken his ankle so bad on one of the airplane jumps. That he'd really done his back: ooh, stop, doc, that hurts. A couple of weeks later he was doing a Kasuals gig, a bandage tied conspicuously round his ankle. Didn't stop him a-moving and a-grooving, though, big smile on his face. Jimmy was out to stay.

With Billy back on the street three months later, he joined Jimmy in the one-room apartment in Clarksdale Jimmy shared with his new girlfriend, Joyce. Betty Jean had mailed back the engagement ring he'd given her months before, when Jimmy made it clear he wasn't coming back to Seattle. Jimmy pawned the ring – along with the Betty Jean guitar – and never seriously considered marrying again, though there would be many women to whom he swore he would love for ever and a day.

Jimmy spent the next few years living some kind of dream. At first it was him and Billy all the way, taking the Kasuals back to the Morocco and anywhere else they could talk their way into, driving around in a broken-down '55 Plymouth with no reverse gear.

Jimmy learned quick that sleeping with the girls he met at gigs provided a sweeter means of getting by than renting some shithole dive with Billy. Joyce was followed by Florence followed by Verdell followed Cynthia, Debra, Lisa, Sheena, Marie . . .

But practising on his new guitar, a cherry-red Epiphone Wilshire, every hour, every day he wasn't fucking or working with the Kasuals. Juke joints, barrelhouses, pool halls, ten-dollar brothels, backhouse gambling dens, roadhouse taverns. Arkansas, Kentucky, Indiana, Tennessee . . . Jimmy in white shirt, black pencil tie, hair done up like Little Richard, ooh-wee, baby!

Joining – for two minutes – Bob Fisher and the Barnesvilles, trading licks with their other guitarist Larry Lee, a good guy Jimmy wouldn't forget. Playing backup with Larry to the Marvelettes. Bunch of foxy black chicks from Michigan, dig, with the big number 1 'Please Mr Postman'. Jimmy offering to be their backdoor mailman, every day hypnotised watching Curtis Mayfield – whom they opened for – make his magic guitar sing.

Jimmy getting noticed. The boy was flash – too damn flash for his own good. But he was good at picking up one-nighters and short-stop tours playing in backup groups for Marion James, Slim Harpo, Carla Thomas, Solomon Burke, even Otis Redding for a week. Chitlin circuit gigs, cash in the claw, no stoopid questions. Riding around the Deep South, learning about life under Jim Crow law: can't eat here, can't piss there, watch your back po' boy, one wrong look at a white woman that's one less nigger on the bus.

Soon the Jimmy gigs outweighed the Kasuals gigs, and Jimmy gradually left Billy and the boys behind. Telling Billy he'd come back for him one day. Sure, Jimmy.

These were hard roads to travel. Bad luck always to be counted on. Getting used to being fired for being too flash, fired for breaking Curtis Mayfield's amp, fired for outshining Bobby Womack

– Bobby's hothead brother throwing Jimmy's guitar out the bus window.

Offered a gig in New York, taking the midnight Greyhound out of Nashville, overnight to who the fuck knew what, checking into the bare-bulb room at the dump on 125th Street, told the next day, what gig, pretty little coloured boy? Who the fuck is you?

It was 1964. The Beatles were on Ed Sullivan, JFK dead at the hands of a lone-wolf Commie assassin, Harlem like some place Jimmy had never even imagined. Stick or twist time.

Then – luck! A gig with the Isley Brothers, hot with their hit 'Twist and Shout'. Hitting the big time at last! Touring all over the East Coast, back down through the Deep South, even over to Bermuda, baby! Pink sand, blue sea, to-die-for black-mama girls! Then back to New York for some *recording dates*. Jimmy with only four strings left on his guitar, the boys chipping in to buy him two more.

Jimmy writing home, the big star, boasting of $100 a week pay cheques and running around in a Caddy – Jimmy adding *just a little* extra cheese to the burger.

Only snag – the white mohair suits the backing band *all* had to wear. The same shiny patent-leather shoes. The same slicked-back hair. 'If our shoelaces were two different types,' Jimmy complained, 'we'd get fined five dollars. Oh, man, do I get tired of that!'

When the Isleys hit Nashville, Jimmy quit. Not to come home, dig – to sign up for a tour with Gorgeous George Odell, the most famous wrestler in America. But only as far as Atlanta, where Jimmy tour-hopped into Little Richard's back-up group, the Up-setters. Richard treated the new kid like his personal valet, only letting him onstage on condition he stay strictly background. No tricks, geddit, kid? But Jimmy couldn't help himself, playing with his teeth, 'forgetting' to put the right shirt on, fucking with his hair, and Richard rained blood and thunder on him, kicking him out of the band – and don't come back, nigger!

Jimmy shrugged. 'I wanted my own scene, making my music, not playing the same riffs. Like once with Little Richard, me and another guy got fancy shirts cos we were tired of wearing the same uniform. Richard called a meeting. "I am Little Richard, I am Little Richard!" he said. "The King, the King of Rock and Rhythm. I am the only one allowed to be pretty! Take off those shirts!" Man, it was all like that. Bad pay, lousy living and getting burned.'

Met a lot of groovy cats, though. Albert Collins, who eventually took over from Jimmy in Richard's band; B.B. King, with whom Richard shared a bill one time, very cool to the thin, young black guitarist, offering kind words; Arthur Lee, rangy young black cat outta LA, fronting his interracial band Love. *Interracial?* Yeah, baby. Looking for a guitarist to play on a song Arthur had written for Rosa Lee Brooks. Some cat who could give him that low-flame Curtis Mayfield vibe. Jimmy stepped up and connected with Arthur in the studio on two truly transcendent soul tracks for Rosa, 'My Diary' and 'Utee'. Jimmy and Rosa enjoying a little love-in on the side.

While he was in LA, Jimmy also picked up some easy money, back playing a couple of shows with Little Richard and recording a sweetheart soul tune called 'I Don't Know What You've Got but It's Got Me', gifting Richard his first R&B chart hit for seven years.

Still following the quick money, Jimmy accepted a gig with the Ike and Tina Turner Review. Did a handful of shows, hated fucking Ike, who hated him right back, and left to join the Drifters. More uniforms, more shut-your-mouth-and-play, but some nice dollars. Then back to Richard, fired for the final time after missing the tour bus after a show in Washington, D.C.

Picking up tricks everywhere he went. The importance of

putting on a *show*, playing with your teeth, playing behind your back, shimmy and stroll. Just like big old T-Bone Walker did it. Just like baad-man Albert King. Fuck the white man's head up; put fire in the black man's soul. And all you pretty wimmin . . . I *know* what you like.

Jimmy's biggest break wasn't anything to do with music. Not really. It came when he met his first real Harlem girlfriend, a star-popping nineteen-year-old beauty named Lithofayne Pridgon – Fayne to her many, many friends. Or 'Apollo Fayne' as she became known to the musicians on the scene, down to the fact that Fayne was so often backstage with one of them.

Fayne had been one of James Brown's favourite Harlem friends, was only sixteen when she became Sam Cooke's New York girlfriend. Was always there when Jackie Wilson was in town. Fayne was a whole scene unto herself. She 'had lots of cop friends, lots of hustler friends, lots of music friends', she'd smile and say.

Fayne wasn't like those other New York girls, though. Born in the Dirty Spoon neighbourhood of Moultrie, south-west Georgia, she'd grown up in 'a full square mile of poor people. Not just blacks, but poor.' The women in Dirty Spoon 'drank moonshine and partied. And most of them didn't have husbands. All the loose ladies were in Dirty Spoon.'

She was fifteen when she met her first famous musician, Little Willie John, who'd just had a hit with 'All Around the World'. It was Little Willie who took her with him to Harlem, where he introduced her to Sam Cooke. Big mistake. Now Fayne was Sam's gal. Her mama even came up from Georgia to take up with Sam's brother.

It was party time for the Pridgon ladies of Harlem. By the time she met Jimmy, Fayne had been on the scene long enough to be one of 'Fat Jack' Taylor's favourite girls. Jack was Harlem's dope kingpin, laundering his dough through an R&B record label, various restaurants and apartment buildings. All kinds of legit shit.

'Everybody was young and energetic,' Fayne would say. 'And so if you saw somebody you liked you kinda just hooked up with them.' As long as it was in a hotel suite or an apartment run by Fat Jack, joints he called his 'sets'. Fayne and what she called her 'young tenders' would party all night and the next day, sometimes for two or three days at a time. Fat Jack the one who 'always provided the finances, the drugs or whatever was necessary'.

Fayne would joke and say she met Jimmy at one of Fat Jack's orgies, which sounded like something Fayne would say just to catch the look on your face, but which Jimmy, though he'd had plenty of orgies by now, would *never* have said out loud, being such a quietly spoken young gentleman and all.

However, they hooked up, the two soon moved in together at the Hotel Seifer, one of those low-rent Harlem joints no holiday-maker or tourist would ever be safe in. But which the locals could call home. Or home from home, as in home to get the fuck away from home.

Jimmy and Fayne lived there, or at her mother's, together and apart, for the next year or so. It was hard to tell, they had so many fights and break-ups.

Jimmy loved Fayne, was devoted to her, looked up to her and craved her approval.

Fayne loved Jimmy, in her own way. But she wasn't about to tie herself down. She let Jimmy know that right away. Jimmy becoming frantic sometimes when they were apart, writing her long letters even as he was having one-night stands with two, three, four women a night out on the road.

'As I write more and more, I feel myself grow so very weak under the power of you,' he wrote in one.

In another, insecure about what Fayne's other male friends

were saying about him. 'Don't listen to the niggers in the street,' he begged her, a futile request.

Another letter, another time, after another fight when he refused to take her out: 'You know how I hate to go out when my hair doesn't look right.'

Jimmy might have been dressed in thrift-store rags, but he felt he had beautiful hair. Getting Fayne to put curlers in his hair before going to bed at night. Getting Fayne to *pay attention*.

Fayne looking at him like, hush now, honey. 'Stop talking crazy.'

CHAPTER FOURTEEN

Mike and London

The trick was to keep moving. Not get left behind. Mike had learned that in the army. Made the most of it in the secrets game. And had applied it with a passion to his career as a club owner in Newcastle. Now, at the start of 1964, he was in a hurry to get in on the action again. There were fantastic deals to be made everywhere in the pop game now, it seemed. In London, the Irishman Ronan O'Rahilly was getting ready to launch his own pop music radio station Caroline – without a licence, from an actual pirate boat in the sea. Bloody genius! The Beatles were number 1 with 'Can't Buy Me Love', though Mike knew damn well you could. Even the BBC were somehow riding the coming wave, launching a new TV station – BBC2 – that you could only get with one of the new 625-line tellies. Mike had two installed at home and one at each of his clubs. There was never anything on them, but he knew image was everything and that the gormless gits who worked for him would be impressed.

Mike was now shagging it back and forth to London every week. He'd palled up with O'Rahilly and some of the other music-biz wide boys running the scene, like Giorgio Gomelsky and Don Arden, seeing them for what they really were – chancers, but with brains. Gomelsky's family came from Georgia; Arden's people were Russian and Polish Jews. These weren't street hoods working off backhanders. They were building empires. Mike saw a lot of himself in them. Except they had a head start when it came to making money out of pop groups.

Don Arden already had Gene Vincent and Little Richard, and was now moving with the times, picking up little combos like the Nashville Teens. He'd also invested in a talented boyo from Aldershot who'd spent the past few years having eleven straight number 1 hits in South Africa – cheeky chappy with the showbiz name of Mickie Most. Don had tried launching the boy in the UK, but no dice. Mickie had skills, though, and Don had taken a chance and got him to produce a record for the Teens – a tiny-tears white-bread cover of 'Tobacco Road'. Well, fuck my old boots, said Don, popping open the champagne at his regular table at Annabel's, when the record went Top 10 and he was suddenly able to book the group all over the country for top dollar.

Like Don, Giorgio Gomelsky had been around for ever already. He knew how to hustle; he'd been doing it all his life. The difference was that Giorgio's mother was from Monte Carlo and sent her son to be privately educated in Switzerland. He'd hit London in time for the skiffle fad of the fifties before he hopped aboard the jazz fling and then the early sixties blues obsession. He opened a club, the Marquee Blues Club, fell in with the same crowd of jazz and blues hipsters that belonged to the Ealing set, opened the doors on another weekend venue, this time in Richmond, which he dubbed the Crawdaddy. The Stones played there and made the place cool *and* famous.

Now he was a big chum with Ronan, and together they were happy to have the Alan Price Set tootle back and forth from Newcastle to London in their little Commer van as often as Mike could arrange it. As far as they were concerned it was implicit in the arrangement that they would also now own a piece of the group's contract with Mike.

The same age as Mike, and thinking about all the same things, Giorgio was also involved with his own group of bad haircuts, called the Yardbirds. The first thing Mike realised when he began talking to Ronan and Giorgio about plugging the Alan Price Set into the London club circuit was that he needed a better, more 'with it' name for the group. Over a drink one night Graham Bond suggested Mike change their name to the Animals. There was no way of telling if Graham – a big, brooding man whose mind was already on the way to being blown apart by drugs – was joking or not. Mike thought about it on a long drive back to Newcastle one night – and decided that, actually, it was a great idea. By the time he phoned Eric and Alan it was now Mike's idea – and the boys were happy to go along with it, once Mike had explained how many new bookings he would be able to get them in the smoke off the back of it.

With the boys in the group now singing the praises of their new London 'managers' Ronan and Giorgio, Mike got the hump and made a bold move. He signed a booking-agency agreement with Don Arden – which Don took as a de facto management contract in his favour, as was his way with these things. Ronan shrugged, took it all in his stride. Mike Jeffery and his tuppenny-ha'penny group would be back. Giorgio looked on; if Mike wanted to get his tits ripped off by that old gangster Arden that was his lookout.

Full of the joys of getting one over on his rivals, always a good day in Don's book, he introduced Mike to Mickie Most, whom Don said was the man to make the first Animals record with. He was. He was also the man who suggested to Mike on the q.t. that the smartest way to land the Animals a deal was by recording them first and then selling the distribution rights to a record label. That is, for Mike to pay for the recording himself then have Mickie shop it around. No need to drag Don into it. Don was an old-school show-runner. What did he know about modern record deals?

Mike didn't need to be told twice. He could smell Mickie's intention a mile off. So Mike coughed up for an Animals recording session in London, produced by Mickie at De Lane Lea Studios near the Strand. In just a couple of hours they had two tracks – plausible A- and B-sides of a single, strutting R&B covers of 'Baby Let Me Take You Home' and 'Gonna Send You Back to Walker', both highlights of their live sets.

Good as his word, Mickie took the acetates to his pals at EMI and got a deal that same afternoon for the record to be released on their Columbia label. Mike was happy about the deal, on a standard royalty of 6 per cent, of which he and Mickie took 2 per cent each, with the five members of the group sharing the other 2 per cent – after Mike had recouped his outgoings and taken his management commission off the top first, of course. Which was only fair, lads, right, as Mike was the one who put the thing together, the one who'd ponied up the dough and took all the risk. Right, lads? Right, Mike!

Released in March 1964, 'Baby Let Me Take You Home' was only a modest hit, skittering to number 21 in the UK charts. Not enough to draw the kraken-like attention of Don Arden, but enough to make Mike and Mickie impatient to have another go. The Animals were on tour, opening for Chuck Berry, after Don 'did the necessary' and bribed them on. They had started doing their own electric version of Bob Dylan's take of the old folk dinosaur 'The House of the Rising Sun', Hilly's brittle guitar chords like static electricity in the air, Eric's mountainous vocal calling down the faithful to prayer.

Recorded in just one take, on the run between tour dates at a small studio in London with Mickie, 'The House of the Rising Sun' became the second Animals single in the summer of 1964, and it went to number 1 in Britain and America – the first British Invasion record to top the American charts that had nothing to do with the Beatles.

Mike bought a mews house in London's Holland Park – millionaire's row – and left Newcastle behind for good. The band soon followed. In November 1964, Mike took the Animals to America for their first tour, launched with a spot on *The Ed Sullivan Show* – the same show that had launched the Beatles into the American stratosphere nine months before. They went straight from JFK Airport to mid-town Manhattan in a motorcade of open-top cars, each showing off a different band member riding alongside a beautiful young model dressed as a cuddly animal.

By then they'd had another Top 10 hit in Britain, this time with a song co-written by Eric and Alan called 'I'm Crying' – which also got into the US Top 20. Two months later, they began 1965 with another huge hit, 'Don't Let Me Be Misunderstood', their white-boy version of a down-and-dirty Nina Simone track from the year before. The B-side was something the grateful group had put together especially for their wonderful manager Mike, about the club where they all met – a track called 'Club A-Go-Go'.

Now they play the blues there every day and every night
Everybody monkeys and they feel alright
Ask my friend, Myer, he'll tell you so
That there ain't no place like the club a-go-go . . .

The 'friend' Myer being Mike's real friend and employee partner, Myer Thomas.

If Mike Jeffery could get any higher at that point, even he couldn't see how.

Two flies in the ointment, though. The first – Don Arden. After helping, from his point of view, bankroll the recording of 'The House of the Rising Sun' and the subsequent US tour, Don was ready to shoot somebody after being informed that Mike and Mickie had outmanoeuvred him when it came to names on contracts. Bits of paper didn't mean shit to the Don when it came to paying his acts royalties. But to be told that those fucking thieving ungrateful bastards had paper to prove that they alone owned the Animals and their recordings, that was crime punishable in Don's eyes by death – or the nearest music-biz equivalent. He made it clear that there would be a brutal reckoning somewhere down the road. They had better watch their fucking backs, upstart little cunts.

Mike affected not to give even the tiniest shit – he had his own heavies working for him. Mickie Most would spend the rest of his life avoiding Don like the plague.

The second more urgent problem Mike suddenly had came from within – when Alan Price upped and left the group without even leaving a note.

Identifying Alan as the most important component in the potential long-term success of the Animals – the one with an abundance of musical talent, the right head on his shoulders and the nous not to blow it – Mike had dealt Price an extra ace from the bottom of the deck in an attempt to keep him onside.

As Eric Burdon later recalled in a 1991 interview: 'We recorded "The House of the Rising Sun" in such a hurry. There was such a rush on it, so we printed it and shipped it immediately. And I remember Mike Jeffery calling a conference. So he comes into the room and he goes, "Fellers, we've only got one problem. We've got to print up this record label really quick. There's not enough room on the label for everybody's name and you all did arrange it, didn't you?" And we all went, "Yeah, yeah, yeah." "So what we'll do is – we'll elect one person and we'll put one name on and then, you know, we'll work it out later, okay?" And we all went, "Okay, who?" "Well now, how about Alan?" "Okay." So Alan Price's name went on there. You know – traditional, arrangement: Alan Price.'

While Mike pulled a fast one on the rest of the group, knowing full well that Alan stood to make a royalty for such a credit, not even he could have predicted that the record would go on to become one of the biggest-selling hits of all time and Alan Price would be the beneficiary of a massive windfall. And that by then he would decide to leave the Animals, taking all the royalties he was now making with him.

Moving quickly to cover his tracks, Mike deflected the fury over Alan's act of escapology by affecting to be as taken by surprise as the rest of the group. A new keyboard player was found and Mike had the group back in the studio making more hits. Then out doing more lengthy tours. Don't worry, boys, we won't make that mistake again!

In fact, Mike was now making the kind of moves that would ensure none of his 'boys' would ever catch him out again. With his own cut from the river of money now pouring through the doors, he added two more nightclubs to his portfolio, on the Spanish island of Mallorca: one that he named Zhivagos (after the Omar Sharif movie *Doctor Zhivago*, which was the glamourous hit of the year), and one in the Bay of Palma he named the Haima at Cala Mayor. He would even invite Eric and the boys from the group out for private vacations when they weren't working, which, of course, was hardly ever. But it was the thought, wasn't it, lads? Right, Mike.

There were always minor aggravations like the court case a pair of wanker property developers – Leslie Elliott and Harvey Lewis – brought against Mike and Mickie, claiming they had financed the Animals after Mike and Mickie had said they were having cash-flow problems and offered to make them directors of a company called Warrior Records. Elliott and Lewis alleged that they had not received their share of the proceeds from 'The House of the Rising Sun'. When the judge found in their favour, Mike and Mickie were up shit creek. But only for a minute. A settlement was reached – for a fraction of what it might have been.

A month later Mike married an actress he'd met, named Gillian French. Mike was thirty-two. Gillian was twenty-one. Gillian's father, Stanley French, had also been in the biz – a theatre manager and sometime BBC talent agent – before he'd snuffed it the year before. Stanley had been a bloody good egg, loaning Mike his Rolls-Royce to swan around in with his daughter. Gillian was having a good year too, landing parts on TV and co-starring in the fantasy-comedy musical *Gonks Go Beat*. It was funny how things worked, because the film also featured Graham Bond, the Nashville Teens and the Graham Bond Organisation's drummer, Ginger Baker – all mates of Mike's. Funny old world, innit?

Good times. Bad times. You had to roll with the punches, as Mike liked to say. There would be one more Animals record produced by Mickie Most – a great song good-old Mickie had found for them through his relationship with the hit-makers at New York's famed Brill Building called 'It's My Life', which was another big transatlantic hit in October 1965. But that was it. Mike let Mickie know that was his lot. It had been great while it lasted, but now it was time for a change. A new direction. One in which Mike would no longer be obliged to give over a percentage to anyone. Not even, as it turned out, the band.

With Mickie out of his hair, Mike set about negotiating a very sweet new deal for the Animals with their UK label Decca, along with a sign-on-the-dotted-line advance of £100,000 – worth around £2 million in today's money. He also told their new US label, MGM, that they'd have to stump up a yummy-in-my-tummy advance. They did, sending Mike a cheque for £90,000 – around a further £1.7 million in the here and now.

Rather than waste all this lolly by passing it onto the group, who would of course only blow it on wine, women and dope, Mike hit upon the brilliant idea of investing the money on the group's behalf. Thoughtful, kind, wise Mike. Always thinking of others – and how to steal from them.

With the personal assistance of John Hillman, a London-based lawyer who specialised in tax, revenue and international law, Mike invested in an offshore company named Yameta. Registered in the Bahamian capital of Nassau, under local law Yameta was able to operate in virtual secrecy. With no legal obligation to even disclose who actually owned the company, it would never even need to offer up the company accounts for government inspection. A list of company directors and the minutes of company meetings were the only paperwork needed, all of which could be kept under lock and key in the Bahamas.

What started out as a simple look into the various tax shelters that Mike knew other groups like the Beatles had exploited, now turned into a dream-come-true scenario in which he could legally ferret away all worldwide earnings made by the Animals – and himself – and nobody need ever be the wiser.

In January 1966, Mike officially bought into Yameta with a cheque for $50,000 – the latest sum he'd received on behalf of the Animals. It definitely felt like the right move – to Mike.

The more he thought about it, the more Mike liked what he discovered. Not only would Yameta receive all earnings on behalf of the Animals, it would also take an administration fee of 10 per cent. Once that and the group's expenses were deducted, the rest would be kept in trust, accruing tax-free interest. Mike formed two other associated companies – Yameta Music and Yameta Publishing.

What only Mike knew outside the band was that Yameta was a subsidiary of something called the Caicos Trust Company – with Mike's new business adviser John Hillman as a director. Caicos owned 90 per cent of the shares issued by Yameta. Later on, Caicos would be renamed the Bank of New Providence Trust Company, with accounts of its own placed with the Nassau branch of the Bank of Nova Scotia and the Chemical Bank Trust in New York. This was getting complicated, even for Mike. But Mike thrived on such details. Thrilled to them, in fact.

Another of Yameta's most prominent directors was Sir Guy Henderson, once the chief justice of the Bahamian Supreme Court, and Ralph Seligman, a distinguished QC. Mike, meanwhile, held no shares in Yameta, nor was he a director. Officially he was just another company employee – a talent scout. This ensured that the funds generated by Mike through the Animals actually belonged to Yameta – from which Mike merely picked up a salary. It was a brilliant scheme, which Mike would later introduce to Chas Chandler after he got into management with Mike, with his new American star-in-waiting Jimmy Somebody.

Mike happily shared all this with Eric and the boys from the Animals. Short-version: very clever and really quite wonderful Mike had found a way for the group to have all their earnings paid into a tax shelter, where it would accrue massive interest – ready for that far-off day when they wished to retire to a dream island of their own.

The feeling of contentment and security – the love – among the group was a real joy for Mike to behold.

CHAPTER FIFTEEN

Jimi and Brian

The Beatles couldn't get enough of Jimi. Paul's steady, Jane Asher, didn't trip on drugs or dig rock 'n' roll, and Yoko wasn't about to trade in King John for some no-name New York sideshow – so no hang-ups the way there were with every other freaked-out, shrivel-cocked white muso in London that summer.

Just George and Paul, already hip to acid, tripping on that hydra-guitar; grave-robber John ready to pounce on the possibilities for his own shit. Ringo bored.

But the Stones were not so cool about the new dick on the block. Keith was still bummed out about Jimi replacing him as Linda Keith's number one bad boy. Couldn't get the picture out of his mind of posh Linda turning skeezer for Jimi's extra inches, even though she still swore blind it never happened.

Mick was on the warpath because baby Marianne not-so Faithfull also had the hots for Jimi – and the feeling was, for all to see, mutual. And speed-jiving Loog Oldham had already passed on Jimi after the shit-show at the Cheetah and wasn't about to bend the knee now to help some rival cat get rich quick.

But Jagger-hating Brian, he was simpatico to the cause. Jonesy was still living with witchy Anita Pallenberg at Courtfield Road, South Ken. Moroccan rugs. Dirty dishes piled high. Wall posters. No bed, just a flop mattress at the top of a minstrel's gallery. Very little furniture, but tall ceilings and enormous windows, furs and satins and silks and velvet strewn across the bare floor, Brian and Anita playing dress-up all day long, getting stoned on hash, acid, opium, Mandrax. Piles of books and comics, hip underground lit, ancient occult texts, Brian's train magazines.

Jimi would stop by, then split if Keith showed up. Jimi and Brian sitting on the floor, tripping on endless chatter about UFOs and ley lines, Stonehenge and the pharaohs, landing lights, oh so bright. One day The Truth would emerge, but Jimi and Brian, they already knew and would be among the first to be contacted. It was obvious.

Other times, Jimi would see Brian and Anita going at it – 'Cunt!', 'Queer!' Blam-blam, pretend you don't know. Brian with a black eye and blood smeared across his face, the sound of Anita's booming Germanic laughter chasing after him like horror-movie thunder.

Jimi liked Brian. Felt some of his pain. Jimi had plenty of fights with women too. But that wasn't the bond. The bond was that they both were outsiders, square pegs in diaphanous holes. Brian, whispering and paranoid; Jimi, beaten hound-dog smile.

Brian, a war baby like Jimi, had been baptised in negro American jazz and blues since he was an asthmatic, malcontent teen. Schooled in classical by his stiff-backed piano-teacher father and starch-petticoat choir-mistress mother, he fell hard for Cannonball Adderley and sandbagged his parents into buying him an alto sax. He was fifteen, but when he played he sounded ninety-nine.

Not long after that he got his first acoustic guitar and then it was all Elmore 'King of the Slide' James and 'Shake Your Moneymaker', and Robert 'King of the Delta Blues' Johnson and 'Hellhound on My Trail'. Followed by penny-a-go cigarettes, underage booze, pregnant girlfriends – *five*, all told – fleeing school in disgrace, busking round Europe, art college – for *two days* – then London, where he went by the handle Elmo Lewis, fell in with the dropouts and beatniks at the Ealing Jazz Club, and played his first gig with the Rolling Stones at the Marquee Club in 1962. He had just turned twenty.

Everything escalated after that. Time tipping over into infinity every twenty-four hours. Five years later it was already almost over for Brian. Suck-cess had consumed him whole. He could play anything and often did, but he couldn't write hits and Mick and Keith left him choking on their fumes.

While Jimi, the novelty act, was being welcomed in by London's nouveau-pop elite, Brian was being shunned, his value diminishing almost hourly as the Stones donned their new personas as rock sophisticates and Brian became the hollow-eyed embarrassment of the family.

Brian affected to be blah. Jimi, eyes darting, took what he could get. It was twenty-four-hour party time at Courtfield Road. Lotta new faces pressing up close. Swish artists, fashion grouters, third-eye occultists, bent actors, slumming aristos, diet-pill-demented models, wannabe street wizards, old-money ninnies with flash cameras they didn't know how to use and zig-zaggy two-seaters they didn't know how to drive.

Jimi *overdosing* on it, man. So high on his luck he never wants to come down. Thinks it's all *him*.

When Jimi picked up his acetate of *Are You Experienced* from Chas, he phoned Brian, flipping out, insisting he come over, take it in. Brian showed later, early hours, with his far-out pal Stash – real name: Prince Stanislaus Klossowski de Rola, Baron de Watteville, aristocratic son of Count Balthasar Klossowski de Rola, one of the greatest living painters of the century. Stash'll tell ya,

Jimi, only dimly aware of this, knows Stash as one of those Eurotrash London hipsters everyone says is coool, baby. One of those intimate brethren of Brian and Anita, McCartney and Lennon, Mick and Keith, Robert Fraser and Christopher Gibbs, Eric Burdon and Pete Townshend, Tara Browne and Marianne Faithfull.

Stash is a meticulously self-realised coxcomb wrapped in silk and velvet, satin capes and antique lace, styled in the finishing schools of Bern, Geneva, Paris, Rome, New York, LA, fond of collecting Elvis records and riding horses, playing drums with mad Vince Taylor and hanging out at Cannes with Fellini. Confidant of Sir David Napley, QC, close personal friend to French writer and alchemist Eugène Canseliet, the direct disciple of the legendary Fulcanelli. A regular at the Ad Lib and Speakeasy, interviewed in *Rave* magazine about his new jacket, headline: from Damascus not Carnaby Street. Stash giving it big time: 'I'd never wear clothes that everyone else could get hold of. In fact, I've just bought a "new" coat made in 1718. It's the only thing I've seen that I like.' Well, fucking obviously.

This night at Jimi's, Stash turns up wearing a kangaroo-fur coat that Brian has just given him. The same coat Brian wore for the cover of *Between the Buttons*. Earlier that day the pair had breezed into the *très chic* King's Road boutique owned by Ola Hudson, the beyond beautiful black American dancer and designer married to in-the-room English graphic designer Anthony Hudson. Brian and Stash swished and soared with Ola, smoking rainbow-coloured Sobranie cigarettes, making a fuss of Ola's two-year-old son, Saul, soon to be renamed Slash, and 'scoring chick clothes', as they called it, bundles of antique women's finery 'that we would fashion as tunics', Stash explained earnestly to Jimi.

Seeing the light briefly flicker in Jimi's eyes, Stash immediately offers to swap clothes with him, but Jimi is too wrecked on the idea of playing Brian his album. Jimi cranking it loud on the player, volume all the way up. Brian, eyes tight shut, tripping on the freak-out section, seeing the pictures in the words . . . '*No sun comin' through my windows / Feel like I'm livin' at the bottom of a grave . . .*'

Stash solemn, inward-journeying. 'Jimi, that's beautiful, man,' says Brian in a stupor. 'So true. How did you know, man?'

Jimi just smiling that smile like a man enjoying the smell of his own farts. Jonesy, eyes rolling back in his head, Stash nodding knowingly, all now revealed. The night drifting into smoke and dawn-light haze. Brian twittering stoned about the 'essential similarities' between Elizabethan ballads and Robert Johnson.

Two days before the album is released, in May, brother Brian and Prince Stash are arrested on drugs charges. Coke and dope. Nothing too crazy. But they both swear the shit was planted by the cops. They get off on a technicality. West London Magistrates not calling the cops liars exactly, but letting the Stone and the Baron exit unsullied. This time. The gallery goons giggling as Stash is rebuked by his own lawyer, Sir David Napley: 'But you, sir, are a gentleman. What on Earth are you doing with those chaps?' Stash all bent out of shape about having his passport confiscated, depriving him of flying to LA to be with his sixteen-year-old fiancée Romina Power.

Brian ran to Jimi. Devastated. Blown apart. 'My fucking lawyers have told me to stay away from Stash!' he screamed. 'They don't even want me around the Stones.' Jimi, offering sweet sympathy tea and milky Mandrax. Brian broken up, man. Jimi, like, getting it and not getting it. Brian so down, man. Blown up. Blown apart.

It's a different scene when Jimi arrives in California two weeks later for Monterey Pop. Invited personally by Paul McCartney, part of a British contingent that also includes the Who and Eric Burdon and the Animals, this is Jimi's first time home since he changed his name and invented a whole new backstory. He's excited, man, but watchful. Nobody knows Jimi in America. Jimi is English now. Nobody cares.

Brian flies with him, first class, Heathrow to JFK, Eric Burdon in the next seat. First stop on the Sunshine Express. Brian gives Jimi the lowdown. American chicks, man – totally different scene to London, ya dig? Like Jimi hasn't noticed. Jimi relaxed, playing along, Brian, man, what a trip, the sunken eyes, the dead blond hair, the ghost face. The English accent the American chicks dig special. The true-devil Rolling Stone, Mick just a hard-on pretender next to him, Keith still a gap-toothed maybe.

Jimi and Brian. Sun and Moon. Land and Sea. Brothers, born nine months apart: Brian the eldest and, later, the first to go. Right hand, left hand. Black and white. Equals. Almost.

Until they get to New York, where Jimi the psychedelic superstar is suddenly back to being plain Jimmy, the raggedy-ass nobody. The suspicious white limo driver nervously eyeing the black apparition in his rear-view on the way in from the airport; the gussied-up old dowager at the Chelsea Hotel mistaking the coloured boy in the scarlet tunic for the bellhop, ordering him to carry her bags; Jimi dissolving back into Jimmy, no longer laughing so easy. Brian and Eric coughing nervously at the check-in desk.

Back on the street that night, Jimi found himself among his people again. Checking out the clubs in the Village, old places he used to hang, new places that had sprung up in his near year away. He introduced himself to Frank Zappa and his band the Mothers of Invention at an eatery. Frank, who knew everything, knew of Jimi's London success. Invited him over to his apartment. But instead of the crazy scene Jimi had envisaged, he found Frank's wife Gail making supper. That didn't stop him getting up and jamming with the Mothers onstage that night, though Zappa left them to it, sitting in the stalls to watch Jimi play. Silently weighing, judging, discarding . . .

Jimi moving on to the Cafe Au Go Go – scene of so many moments good and bad for Jimmy – where Richie Havens is playing a set. Richie recalled Jimi as the midnight-lightning kid who had so blown away his own guitarist, Mike Bloomfield, the year before that Mike couldn't get out of bed for two days. Richie is supercool, slapping Jimi's back and telling him how happy he is to hear of the boy's adventures in London. Jimi lapping it up while still thinking about the new gizmo the Mothers have gifted him: his first wah-wah pedal. Wait till those cats in London get a hold of some of that.

Then . . . wake-up call. Then . . . Monterey. California, baby! Wear some shit in your hair . . .

Jimi coasting on the psychedelic coast. Floating around, checking – it – out.

Monterey: the world's first mass counterculture freak-out, with its poster of an exotic, psychedelic bare-breasted hippy love goddess.

Monterey, with its coloured love beads, incense, dope, warm wine, Owsley acid, free love, low rides, underground literature, subcontinent raga, consciousness-expanding vibes, occult head-trips, anti-war, anti-flag, supernova far-out paint jobs, flowing chakras, meditation mats, Hells Angels tattooed sentinels walking tall in the sun with Sergeant Pepper, all cool, baby, letting it *all* hang out. No jive, no big deal, Grateful Jefferson Dead Airplane Jimi craving total mountain-high psyche out.

Before the show: Jimi and Janis in a toilet stall backstage, fucking so noisily it is bumming out passers-by. Janis fantasising about Otis Redding, Jimi getting rocks for Michelle Phillips. Neither 'J' famous enough yet to make it happen.

Jack Casady from the Airplane gives Jimi two tabs of brother Owsley's powerful Monterey Purple. Jimi, born high, swallows both. This, on top of the STP Jimi and Brian already dropped together that will keep them tripping for seventy-two hours. By the time Jimi reaches the stage the bonfire has engulfed him. Brian's mumbling intro – 'the most exciting guitarist I've ever heard' – lost in the trillion-vision head rush.

Jimi showing off with 'Killing Floor', the Howlin' Wolf juju not even Clapton has mastered. Jimi doing at lightning speed what Led Zeppelin would slow to a drag and turn into a career move two years later. Zeppelin, whose Jimmy Page would later claim he'd never seen Hendrix. Jimi in the shadows, glowing like radiation. 'Tee-hee, Little Jimmy, you a tall tale . . .'

Jimi taking his beloved Dylan's 'Like A Rolling Stone' and turning it to scree. Jimi talking speed-acid space-jive . . . '*Yeah, dig, brother, um, it's really out of sight here . . . didn't even rain . . . no buttons to push.*' Little guitar splash. '*Right now we're going to dedicate this song to everybody here . . . with hearts, any kind of hearts and ears. Goes something like this here.*' Little guitar stabs. '*Yeah! Yeah! What I say now . . .*' Guitar rolling into the main riff, slowing to a turn. '*Yeah, it's as I said before, it's really groovy . . . I'd like to bore you for about six or seven minutes and do a little thing you know . . .*' False laughter. Sky-dog, acid-rush, full-bore. '*Yeah, please excuse me for a minute, let me play my guitar, right . . .*'

Noel, getting nervous: 'What's he fucking doing?' Mitch, head up instead of down, just keeping keeping on. Fuck Noel.

'Right now, gonna do a thing . . . by *Bob Dylan.*' Jimi pointing at Noel, laughing: 'That's his grandmother over there . . . Just a little thing called "Like a Rolling Stone".'

Jimi makes it through the number, turning it to scree, remembers most of the words, gives it some special sauce, then falls out, the crowd distracted, the band a step behind, tuning up, living with it, getting juiced in it, Jimi still talking, rambling, rumbling, gambling, ambling. Three more numbers whirl by, almost out of reach, Jimi whispering on the guitar, Jimi beseeching, Jimi defiant, then despondent, haywire in drama, onlookers running hot and cold.

By the time he gets to 'The Wind Cries Mary' he is fork-tongued embarrassed. Eerily exposed. Eyes blinking. 'Right, now, we got a song named "Wind Cries Mary", thank you very much. We have a song named "Wind Cries Mary", we gotta keep going real quick, goes something like this . . .'

Those lush, paint-splashed-canvas chords.

'The next single here, I hope . . .'

Jimi pulling it together like hypnosis, baby, the wind and the names it has blown in the past. Pretty so much, thank you, baby.

'We only got two more songs to do. We have two more songs to do. And, uh, we're going to try to do this . . . "Purple Haze", man, I think it's about going to come out the same time. It's gonna be a double A-side – hey, what's happening? Hey! Hey! Yeah, okay then! Hey! Hey, man! Goes somethin' like this here. One, two, three, four . . .'

Hammer down. Wheels up. Jimi hits the sky. Jimi in the eye of the trueborn-one tomorrow yesterday, whoa, yeah.

Hey! Hey, man!

There is a long pause before the last number, 'Wild Thing'. Two and a half minutes of Jimi talking fire crack. Joking, ha, yeah. 'What's he *doing*?' Fuck, Noel.

'Man, I'd like to say this before, you know. Well, you know, everybody says this, man, but . . . this is something else, man. Like, it's no big story about you going, you know, we couldn't make it here so we're going to England, and America doesn't like us because, you know, our feet's too big, and we got fat mattresses and we wore golden underwear. Ain't no scene like that, brother. You know, it's just . . . dig, man. It's, you know, I been around, went to England, picked up these two cats. And now here we are, man. It was so, you know, groovy to come back here this way, you know. And really get a chance to really play, you know?'

The crowd digs that one. Whistling, clapping, the crowd always digs a stroke.

The band flex for the final number, but Jimi's not finished.

'You know, I could sit up here all night and say thank you, thank you, thanks to you, but . . . I'd rather just *grab* you, man, and just ooh-ah . . .' Kissing and mow-mowing the mic, a cat gobbling meat. 'One of those things, man, you know, one of them scenes. But dig, I just can't *do* that. You see what I mean? So what

I'm going to do, I'm gonna sacrifice something right here that I really *love*, okay? Oh, and . . . Thank you very much to Bob Dylan's grandmother. Anyway, I'm gonna sacrifice something that I really *love*, man. Don't think I'm silly doing this, you know, cos I'm not, I don't *think* I'm losing my mind. Last night, man, ooh, *God*!'

'*What's he fucking doing?*'

Fuck off, Noel.

'But anyway, wait, wait a minute, honest . . .' *Laughter.* 'Anyway, man, but today I think it's the right thing, alright, so I'm *not* losing my mind. This is for *everybody* here, man. This is the only way I can do it. You know, so we're gonna do the English and American combined anthem together, okay? Don't get mad. Noooooooo! Don't get mad. Everybody, I want everybody to join in too, alright? And don't get mad. This is it now. This is nothing I can do more than . . . this. Ooh, play this beautiful piece . . . ah . . .'

FEEDBACK!

Motorcycle screams!

DRAGON WINGS!

More. More. More. More. More. More.

ARMY SIRENS! BLUE FLASHING COP LIGHTS!

UFO static. GOVERNMENT forces. MOUNTAIN people.

A minute, sixteen of this before the purple noise zeroes out momentarily – then . . .

BLAM-BLAM.

BLAM-BLAM-A-BLAM-BLAM.

BLAM-BLAM-A . . .

Christ on the cross, JFK in the ground.

Jimi stone-cold crazy now.

'Wild thing,' he sings.

'You make my heart sing,' he sings.

'You make *ever-y-thing*,' he sings.

'*GROOVY!*'

The mountains continue to judder and quake as Jimi the spirit-jinn leads the band, the crowd, the backstage through the song, what used to be a song.

Jimi fills the stage and begins fucking the universe, humping his goddess-guitar, riding her like an angry Angel's hog. Kicking her out of bed, onto the stage floor.

He saunters to the back of the stage, digs out a bottle of lighter fuel, squeezes it ejaculatory over the guitar, thick long spurts, the guitar dripping in Jimi's inflammable cum. He keeps it up, bumping, grinding, pissing down on the wretched, screaming thing. Piss and cum and sweat and spit, the jinn hosing his slut-goddess down. Then falling on his knees again, leaning over and kissing his old lady smack on her sweet, cum-sodden baby-belly.

The demon ritual unspooling madly now, he takes out a box of matches, strikes one, it hisses into being as he tosses it onto the broken axe, which jumps into flames, Jimi ecstatic, bidding it to come hither with fluttering hands, Odin directing his blood sacrifice.

Reaching for the lighter fuel again, he squirts what remains onto the flames, making them jump higher. More and more and more until the fuel runs out and he chucks it down on the stage, spent, no longer of use to the god of sex-fire he has summoned. Fire-fucking demon orgy cosmic knowledge ritual flaming planets colliding hell-love worlds abandoned, fleeing alien ships crashing through stars.

Burn, baby, burn!

Then, impatient for the climax, Jimi grabs the burning witch by the neck and begins slamming her into the ground, the stage catching fire now too. Microphones topple in the commotion, the fire sputters out, blown away by the cyclone of Jimi-Jinni's fury. The neck and head leave the body. Jimi tosses them into the crowd. The body left, agonising dead-star howl, writhing, rattling on the floor, then it too expelled into deep space. The crowd staring wildly, lids flapping open, too exposed to the radiation to react.

Vietnam apocalypse-Mekong-Delta-blues, acid-priest end-times rock revelation.

Burn, baby, burn!

Jimi doing his obscene tongue-flapping thing at a time when pussy-licking is considered outsider, the men who offer it depraved and the women who crave it even more disgusting and loathsome. Jimi as whitey-baiting leper messiah. Chicks digging it special, white Toms shaking in their skin. Not like the night before with Brother Otis, white middle-class kids jiving and acting poor-boy black, yelling, 'Lord, have mercy!', 'Right on, brother!' Otis coming on like a black Elvis-Sinatra, finger-popping double-breasted suit, smiling, sweating, singing about 'girls in mini-skirts', burying the hate in dollar signs.

None of that shit tonight. Jimi laughing, tripping. Jimi white scare-mongering, giving it away for free. Jimi bringing home his destiny. Stone free at last.

Pete Townshend looking on from the wings, shattered, hateful, terrified.

Burned.

CHAPTER SIXTEEN

Monkee Noises

After Monterey, the London honeymoon was over.

Anointed as the new musical figurehead of the American underground just as it was beginning to swamp mainstream culture, Jimi tore it up coast to coast, right on in all the right places, far out in all the heaviest new scenes. The newest, coolest baad-ass on the block, have you heard him yet? Have you *seen*? But it wasn't the attention of Janis Joplin or Stephen Stills or Mama Cass or Jim Morrison or even Brian Jones that stayed with Jimi the most now when Chas pushed him into shitty little Mayfair studios in New York in July to try to finish making his second album, to try to keep Chas and Kathy and Mike and Mitch and even Noel happy, to pretend to show how much he still really, really cared and appreciated all the love, baby, so much love, from his new white English family.

It was the vision of a believe-it-when-you-see-it beauty he had unexpectedly reconnected with at a party in Laurel Canyon after his show at the Whisky. Her name was Devon Wilson, and Jimi, you better believe it, was now under her spell.

One of those New York party girls he had met through Heather White back in his early days in New York, Devon had always been one of those out-there young chicks who'd lived a long time in her bones before *you* came along. Tall, sexy, proud, Afro hair – bold as love for all to see.

But Jimmy do-I-know-your-name? was a nothing back then. While Devon could call on some real marquee headliners for endorsements: Quincy and Miles, to name just two. Plus a lotta other deep-pocket cats happy to pick up her tab since she'd shown up in Vegas as a fifteen-year-old runaway back in 1959.

Born Ida Mae Wilson in Milwaukee, in 1943, Devon was a classic Libra, ruling planet Venus. Running from home at fifteen for reasons you didn't need to know about, daddy-o, she had wielded her Lady Justice sword to somehow get her the near-2,000 miles of road to Las Vegas, where she made it turning tricks on the Strip. Working the neon-sprayed turf between the Desert Inn and the Sands, but the wrong colour for the high rollers inside the casinos to be seen out with, Devon, as she glamorously rebranded herself, worked her way up from rube thrill-seekers looking for a weekend burn, through craps dealers and slots jockeys, hoofers and hustlers, to older, better-connected dudes with plenty of cash to splash and a yen for underage pussy.

But if you knew that much it wasn't because you got it from her. Devon never talked about those hard-knock early days. By the time she met the young, raggedy-ass Jimmy James in New York she had invented a whole new persona for herself. Using a steady gig at the Playboy Club as her base, Devon was one of the first of what later became known as the super-groupies, parlaying her on-off flings with Brian Jones, Jim Morrison, Eric Clapton – insert famous rock name here – . . . into a social status that saw her name on the hippest guest lists in New York, from the Scene and the Cheetah to backstage at the Garden.

'I went out with Brian Jones first,' she told a friend. 'I was closer to him than any of the others. He was the true Rolling Stone.'

It was Emeretta Marks who introduced Devon to Jimmy. When they met again in LA, Devon affected to hardly remember the boy. But Jimmy – now Jimi – knew exactly who this fox was.

It wasn't just the sex – though there was that too, always, when it came to Jimi and his lady friends – there was something else about Devon that had Jimi hooked. Something more . . . *evolved*. Not like Linda Keith, whom everyone could see was slumming it with Jimi. Not like Kathy, who straightforward legit loved Jimi. Devon was simply *other*. Whatever weird world Jimi now found himself living in, Devon acted like she'd already been there a lifetime. Openly bisexual, she wasn't remotely jealous of Jimi's other sexual trips and she didn't bother hiding her own many other sexual adventures.

Devon understood the game, was smart. Not school smart. Street smart. Devon knew things, knew people, got the deal without having to be told. Dug whatever groovy scenes were going on around her and shape-shifted into them with supernatural ease.

Seeing how burned out Jimi was that night in the Canyon, Devon took him by the hand and led him to her car, and a few blocks over to the house she was living in, the same four-bed cottage, she said, that Harry Houdini had once lived in. Jimi majorly impressed. Devon took the phone off the hook, where it stayed for the next thirty-six hours.

Devon would come floating like a cloud into Jimi's life more and more over the next three years, and despite the changes she would put him through – watching her dissolve into a junkie, bloodying his own bruised karma, frightening others away – he was nearly always glad to see her. Not that Devon ever gave him much choice. She was the kind of chick who, when she punched your doorbell, kept her fist on the buzzer until you or someone like you opened the damn door.

Jimi and the Experience were back in New York in July, sweating it out at Mayfair Studios, which was *not* working out, when Chas got the phone call from Mike Jeffery. Labouring over a new track, 'Burning of the Midnight Lamp', which Jimi had written with his second album in mind but Chas had now earmarked as their next single in the UK, the mood was uptight, Jimi putting the group through thirty takes before letting them go for the night – then overdubbing parts on his own, Chas struggling to stay awake at the controls.

They'd finally got back to the hotel and were having a nightcap in the bar when the concierge approached Chas. There was a call for him, long distance.

'I've done it!' barked Mike down the crackling line from London. 'A great deal, a nationwide tour!'

'Oh, yeah?' said Chas, weary to his studio-ground bones. 'Who with?'

'The Monkees!' said Mike, high-five triumphant.

Chas nearly fell off his bar stool. 'Are you out of your fucking mind?'

Mike laughing. Not getting it. Seeing only large denomination dollar signs.

Chas getting more steamed up. 'Fuck off, Mike! Jimi can't tour with the fucking Monkees! It'll blow everything!'

Mike truly perplexed. Blow *what*? The Monkees were bigger than the fucking Beatles in America that year! This was better even than getting him on with the Walker Brothers when they were trying to break him in Britain. Jimi opening for the Monkees – this was a fucking masterstroke, you fat Geordie cunt, behave yourself!

Jimi, torn between a genuine distaste for what he saw as the contrived, formulaic teen pop of a manufactured puppet group like the Monkees – he'd been quoted in a British music weekly as being 'embarrassed that America could be so stupid as to make somebody like that' – and the very real opportunity to make some serious dough, said nothing. Let Chas lose his shit with Mike. Jimi would do what he always did when confronted with bad static: ghost into a corner and watch and wait.

Plus, you know, man, Jimi had hung out with Micky Dolenz and Peter Tork and all those cats, at Monterey and later in LA. They were cool guys. Telling Jimi how they were determined to start playing their own stuff on their records. Jimi tries saying some of this to Chas when he gets off the phone. But he is too far gone, load blown, knowing Mike always gets his way.

Less than a week later Jimi and the band fly out for the first of what is supposed to be sixteen huge arena and stadium shows, opening for the Monkees. Now *this* is a trip, man! The Monkees have had the number 1 album in America for twenty-three consecutive weeks, starting from January. They will go to number 1 again in the album charts for five straight weeks, beginning in December. At the time of the tour with Jimi, the Monkees have just had their third straight number 1 single in America with 'A Little Bit Me, a Little Bit You', and have just released a new single, 'Pleasant Valley Sunday', also now zooming its way to the toppermost of the poppermost. They have been on the cover of every issue of the country's biggest-selling teen magazine, *Tiger Beat*, for over a year.

Chas might be down in the dumps but Mike knows he has pulled a stroke getting Jimi's wagon hitched to this skyrocket.

But here's the fun part. Jimi's opening show on the Monkees tour is in Jacksonville, Florida – home to rednecks in pickup trucks with gun racks, respectable family homes flying rebel Confederate flags, stores selling gator-meat sausages. The only coloureds on view the ones with big white smiles calling you 'sir'.

When Jimi hits the stage he is greeted with disbelief bordering on bloodlust. What is this fucking *circus clown*, this jumped-up fucking *pickaninny* doing waggling his dirty motherfucking tongue at our sweet little Selma? Somebody's gonna have to pay, and if this guy Jimi-what-the-hell doesn't get off the stage real fucking quick it is surely, oh Lord, going to be him.

Meanwhile, the kids chanting: 'We want Davy! We want Davy!'

They play a quick set, stick to the obvious crowd pleasers – 'Joe', 'Purple', 'Mary' – and get the hell off the stage before something really bad happens.

Afterwards, back at the hotel, Jimi acting relaxed, long practised at hiding the generational humiliation and suffering, the up-close intimidation, the deep-down-inside fear. Mitch and Noel, though – especially Noel – are freaking out.

Next stop: North Carolina. Fuck, fuck, fuck.

Lookie here, what's come to our good, God-fearing town?

Virginal teenage daughters of gun-toting, white-hate Injun killers mixing with Colgate-smile moms and pops taking their kids to see them nice young fellers off the TV show. Only to be confronted by . . . well, what the fuck would you call it, Travis? Some black, hippy drug-fiend homosexual making hell-shit noise like he be begging to be strung up! What the fuck is the world coming to, sheriff, I gotta put my kids in front of some fucking jigaboo degenerate singing about drugs and queers and fucking right there in the street in God's own good daylight?

The Monkees are travelling in their own security-guarded private plane with their logo painted down the side. Jimi and the boys are schlepping commercial. Laughed at and pointed at, catcalled. 'Is you a *boy* or is you a *girl?*' Smell of gut-rot whisky, stench of gang hate.

HAW-HAW-HAW-HAW-HAW!

Thank God for New York, where the tour arrives mid-July for a four-night Thurs-thru-Sun run at the 14,000-cap Forest Hills Stadium, in Queens. Jimi and the Experience are in the same hotel as the Monkees – the Waldorf Astoria. New York's finest. Liz and Dick drunkenly hurling plates at each other in the presidential suite, Jack Jones crooning 'Lady' in the ballroom.

Jimi is now so shut down emotionally about the Monkees shows that he just stops trying. Even at Forest Hills he barely reaches out, does his twenty-minute minimum requirement and

skedaddles. Jimi's had it, man. He could handle the southern rac-
ists; he could deal with the confused young kids impatient for the
Monkees, not caring what this weirdo is doing there. But copping
to this shit in New York – where people fucking know me, man.
Naw, forget about it.

He tells Chas, and Chas, already seeing it coming, has urgent
words in private, and it is agreed with Dick Clark, the promoter,
that Jimi will leave the tour after the fourth and final show in
Queens.

There is a bullshit press release hurriedly sent out on the wire,
explaining why Jimi couldn't continue. 'We decided it was just the
wrong audience,' he told a guy on the phone from the *NME*. 'I
think they're replacing us with Mickey Mouse.'

But back in the Monkees' suite at the Waldorf later that night,
Jimi is hanging with Micky and Davy, passing around these little
white pills some cat Jimi knows from the East Side has shown up
with. Lab-built synthetic psilocybin, powerful psychedelics, none
of that strychnine-laced street shit. Everyone swallowing them
with beer then going off into the night on their own separate trips.

It wasn't just bellyaching about the Monkees. Jimi was starting
to assert himself now in ways Chas and his other new London
friends and muso buddies hadn't yet grasped he had in him. Not
knowing the hungry alley cat who had fucked and fought, lied
and bought his way out of his father's noxious clutches, out of the
army's horrifying systems, up through the ranks of a zillion different ringmasters and musical half-asses, hustlers and whores,
biz-thieves and slick fixers. Not knowing how desperately *angry*
Jimi really was. How much of a goddamn *hurry* he was in just to
get it on, all of it, right now, here today, too bad who gets in the
way.

You could hear it all over what now became his second album,
the exultantly titled *Axis: Bold as Love*.

Recorded under the same sweatshop conditions as his first album, on the run between tours, here in London, there in New York, no clear plan other than for Chas to hold Jimi still long enough to get something down on tape. To feed the record machine, make hits while the sun still shone. Before the fickle fans changed their minds, or grew too old and uptight, and you were left like the Animals, sniffing around for scraps, living off fumes.

Happy enough at first to carry on playing the game, so much of it overlapping with those first records, those unexpected knock-on-wood hits, Jimi initially returned to familiar themes.

Sci-fi – the goofing around on the intro track, 'EXP', Jimi's voice slowed down to sound like a comic-book extra-terrestrial. Into the deceptively low-key 'Up from the Skies', Jimi's wise, friendly alien asking the human race important questions: '*I just want to know about / The rooms behind your minds . . .*'

Funky fun for sure, but without the signature sexual heat of the guitar: Jimi nursing the flame in his palm. The unexpectedly subdued mood sustained through the early motions of the next track 'Spanish Castle Magic', ostensibly a fond recall of the roadhouse Jimmy used to sneak off to as a teenager. The guitars beginning to build like a jumpy fire on another cold-ass night in hell. '*Don't think your time / On bad things / Just float your little mind around . . .*'

And again on 'Wait Until Tomorrow' – dig, a funky little strut about being shown the stop sign one too many times by some chick talking sweet love but never letting you get your hot hands on her 'golden garden'. It's a nothing, old-timey blues lyric, but the beautiful swirl of Jimi's unicorn guitars and Mitch's circling campfire percussion make it deliciously ticklish.

Still no 'Foxey Lady', though. No 'Fire'. Instead there are pale-sky versions of *Are You Experienced*-era tracks, more immaculately rendered, but in so doing making a farce of the original intention: 'Ain't No Telling', beautifully executed, empty as a seashell; 'Little

Miss Lover', same thing. Jimi does Jimi, blah.

Chas yanking open another pack of cigarettes, waiting for Jimi to stop fannying around and get on the good foot. Lay something down thunderbolt hot. Chain-smoking, hoping-praying for a hit.

It would eventually arrive with the dread voodoo alarm of 'If 6 Was 9'.

Now this was more like it, Chas told Jimi. Jimi ignoring him, deep into what he was trying to say, not what Chas was trying to sell.

Here was Jimi appearing to subvert everything that had made him famous so suddenly. Everything that he supposedly stood for, epitomised, flew the freak flag for – and now, shockingly, openly questioned.

If all the hippies cut off all their hair
I don't care . . . I don't care . . .
Dig, cos I got my own world to live through
And I ain't gonna copy you . . .

Set against a split-second-timing riff, heavy as winter mountain snow, it sounded on the surface like an anthem for the hippy nation. But the words – the very title – turned that idea upside down. Made you think twice. Made you keep going back to check again. Find reassurance in the tagged-on coda about 'white-collared conservatives' pointing their 'plastic fingers' at 'my kind'. Into four minutes of rhythmic rumble as the multi-layered guitars investigate and probe while Jimi whispers and mumbles over the top, copping out on the original idea, turning personal protest – against hippies, against fixed ideas, against whatever it is other people want from him – into professional musical platitudes.

'If 6 Was 9' summed up so much of the intrigue about *Axis*, while also serving as a classic widescreen rock showstopper. It was the same for most of the tracks. Brilliantly realised productions of perfectly manicured raw sounds. 'You've Got Me Floating' was yet another. Was it really about some chick that's got Jimi's head spinning?

Well, you can believe that if you want to, man. But all that inhibited emotion in the guitars and drums, that love-love-love thing going on while Jimi sounds like he'd like to smash your face. That pay-off line: '*You got me floatin' – float to please . . .*' Those wasp-stinging guitars slicing at the air. That's about a *chick*?

'One Rainy Wish' was this album's 'May This Be Love'. More adventurously conceived, more skilfully executed, a diamond in the rough on anybody else's album that year. In this context: killer filler.

The only outright bummer, the well-intentioned but musically redundant decision to allow Noel to write – and sing – a track on the album, 'She's So Fine'. Millions of pissed-off record buyers doomed to spend the next two decades leaning over their turn-tables, carefully lifting the stylus to escape the mediocrity. What a drag.

The only genuine moments of timeless wonder on *Axis* come in three utterly unprepared-for moments, beginning six tracks deep into side one with the transcendent 'Little Wing'. Butterfly-like guitar, soft conversational vocals, the whole cathedral-like musical edifice deliciously, deceptively short and featuring no chorus, just thirteen lines of Jimi's riding-with-the-wind poetry, 'Little Wing' expressed more in just two and a half minutes than most artists were able to demonstrate in their whole careers.

Musically, its bell-chime guitar was an improved version of another 'track for cash' Jimi had played on in 1966 with ex-King Curtis sax player Lonnie Youngblood, called '(My Girl) She's a Fox' – a close-but-no-cigar musical identikit of 'My Girl' by the Temptations, unreleased at the time.

What Jimi did with it for 'Little Wing' was something else,

though, another headspace, transmuted into one of several Jimi songs to come, about the idealised guardian angel that he said came to him at certain auspicious times. Mother figure, sister-lover, God in female form, a celestial spirit he was always careful to let fly away again.

As he tried to explain in a later interview, 'Little Wing', for Jimi, was 'like one of these beautiful girls that come around sometimes. You ride into town for the drinks and parties and so forth. You play your gig. It's the same thing as the olden days. And these beautiful girls come around and really entertain you. You do actually fall in love with them because that's the only love you can have. It's not always the physical thing of, "Oh, there's one over there . . ." It's not one of those scenes. They actually tell you something. They release different things inside themselves, and then you feel to yourself, "Damn, there's really a responsibility to some of these girls," you know, because they're the ones that are gonna get screwed.'

He paused, had a toke, resumed the reverie. '"Little Wing",' he said, 'was a very sweet girl that came around that gave me her whole life and more if I wanted it. And me with my crazy shit couldn't get it together, so I'm off here and there and off over there . . .'

Kathy? Devon? Diana? Jimi flashing on some way of copping to how he could never, would never repay them? Riding with the wind . . .

The second transcendent moment came with 'Castles Made of Sand', another short track evincing much larger vistas, more gorgeously restrained guitars, almost spoken-word vocals, lyrics inspired by personal memories of Buster's childhood torments, rescued by an overarching belief in letting go long enough for the eternal light to shine through. Though never for quite long enough. Love was not all you needed, but without it you had nothing worth treasuring even as it fell into the sea . . . eventually. Jimi reaching for the eternal, watching frozen as it slips through his fingers.

The final, pivotal moment came at the end of side two on the demi-title track, 'Bold as Love'. Another epically proportioned musical tableau – suave Curtis Mayfield vocals and inky guitar, full-spectrum Dylan-deep lyrical imagery, plus every trick in the psychedelic studio handbook, as devised on the spot by Jimi in blissful harness with his new production ally and musical mountaineer, engineer Eddie Kramer – this was a super-confident Jimi Hendrix operating on a new, much higher level of musical consciousness.

It didn't matter what it was *about*. It was where it took you. It was where it placed Jimi now, far ahead of the hits. Beyond the call of the radio, the selfish demands of the crowd.

Whereas the Beatles had the deluxe-class production expertise of George Martin to help zoom their aura into another dimension, and the Beach Boys had the fragile, overwrought freak-of-nature genius of Brian Wilson to build their rocket ships, Jimi only had himself, yeah? But with the wherewithal and the sheer balls to know that if he bowed to his betters and followed Chas's advice – 'Art for art's sake, hit singles for fuck's sake, Jim!' – he would have been no better, in the end, than the Monkees.

Instead he took a step into the unknown – risked his career – while having to endure well-meaning Chas's big, serious face looking out at him dolefully from behind the control-room glass. Noel's moaning because of all the takes they were being made to do and his desperate attempts to draw a moustache on the *Mona Lisa*, pushing to have more of his own terrible songs on the album.

When it was over Jimi didn't know what he had. By the time *Axis: Bold as Love* is released in December 1967, four days after his twenty-fifth birthday, Jimi is on another of Mike's fucking big idea package tours, having Chas patiently explain to him that the reason the album isn't selling as well as *Are You Experienced* – peaking at number 5, compared to *Are You Experienced* at number 2 – is because he hasn't had anymore hit singles, see?

Jimi hates the cover too. Some bullshit gimmick in which he and the other two are rendered as different 'visions' of Vishnu. Since the Beatles appointed the Maharishi their 'personal guru' that summer, everything was now TM this and Eastern mysticism that. Jimi offended, man. Fucking pissed. Dig, if they wanted to have an *Indian* cover, why didn't they use something that showed his Cherokee blood?

Jimi tells every writer he talks to: 'The three of us have nothing to do with what's on the *Axis* cover.'

Released – with the same cover – in the US in January, *Axis* is an immediate hit, jumping to number 3. Again, it doesn't sell as many copies over there as *Are You Experienced*, but nobody from the record label is riding his ass about hit singles.

Jimi can't wait to split the London scene and get back home again. That scene is so *small*, man. It gets so *claustrophobic*. Chas living, like, a block away or something, right, coming by the apartment every day. Kathy, still cool, just not digging America. That's cool, baby. You got your thing. I got mine. Then hearing about Linda Keith, OD'ing at Brian Jones's pad. Wow, man. The cops involved, newspaper headlines, very bad scene, dig – Linda *fucking up*. Everybody knows Linda likes coke, man, and acid, and, you know, whatever and so on and so forth. But turning blue at Brian's pad, man? Where's that at, man? Some things you just don't do, okay, right?

Jimi wanting to keep it all on the down-low now, geddit, do his American shows, make his next album – in *America* this time – and just, you know, *do my own thing*.

CHAPTER SEVENTEEN

White Lightning

Coventry Evening Telegraph, 20 November 1967
More than 3,000 youngsters attended two houses at the Coventry Theatre. He can play guitar with his teeth, lying on the stage, or behind his back – and do it better than most in a more conventional position. The result was a stunning, completely individual performance, which included hits like 'Hey Joe', 'The Wind Cries Mary' and 'Purple Haze', and the wildest version yet of 'Wild Thing'. But the teenagers who stood on their seats for Jimi Hendrix were unmoved – and I guess somewhat bewildered – by the Pink Floyd, a group for whom the new wave is more of a spring tide.

Can you even fucking begin to imagine, man? After Monterey: after San Francisco and LA. After Peter Tork's major hang in Laurel Canyon: after Steve Stills's mansion pad in Malibu. After magical Devon and Houdini's far-out freak zone, man, tripping on the Owsley seven-day weekend and the 'Burning of the Midnight Lamp' flame-on. After the fucking *Monkees*, man, are you fucking *kidding*? After killing on the East Coast, after take-after-take-after-take-after-take-after-take back in the studio, with Chas breathing heavy down my neck, man, and that little bitch Noel pulling his faces and drinking his shitty brown beer, man, after all the hassles and bullshit and money I'm making you, man. After *Axis* and Paris and Amsterdam and the Albert Hall and all the TV and the radio, after the *Melody Maker* award for 'World Top Musician', big reception at the Europa in London in September, stepping over believers everywhere I go, man.

After all of *that*, you want me to go to Coventry? Do they even know what year it is, man? *Coventry?*

'That's right,' said Mike. 'It's all arranged.'

Another goddamned package tour?

'That's right,' said Mike. 'Only this time you're the headliner. Forty minutes a night, two shows a night, a thousand pounds guaranteed. You can do it in your sleep.'

Jimi in a time loop, a tailspin, all tapped out: everything he'd done in the year since he hit London. Everywhere he'd been, everything he'd seen. Everybody that now knew his name, his face, the whole crazy voodoo trip, man. And he's going out on another *package tour?* Wait – is Engelbert on the fucking bill again too?

'No,' said Mike, the air thick with the fug of cigarettes and joints. Pink Floyd, the Move, the Nice, Amen Corner . . . all very cool. Easy-peasy: money for old rope – and good cost-free promo ahead of the release of the new album.

Jimi going home to Kathy, drinking whisky and cola, smoking Rocky Marciano and Marlboro reds, dropping three or four trips at a time, the way you did when you tripped every day, one more than yesterday every day until you finally stopped – if you finally stopped. Jimi didn't like to stop. Swallowing leapers to help maintain. What if the aliens came down now to finally say hi when you're out cold? Think about that, man. How bummed you'd be. Best to just keep on keeping on, ride on, ride on.

Three weeks, twenty-nine shows – a cheap-thrills hits package. The Move had had three, Jimi four, including 'Burning of the

Midnight Lamp', which only just squeaked into the Top 20, Jimi bent out of shape over it but never letting on cos it's all cool, it ain't just about having hits, you know? Pink Floyd had just one, Amen Corner had one and a half. The Nice: nada.

Jimi digging the scene for what it is, going out and doing his party favours, crotch-thrusting, tongue-waggling, playing with his teeth, behind his back, lying writhing on the floor. Those forty minutes fly by, Jimi tripping throughout the entire three weeks.

Jimi had picked up a new English roadie for the tour, a young guitarist named Ian Kilmister who had known a little success of his own in a northern ballroom party band called the Rockin' Vicars. Ian – later better known as Lemmy, after his habit of always asking people to 'lend me' a quid – was destined to become a force of super-nature in his own psychedelic pioneers Hawkwind (then later punk-metal game-manglers Motörhead). Just twenty-one, he had hitchhiked to London and managed to blag a room at Neville Chesters's squat in Kensington. Ian had met Neville when he was working for the Who, 'trying to put guitars back together after Townshend had finished smashing them'.

Ian had phoned Nev from a red call box asked him if he could kip on his floor a couple nights and Nev had said, yes, come on over.

Ian didn't know till he got there but Nev was now working for Jimi and shared the flat with Noel. The place full of guitars 'in different degrees of destruction that Neville was trying to put back together out of the bits – cannibalising Rickenbackers'.

Ian lit a cigarette, blew smoke in my face and continued. It was thirty years later and by now he was Lemmy. Seeing Hendrix play for the first time was the big turning point, he said. 'I couldn't believe him, you know? Nobody could believe him. Nobody knew you could do that with a guitar. The big thing before that was Clapton. That was as high as you could get. Hendrix used to fucking do a double-somersault and come playing it behind his neck, fucking biting it! I watched him many nights and he wasn't just pretending, playing it with his fingers. He was playing it with his teeth! And he used to fuck the amplifiers and drag it around the floor. Lighting it on fire . . .'

Ian was still wondering how to go about finding his own pad when, out of the blue, Neville mentioned they were looking for a second roadie for the next Hendrix tour. Luck! 'I hired on for £10 a week and all your meals and whatever. It was madness. Two shows a night. Just do your hits. Bang, bang, bang. Great fun.'

His job was simple enough. 'Neville took care of all the electrics. I just humped all Hendrix's gear. When he was playing I'd watch him onstage from a chair in the wings. You could never tell how he did it. He loved to fuck off all the guitar players in the audience. Graham Nash sitting backstage with his ear on the stacks all night – none of this glad-handing you get backstage now with the fucking canapés. In those days people wanted to learn and improve.'

Even being around Hendrix offstage was a lesson. 'He had this old Epiphone guitar – it was a twelve-string, strung as a six-string – and he used to stand up on a chair backstage and play it.'

Jimi was 'a prince, a really good guy – old-fashioned. Get up when a lady enters the room. Pulling chairs out for chicks.'

Jimi had superman stamina.

'If you wanted to see some athletic fucking, Jimi was the boy for it. I'd never seen anything like it – there were always lines of chicks going nuts outside his dressing room. It was like, "Take a number and wait." I used to score acid for him and his dope. I'd get him ten hits of acid and he'd take seven and give me three. They say acid doesn't work two days in a row, but we found out if you double the dose it does.'

After Monterey, Owsley had gifted Jimi thousands of tabs of his triple-strength White Lightning. The ones with the little owl faces stamped on them. They weren't illegal yet. But what he hadn't swallowed in handfuls he'd given away like candy, or simply ditched when he got on the plane back to London. Now he felt like he needed to do acid every time he played.

When the tour ended in Glasgow, just before Christmas, Ian was bereft. Jimi's next stop was Scandinavia – Sweden and Denmark in January – followed by a three-month tour of the US. No need for any English roadies. Ian left Hendrix determined to get his own like-minded band together. A lot of people who saw Jimi on that tour felt the same way.

Jimi in a wide-brimmed hat with a feather and crushed red flares.

'A lot of the guys were getting stoned,' recalled Bev Bevan, drummer with the Move. 'It was a very peaceful tour.'

'It was like a huge school trip,' Keith Emerson of the Nice said. Keith carried knives onstage: driving huge hunting daggers into his keyboards; throwing them into the side-mounted speakers; whipping them with an actual whip. The man had a whip.

Bored, Jimi bought a home-movie camera. One night Keith is doing his knife act, throwing them towards the speakers, when at the last moment he sees Jimi poking his camera between the speakers. 'I kind of froze mid-throw. Jimi had his tongue out and was beckoning me to actually throw them at the speakers while he was in the middle, while he filmed it. I thought, I don't want to be the one who puts him in the history books.'

But Jimi is already in the history books.

'I remember Newcastle City Hall,' breezed Amen Corner sax-player Allan Jones. 'Jimi was very often out of tune, because he used to bash his guitar around like crazy. And he may have been a little bit out of it and didn't quite tune up his guitar properly before he went on, or whatever. And he was constantly going out of tune.

'This night, he actually took the guitar off his shoulder and threw it at the Marshall stack. The place just erupted and went fucking ballistic!'

Schoolboy shit. 'I remember the Move playing once, and I rode a bicycle across the stage,' Noel Redding liked to recall. 'Another time we put stink bombs in Bev Bevan's bass-drum pedal.'

Oh, how they laughed.

Jimi seeing the other side of acid in Syd Barrett of Pink Floyd: his brains already blown out. Syd standing there motionless, the band filling, long crazy head-trip instrumentals, like it's all part of the plan. Put a mark onstage for him to stand. Arty student think music.

A sold-out Royal Albert Hall as the Experience powered through 'Foxey Lady', 'Fire', 'Burning of the Midnight Lamp', 'Spanish Castle Magic', 'The Wind Cries Mary' and 'Purple Haze'. Jimi, Noel and Mitch just showing off now. Power-trio trip, world bow down, yeah.

Keith Emerson before he died: 'Everybody involved in the tour, they'd all come back in the wings and watch him because every night he played he'd do something completely different. A lot of times he astounded Noel Redding and Mitch Mitchell, because they didn't always know what he was going to do. He was certainly trashing a lot of speakers. I remember him playing the Flying V guitar for the first time, and he threw it and it actually landed like an arrow into the speaker cabinet, and us backstage watching from the wings were just completely, wow!'

The night in Bristol: dozens of fans crash the dressing room. Eager autograph hunters. One of them to Jimi loudly so that everyone hears: 'I think Eric Clapton is much better than you.'

The room freezes. Jimi turning round: 'Well, I think Eric's a far better guitar player too.'

Another lost night, Jimi swinging his guitar around his head, the seven furies, brings it down and it smashes into Mitch's bass drum. Mitch in tears afterwards. Jimi still tripping-tripping-tripping. 'You shouldn't have done that! You've got no respect for my drums!'

It was true. Jimi gliding, spiralling. Jimi wasted.

Two nights before the end of the tour in December, at the Nottingham Theatre Royal, the elastic band snapped. Jimi just gone, barely even trying, the guitar hopelessly out of tune yet Jimi barely noticing or caring.

Jimi giggled, but it was like some private joke only he was in on, him and the ho-ho-ing voices in his head. The faces that surrounded him in his everlasting dream, the rainbows and the caves and the wild-money river and pet-hate loves and lies and beautiful people, only none of them mine, really mine, ya dig?

Jimi giggled and did all his party tricks – pulling at the guitar strings with his teeth, swinging the guitar around his neck and playing it behind his back – but he couldn't get the music to really move, to focus and breathe and conjure fire. He wasn't really trying.

Almost a year ago to the day he and Kathy had moved into the pad in Montagu Square. Then 'Hey Joe' had come out, been a hit – a hit! And Jimi had been on the move ever since. Not like the old days of being second or third banana, one step ahead of the rent, the law, the baby mamas, all that shit – but this time as the big kahuna. 'Hey Joe', 'Purple Haze', 'The Wind Cries Mary', *Are You Experienced* – all hits, my brother! Big-ass hits! Then Monterey . . . big in America, baby, land of getting it on . . . the Fillmore, five at the West, the Scene in New York, getting thrown off the Monkees tour for being too *baad* for the little girls, the groovy Salvation back home in New York, *five* there, the Ambassador in DC, five *there*, then back to LA and, dig, can you say the HOLLYWOOD BOWL?

After that, who cared, baby? London, Berlin, Stockholm, no hang-ups, no white-woman, black-man prejudices, being voted

'World Top Musician' by *Melody Maker*, overnight at the Europa Hotel, many good friends and groovy bad ladies, many good times and trips and ups and downs and all-arounds, the best dope, the finest pussy, many good friends living the dream with you for you because of you, think you don't really know when you really do.

Filming the gig at the Albert Hall a week later, a stately performance for the educated white-rock classes, turned on, moneyed, coming to dig the Wild Man of Borneo act for the first time, getting something else, something more, Jimi digging it special, a champagne evening, one for the collection, barely remembering it a week after that.

Jimi is public property now. No longer a secret. Mike and Chas smiling contentedly from the wings. Everything going to plan – almost – everything right on groovy gravy.

Almost.

CHAPTER EIGHTEEN

Jimi and MLK

US tour, February–April 1968.

Jimi roughing it, flying commercial NYC to SF, down to LA, back up to Seattle, Colorado, Texas, Philly . . .

On 24 February, *Axis* finally reaches the US Top 20, but it's taken six weeks to get there. The single from it, the dusty shuffling 'Up From The Skies', is a stiff. Jimi soured. He knew that wasn't the one. Shoulda gone for 'Little Wing', 'If 6 Was 9', 'Spanish Castle Magic'. Telling everyone he was now 'beyond singles', then putting up with Mike Jeffery telling him his ass is grass if he doesn't keep having hits. Everyone nodding, mumbling, sucking on cigarettes, that's right, man, far out, fading from his sight even as they sit.

Three days later Jimi's in Chicago, crashed at the Hilton, giving his sweet time to the Plaster Casters. These young chicks, professional groupies, led by twenty-year-old Cynthia Albritton, aka Cynthia Plaster Caster, and her girlfriend, Dianne, who make plaster casts of rock stars' cocks, which they call 'their rigs'.

Using alginate – dental mould – Dianne, the 'designated plater' – the chicks tripping on post-Beatles English jive – goes down on Jimi, while Cynthia gets busy with the goo. With Jimi standing tall, Cynthia pours the sticky white stuff into a vase and tells Jimi to fit his rig into it. Then, hold it for a minute, the chicks agog. Dianne has never even seen a guy's rig before, only in skin comix. Cynthia pulls out a clipboard and starts taking *notes*. Jimi starts laughing.

'We were not prepared for the size of it,' she writes, a new-age Darwin sketching Black Adam. 'We needed to plunge him through the entire depth of the vase.'

Jimi stays with it, no problemo. But when the mould hardens and they pull his cock out, some of his pubes have collected in the gum-cement and Cynthia has to yank them out from the cast one at a time. Jimi still laughing, starts to lose his erection but now he wants to come. Frustrated, he grabs the vase and sticks his cock back in, standing up fucking it like he does his guitar onstage. Chicks looking on, trying to be cool. Failing.

Then Gerry Stickells sticks his head round the door, takes in the scene, straight face, and says, 'Just, uh, let me know when you're ready.'

Everybody falls about the place.

Jimi comes then asks Cynthia what she's going to do with the casts. 'I told him I wanted to put them on display, and he was cool with that.'

Later, she gives the cast number 0004 and exhibits it under the title, the *Penis de Milo*. 'It was a magical process that only lasted a half-hour.'

'I understand why everyone wanted to sleep with the guy,' said Pamela Des Barres, the LA groupie who hooked Cynthia up with Jimi. 'He played like an all-encompassing rock orgasm. He reeked of sex. You wanted to strip to keep up with him when he played "Foxey Lady".'

Jimi unloads and the girls head over to Noel's room – he has also agreed to make the scene. But he can't keep hard, and the girls have to virtually screw his dick into the mould. That's okay, though, because Cynthia has a thing for pale-faced, skinny Englishmen and fucks him back to life afterwards.

Later, on the phone to Pamela, the super-groupies giggle and compare notes. Miss P, as she is also sometimes known, also has a thing for scraggly haired English rock princelings, and had a scene with Noel before he got to Chicago. She tells Cynthia what she tells her diary: 'He put me in a hundred positions and did stupendous things! It was like being in a web – wanting to get more tangled.' Afterwards, Noel told her: 'That, my dear, is what you call a fuck.'

The tour circles back to New York. Gyms, auditoriums, clubs. Freak-flag houses. Onwards to Washington, Massachusetts, Canada . . .

In Ottawa for two shows at the Capitol Theatre, 2,300 capacity, on 19 March, Jimi tries to hook up with Joni Mitchell, who by chance is playing a small place down the street from his hotel. Jimi has met Joni once before, in the Village, back when they were both still dreaming. Now Joni has an album out too, and Jimi wants to reconnect.

Now keeping a tour journal, Jimi writes:

Arrived in Ottawa, beautiful hotel, strange people. Beautiful dinner. Talked with Joni Mitchell on the phone. I think I'll record her tonight with my excellent tape recorder (knock on wood). Can't find any weed. Everything's plastic. Beautiful view. Marvellous sound on the first show, good on the second. Went down to the little club to see Joni. Fantastic girl with heaven words. We all go to party. Oh, millions of girls. Listen to tapes and smoked back at the hotel.

The following day's entry:

We left Ottawa city today. I kissed Joni goodbye, slept in the car a while, stopped at a highway diner, I mean a real one, like in the movies . . .

The journal then records how that night he and the band went to 'a very bad, bad, bad tasting restaurant':

Thugs follow us. They probably were scared, couldn't figure us out. Me with my Indian hat and Mexican moustache, Mitch with his fairy-tale jacket, and Noel with his leopard-skin hat and glasses and hair and accent . . .

Ohio, Cleveland, Illinois, Maine – colleges, theatres, electric ballrooms. Forty-eight shows in fifty-nine days, everyone bent on coke, speed, ephedrine, weed, acid, bombers, ludes, whatever it takes to keep it together. Liddle bidda brown, help you come down. Onwards to the Civic Dome in Virginia Beach, a thousand capacity, two shows, afternoon and evening.

The boys all sitting in a dark bar, savouring the off-duty evening quiet, spread out on the fake-leather banquettes, Jimi and the band and the cats from Soft Machine, tour openers. The tired-faced old gal carrying the drinks tray gives 'em the news. She's just heard on the radio – Dr King, shot and killed in Memphis.

The boys go into shock, don't know what to say, how to react; look over hard at Jimi, trying to read his mind. Jimi stonewalling, living through this movie a thousand times before, one razor cut at a time. Jig, porch monkey, powder burn, spook . . . Jimi turning his face away. Jimi home-schooled that way. At home, on the street, in the army: on every block in every town in the world.

Dig, down the end of the bar, some good-ole boys high-fiving and yukking it up, drinking to the health of the killer, known to be white. Jimi 'just staring away into space as if nothing had happened' recalled Mark Boyle, lighting cat for the Softs. Jimi, his back rigid signalling for them to leave – which they do, quietly, easy, no sudden moves.

Dr King dead by public demand. Dr King dead by public

lynching. Watchoo say to that, young negro? How you gonna roll out that number for your whitey fans?

The following night in Newark is the kicker. Jimi down to play two sets at the Symphony Hall, a 3,500-capacity theatre on Broad Street in the heart of what the cops call niggertown. Arriving in his white limo, Jimi is made to sit upfront next to the white driver who is shitting his pants, white boys Mitch and Noel cowering nervously in the back. Roadies Neville and Hugh, also suddenly and very conspicuously white, back the equipment truck up to the stage door and tiptoe out. In the near-distance the sound of gunfire, explosions, street thunder, the smell of house-burning smoke.

In the twenty-four hours since the assassination of Dr King black anger has engulfed over a hundred American cities. Riots, looting, burning, fighting, killing, met full on by the crossfire of armoured police and military vehicles. The White House calls in the 3rd Infantry to guard it and marines mount machine guns on the steps of the Capitol. The military occupation of Washington is the largest of any American city since the Civil War. Mayor-Commissioner Walter Washington imposes a curfew, bans sales of booze and guns, but it's too late to save more than a thousand buildings from being engulfed in righteous flame, almost as many shops and storefronts. Whole blocks reduced to rubble. When the shit finally dies down they estimate that over $27 million worth of damage has been done. Whole blocks reduced to rubble.

Word comes through to the gig. Harlem and Brooklyn are on fire. Jimi nervously smoking a joint; the others, silent and terrified. Trenton, another black New Jersey township, an hour's drive away, is out of control. Hundreds of downtown businesses ransacked and torched. Nearly 500 crazies, mostly young blacks arrested for assault, arson, looting and saying, 'Fuck this shit!' to the mayor's emergency curfew. Twenty cops down, as many fire fighters hospitalised for smoke inhalation, charred limbs, cuts and head wounds inflicted by rioters. People out of their minds deliberately throwing alarm switches on cars and stores then throwing rocks at the fire teams as they show up.

Word comes through to the gig. Newark, one of the first majority-black cities in the US, is going the same way. Event organisers at the venue, frightened for their lives, tell Jimi to make the two shows one, and to keep it short so everyone can get the fuck out of Dodge before it gets too dark outside. Uptight brothers coming backstage, whispering in Jimi's ear: the Man is out to get all the pro-black politicians, all the famous black faces. First JFK, then Malcolm, now MLK, maybe Jimi next, ya dig, brother?

Inside the Symphony Hall it's all pockets of people. Some sections empty, other sections crowded with people huddled together. Jimi's audience is white but with enough black faces to make the room hum and tremble. Soft Machine step gingerly onto the stage and gently whoosh into their set. Their ethereal English-church rock goes down well enough, like a sigh of relief.

Then Jimi and Noel and Mitch step out, tense, to big applause. According to the set list they'd been hocking around the coast, the opener should have been 'Fire'. Not tonight. Are you fucking kidding me?

Instead Jimi walks slowly up to the mic and says, 'This number is for a friend of mine.' He starts to pluck something out of the air and plays it for everyone, himself most especially – himself and his good friend Martin. Everyone gets the reference. Everyone tripping out. Jimi reaches within, his guitar a wand, sending out a blood light, the boys going with him, just a few steps behind. Phosphorous plumes and catches, minds ignite.

The song has no name. The song is not a song, it is a lamentation, improvised, a blue flame bouncing soul shadows off the walls. Setting light to the air, swimming in emotion. Within minutes most of the audience is in tears.

'The music had a kind of appalling beauty,' said Mark Boyle.

'It was quite a moment,' recalled Soft Machine drummer Robert Wyatt. 'What was striking was that rather than intense anger, his response was intense sadness. We were all a bit lost for words.'

Jimi played his piece. Twenty minutes, thirty minutes . . . no gaps. No hits. Soul bare. Then, when he had finished, he laid his guitar down on the stage and walked off without another word. There was no applause, just a general push for the exits. Newark was a ghost town, empty streets about to fill up.

Years, lifetimes later, Noel Redding recalled the night as 'an occasion when the whole black thing hit Jimi in the face. He couldn't turn away. Jimi was never heavy about being black. He was into being Jimi – human being, pop superstar. When his blackness became an issue, he dealt with it, but he never put it out front.'

Not out front of little Englanders like Noel, he didn't. What would be the point? Five years on the chitlin circuit playing Jim Crow deathtraps that refused black people places to eat, to shit and piss, to sleep, weren't even much of a lesson to Jimi. He'd been born into that world, was as much of that world as the race-hating sheriffs boasting of the 'nigger notches' on their shotguns.

When his own tour manager, Gerry, would say, 'To me Jimi wasn't a black man – he was a white man. He didn't think like a coloured guy,' he meant it as a compliment. But that was not the case. Jimi wasn't just a 'coloured guy' – he was a black star, a symbol of whatever anyone else wanted him to be. His blackness forced the issue. So that even high-minded white libs like John Morthland in *Rolling Stone* could write that Jimi was knowingly playing the part of what he called 'the flower generation's electric nigger dandy, its king stud and golden calf, its maker of mighty dope music, its most outrageously visible force'.

White hate dripped untreated in deep, stagnant pools. Jimi lived it, even as he denied it to his new white friends. Like the cat in the right-on *Village Voice* that year, Richard Goldstein, writing, 'Jimi Hendrix is a jiver, in the most threatening sense. Disguised as the corrupt Black Prince – Othello's Revenge – he is a mirror image of our own inner darkies, struggling to be clownish, sexual and free. Maybe that's why Jimi Hendrix is so much less relevant to black culture. Ultimately, his is a message blacks got long ago: everybody is his own spade.'

What's Jimi meant to *do* with that information, man? Sometimes the mask slips – like the day after Monterey when Pete Townshend approached Jimi at the airport and told him, all friendly, like, 'I'd love to get a bit of that guitar you smashed.' And Jimi – still bent out of shape after the backstage meltdown over who went on first at the show, him or the Who, but also just wasted, man, tired of all the bullshit, making nice for the soft white kids – gave the skinny young Englishman the stink eye and sneered, 'Oh, yeah? I'll autograph it for you, *honky*.'

Townshend folded, like he was the one hit by a bullet. 'I just crawled away,' he said. Sure you did, Pete, like they all did when confronted with the real black deal.

There was one more show, at the Mob-run Westchester County Center in White Plains, New York State, but Jimi blew through it and split for the city – get me outta here, quick – news coming in over the car radio of the death of seventeen-year-old Black Panther national treasurer 'Lil Bobby' Hutton, shot to red ribbons by the cops in Oakland.

The following night Jimi is on the loose again, alone, just Jimi and a dozen of his very good friends, mostly chicks, dealers and chicks and some other good people, awright. They hit West 8th Street, the Generation Club, where Buddy Guy is wailing on 'Stormy Monday', his own broke-heart electric eulogy to the Dead King. Buddy ripping his guitar apart, making it froth and cry. Beg mercy. Jimi looking on, head bowed, trance-like.

When Buddy invites him up for a blow, Jimi sways gently,

biting his lip, lays down a prowling alley-cat thing, Buddy biting chunks out of it. No tricks, Jimi wouldn't dare. Where you think he stole the whole playing-with-your-teeth thing? Who you think he got the playing-it-behind-your-back shit from? Jimi just jamming while Buddy's magic black Strat holds down the floor.

Long time later, Buddy remembered, 'Jimi had a wild look but a shy manner. When it was time for him to solo, I heard him as a good bluesman who like me went looking for new sounds and didn't mind if he got lost along the way. After the set, he thanked me. "You're one of my teachers." I was flattered, but I couldn't remember getting paid for any lessons. I wished him luck and never saw him again.'

CHAPTER NINETEEN

Robert and Jimi

Robert Wyatt was the drummer and singer in avant-garde British band Soft Machine – one of the central groups in what became known as the Canterbury scene – who opened for the Jimi Hendrix Experience on their 1968 tour of the United States. I spoke to him on the telephone.

Do you still have clear memories of the US tour Soft Machine did, opening for Hendrix in 1968?

Oh, yes. It was most of '68, really. We started out on the West Coast then went all over the place. It was fantastic. Part of it, to be honest, was because we didn't have a wannabe guitar hero in our band. For Hendrix it was like those old Western films where the local gunslinger would come out and challenge the famous gunslinger if he was coming to town, try to outshoot him. He was very polite, Hendrix, but he got a bit tired of it; all these guitarists raving away in front of him, saying, 'Look what I can do!' And we didn't have one in our band so it was like a different species. So luckily, although he got some flak for having us on the bill, he said he liked the fact that we were trying something different. And he was like that. He liked people who were trying something different. That said, we got a lot louder during that tour, used a lot more fuzz boxes and stuff, and we were inspired by the theatrical physicality of what he did.

In that context, as a live performer, he was legendarily a real showman quite often. On other occasions he would give a more studied 'in-concert' performance. Which was he on that tour?

He was mature about this, I think, and very kind to audiences. If he was playing to an aircraft hangar of fifteen-year-old Texans, he would play the nearest he could to recognisable rock riffs around the tunes he was doing, and really smack 'em out so the kids right at the back of the hall would hear that clearly. If he was playing, like, nearer New York or the coast, where there's a lot more avant-garde activity, it got more and more psychedelic, as it were. He'd sometimes spend the beginning of the set doing a whole load of feedback stuff before he came to the first tune. It depended entirely on the audience, as far as I could see. He wasn't indifferent to the audience. In that sense, I'd say he was a very conscientious, old-fashioned entertainer, funnily enough.

Others have spoken of this aura that surrounded him. Did you notice anything like that?

I truly did. I absolutely did. It's like . . . I don't know what you call it. It's not a judgement thing about how good or bad people are. It's a certain thing you get in a room when there's a kind of . . . fuzzy thing going on around, an electrical thing going around. The only person I've met recently who has anything like that is Björk, actually. When she's in a room, there's an electrical thing going on, and Jimi had that. But he seemed to actively act against it. He was ultra-shy, almost to the point of, like, stuttering. He wasn't in your face at all. His face would sort of look away and down when he talked to you. I found him very diffident, and he'd sort of whisper, in a slightly hard to hear way, in conversation.

I think one of the things I liked about him that gets overlooked, understandably, is his singing. He considered himself a rubbish singer but thought, well, somebody's got to do it. He was a wonderful singer. He was kind of throwaway in what he did. He wasn't like a singer in a gospel base or anything like that.

He was more in the half-talking thing, like John Lee Hooker or something. It was quite light as well. And there was a thing here that people after him didn't get. Which was that long, long guitar solos – pushing your hands up and down the frets and making higher notes look difficult to play, which they're not, just move your fingers – he actually didn't do. He was very worried about being boring. People think of the sixties as a very ideological time, but the only thing I can think of that he really hated was being bored. He had a very low boredom threshold. He was terrified of boring himself, too.

So if you listen to something like his playing on 'All Along the Watchtower', you'll see that every chorus, he changes what he's playing on the solo. The rhythm thing comes up or the single note thing comes down a bit. He shifts gear a lot, just to keep his own interest going, I think. He wouldn't just wail up and down the strings for hours.

Was that part of his personality too, so that even without the guitar, when you were with him in person, he would be restless?

He was reticent. He didn't hold forth. I never heard him hold forth on a subject. But, I mean, when I was with him, it would be other blokes around, and there'd probably be two Swedish girls with legs as long as the Eiffel Tower waiting patiently at the door, who were maybe more interesting to him than sitting around talking to a bunch of blokes. I'm a bit suspicious of people who say they sat around with Hendrix, talking for hours. I think, you might have, it's possible, I suppose . . .

Soft Machine were actually signed to the same management company as Hendrix. Was that how you first met him?

That's right, yeah. We were signed up not long beforehand. The first time we met Jimi was at a rehearsal room. I suppose the management had booked the same rehearsal room. That was the first time I heard all three [of the Experience] playing together.

Were you already familiar with any of his records?

No. I remember Chas Chandler coming in to the office and – I can't do the wonderful Geordie accent – he said, 'I've just found this fucking guitarist. He plays the guitar with his fucking teeth! He's unbelievable and we're gonna get him!'

Coming from your background as a musician, which was principally a drummer of modern jazz, what was your take on Hendrix as a musician?

Well, I don't sit in judgement of people. I prefer the David Attenborough approach. You know, what is that organic thing? Not do I like it or not? So going into a rehearsal room with the Jimi Hendrix Experience, it was like going into some strange wind machine, being blown around the room. It was quite extraordinary, just the physical impact of what he was doing. It seemed to be moving around the room and he did play loud. I did know Noel Redding from before, because he'd been a bit of a guitar hero in Folkestone, in east Kent, which is where I come from. And indeed I knew Gerry Stickells, Hendrix's road manager, whom Noel got the job through. But the key for me – the jazz link – was actually Mitch. People talk about Hendrix but for me the Experience remains the quintessential Hendrix band, much as I admire Buddy Miles's drumming and so on. What I admired about the Experience was that Hendrix used Mitch at all. Because there were quite a few drummers who could lay down a very funky rock beat at that time. There were some terrific drummers around.

But what Mitch did, he took risks around the kit. A bit like Tony Williams or some of the jazz drummers would do; very, very fluid. But because he was so quick-witted he could find the place Hendrix was going. I think Noel, sometimes, when Hendrix and Mitch were both at it, you'd talk to him afterwards and he'd say, 'I didn't know what the fuck was going on, I just went dum-dum, dum-dum till they played the fucking tune again!'

There were definitely two lead instrumentalists in that line-up . . .

Yeah. That was my jazz connection, because John Coltrane

had only died in 1967, and all those jazz fans were kind of reeling from the shock of that. Then, somehow, we were seeing it through a sort of rock-music equivalent, which we'd never expected. I suppose you could say Ginger Baker and Jack Bruce had some of that, but this really was something else, in terms of recklessness. You really didn't know where he was gonna go, and you got the feeling that Mitch and Noel didn't know where he was gonna go either.

When he started out he hardly had any tunes. I know he did 'Hey Joe' and he had a couple of other things, but they had to do a lot of improvising really because they hadn't had time to build up much of a repertoire before they became stars. So that caused them to stretch out and improvise a lot. And he used Mitch, he didn't use a rock or soul drummer. Mitch had just played with Georgie Fame, in a very tight R&B band. They were jazz musicians in a sort of R&B, soul tradition. So Mitch really knew about both. They say jazz isn't a style; it is an attitude. Hendrix had that risk-taking thing. Whereas with classical or pop music, everyone knows where you're gonna go. It's just a case of doing it right.

Similarly, in jazz at the time, artists like Coltrane or Miles Davis might take a standard like 'My Favourite Things' and turn it into a nine-minute exploration of space.

Exactly right. And sometimes it was very unlikely material. With Hendrix it was hard to imagine him sitting there listening to 'Wild Thing' by the Troggs, but he did. Then took it somewhere else and made magic out of it way beyond the original.

Or 'The Star-Spangled Banner' . . .

Yes, that was something else, wasn't it?

Especially in those days of student revolt and opposition to the flag.

He was quite defensive about that, though. I saw a clip of him on television being asked, 'Wasn't that an insult to the flag?' And he said, 'I thought it was beautiful.' Although the revolutionaries of the day would have preferred otherwise, he was not politically a revolutionary. I don't think he was really interested in politics. His only education in politics seemed to have come from being in the forces, and he had a very conventional American view of the world. But I just thought he liked the hippy thing of taking risks and being a bit out there, more than the tight groups he'd been in before, like the Isley Brothers and so on.

When you heard he'd died, how did you receive that news?

I can't remember. I sort of look back and think, goodness me, we thought we were on the road at the beginning of some bloke's long career, and that was it! It was like a comet. I don't feel sorry for people when they die because after all they're dead and they don't feel anything. And I do believe, honestly, that towards the end, after his Band of Gypsys thing, he was floundering a bit. I don't think he quite knew what to do next. So that may have contributed to his being a bit more careless to himself than he should have been. But I didn't know him well enough. It's very presumptuous of me to speculate any further on that.

I tend to think that often people who've died very young, sometimes they get more in than most of us manage in a lifetime. I mean, if you listen back, just to the recorded stuff, never mind the bootleg concerts and all that stuff, just those records, they're quite wonderful. Sometimes when you read about someone being Hendrix-influenced, you listen to those records and you still think there's something much more going on here. There's a lightness of touch, a fluidity. There's light and shade. It's a very different thing he's doing. It's not driving like a tank through your room, which is what heavy metal does. I saw Blue Cheer in San Francisco, and it was like watching tanks driving around the room – pretty impressive! But it was very delicate what Hendrix did, in a way. It was very loud, but he used the volume as a tool to become part of the colours. The sonic effects from the feedback and so on could really be used as colours. And you could really feel that with what he was doing. It was like some great, swirling abstract painting with very bright colours in it.

I think his management, rather irresponsibly, pushed that wild-man stuff because they thought it would sell a lot. The old cliché, you know, your mother wouldn't like it, lock up your daughters and all that. He was actually very professional and responsible compared to a lot of rock musicians I knew at the time. Almost like a grown-up among adolescents a lot of the time. But when he was doing his show, he did his show. And although it was much more for a rock audience, which was mostly white at that time, as opposed to the soul audience, I think he learned a lot about keeping and holding your attention from the bands he'd been in before. He was an incredibly nice man, polite, decent. All that wild-man stuff is showbiz stuff. He could do it, just like Pete Townshend can whirl his arms around. But he too is a civilised man.

One final memory of being with Jimi?

I remember, at the end of the American tour we did with him, we were in Los Angeles, sitting about the pool together, and I had a guitar and was trying to write a tune – which actually ended up being 'Moon in June' [from the later Soft Machine album, *Third*] – and I was trying different chords. Hendrix was sitting there watching. Then he said, sort of whispered, 'You can get that a lot easier if you go from here to there,' pointing at the fret board, 'unless you really want to do it that way.' And I said, 'Yes, I really want to do it my way.' I thought, I just turned down a guitar lesson from fucking Jimi Hendrix! I now have that memory etched in my mind for ever. I can never sing Edith Piaf's 'Non, Je ne Regrette Rien' again . . .

CHAPTER TWENTY

Jimi and the Mountain

Dr King's death meant you couldn't be neutral anymore, not if you were black. Not if you were black and American and living and working in New York, just a pimp's fancy stride from Times Square. Not if you were Jimi Hendrix and every street you walked down the brothers assailed you.

'Which side you on, brother?'

'You coloured, nigger?'

Waving mimeographed copies of 'What We Want Now!' by brother Bobby Seale and brother Huey Newton. Or their other hot Black Panther screed, 'What We Believe'.

'You got five dollars for the cause, brother Jimi?'

Sure, Jimi's got five dollars. On his way over from his West 44th Street hotel to the newly opened Record Plant, eventually just moving into the studio, sleeping whenever the drugs wore off long enough to let him sleep, on the plush couches, the first home-from-home studio in America, can you dig it? Jimi making real music of the soul. Music of the soul on fire. Music of the soul reaching out beyond the sky, no limits, new worlds beyond, flirting with time, reshaping space, shooting up stars.

Jimi on a motherfucking roll now, brother.

The first taste of what the album's release later that year would bring came in June, after Jimi was flown back to Europe for some urgently needed money shows and to record an appearance in

England on the TV show *It Must Be Dusty*, starring Dusty Spring-field. Dusty was a stone fox but preferred chicks. That was fine too, baby. Dusty had a sweet soul sister's voice and a good heart and was trying to hip her act up, doing Jacques Brel, digging Rod McKuen. Having Jimi Hendrix on her show.

Dusty cueing Jimi up with the intro: 'About a year or so ago I went to the theatre on a Sunday evening. They used to have some big raving Sunday concerts at a certain theatre on Shafts-bury Avenue [the Saville Theatre show where he opened with 'Sgt. Pepper's Lonely Hearts Club Band'] and I saw three people who I thought made the best sound in the world coming from three people. This marvellous man on the guitar and equally mar-vellous fellows on the bass and drums. I think they're fantastic. Ladies and gentlemen, welcome the Jimi Hendrix Experience.'

Cut to Jimi, close-up of his face, saying, 'Thank you very much. This one is dedicated to Brian Jones.' Brian had just been busted again for dope and was back to being a weeping, stoned mess. Few of the good folks watching at home got that, though. Brian who?

Cue music. Jimi in psychedelic-petal shirt: waistcoat and silver jeans. Mitch: *sans* Afro. Noel: still growing his, getting good at the sides and on top. Cool Noel in silver jacket and spymaster shades.

They slip-slide through 'Stone Free', Jimi all flowing aqua guitar, then a quick on-camera schmooze with Dusty. 'Can I have the name of your hairdresser, please, Noel?' Giggly Dusty falling back on the old boys-with-long-hair-look-like-girls jam, still going down well with the straight TV audience in the summer of 1968.

Then: 'Hey, watcha been doing, Jim?'

Jimi cool-weary. 'We've been working on our LP. We've just come off this Italian tour, you know?'

'Yeah? Tearing the place up?'

'Well, you know, doing our thing – whichever that is.'

'Yeah, some – *thing* ... Yeah, great ... Well, listen, we're supposed to do a duet now and you can pick any number you want, provided you pick "Mockingbird".'

A scripted little gag; hooray for Dusty!

'Great.' Jimi playing along – a good pro. 'I'll tell you what we're gonna do. We're gonna do "Mockingbird".'

Zero studio audience response as Jimi glides into a swinging-dick version of the intro to 'Mockingbird', Dusty grinning, grooving along in her sexy-maid sideways shuffle. Dusty in her big blonde wig, half beehive, half hip older sister, pure soul delivery; Jimi adding edge, showing off his chitlin roots, happy to play nice for the armchair straights.

Then, no intro, just straight into 'Voodoo Child (Slight Return)', first time heard anywhere outside the recording studio. Four minutes of pure Hendrix fist-high fury, brought to an abrupt, unplanned climax when the floor manager signals for him to quit. No one can believe this was planned. Shouldn't he be doing his new single or something?

Yeah, some – *thing* . . .

The next morning Jimi is woken earlier than usually allowed by a phone call. Bobby Kennedy has been shot in Los Angeles. *What, man?* Kennedy is in the hospital and everyone is praying he makes it, but fuck, man, the guy was shot three times at close range, dig?

Say what? Kennedy ain't King but he's close enough for a white politician. Close enough to the cause for the black man to see the pattern. Bobby wasn't Malcolm or Dr King or Ali or even his brother JFK. Bobby was *rich* and *white*. Somehow that made it feel even worse, more brazen and terrifying. They would do this to their own? Yes, sir.

Jimi has to get ready. He's flying back to New York the next day. He's about to step onto the plane when news of Kennedy's death is announced. He arrives in New York around the same time Kennedy's corpse does. Jimi goes out that night to the Fillmore East, where he gets up and jams with Electric Flag, around the same time that Bobby is being laid out for viewing at St Patrick's Cathedral in midtown Manhattan.

Jimi didn't go to view the body or pay respect. He didn't need to. He got the vibe like everyone else. After King, Kennedy had been calling for 'social and racial justice'. A lot of white liberals had been doing the same for years, but Bobby went with Peter Edelman to visit black sharecroppers in Mississippi and poor whites in the Appalachians. Bobby was the seventh son, who'd had to fight for his father's attention. Rich man's son Bobby knew what it was like to have to make it from the outside. Now Bobby was going to run for president – and that's when the big white guns came out.

Now who was going to look out for us? *Nobody, man! You crazy?*

Three days later Jimi was in the Record Plant laying down 'House Burning Down'. Not for Bobby, but for what happened in the wake of Dr King's assassination, when blacks across America began setting fire to their own neighbourhoods. Jimi for the first time as militant black soldier, smoke-trailing guitars, martial drums, the sky hellfire red, sending a warning.

'*I said the truth is straight ahead so don't burn yourself instead / Try to learn instead of burn, hear what I say, yeah, yeah . . .*'

Sessions for a new album had begun even before *Axis* was released, back in London at Olympic Studios at the rainy end of October '67, and again in the surprisingly mild lead-up to Christmas. Jimi was lost in an unreliable reality now, post-boom, over the first flush, unsure how to get where he needed to be, or even know where he needed to be. Noel was pushing, pushing to have more of his songs included. So they stretched out the early sessions while Jimi hid behind his acid mask. They fucked around with one of Noel's sketchy ideas called 'Dance', but the rhythm was too lugubrious for its title. Mitch was down to sing it. Jimi didn't mind the idea of someone else doing the singing occasionally. He hated his own voice. But there were no real lyrics yet, and the thing was only saved in the end by Jimi jump-starting it and making it into an okay, no-biggie instrumental, to which he gave a new joke title, 'Cat Talking to Me'.

Mitch would get his stab at singing on another unused thing called 'Dream'. Mitch had a nice voice – for a drummer. But the song was another nothing. Jimi later took his riff and lit it up properly for a groovier little thing he came up with called 'Ezy Ryder'.

The only real non-Jimi demo that would make it onto the final album was Noel's 'Little Miss Strange', which was just a rewrite of the song Jimi allowed him to have on *Axis*, 'She's So Fine'. Noel with his clichéd psychedelic devil-in-*diz-guise* glory-grab, enlivened only by Jimi's extra splashes of candy-striped pop.

Chas oversaw the early sessions, looking for more sheep in wolf's clothing transistor-radio-sized rock-pop. But Jimi struggled with that now, moving towards the engineer Eddie Kramer, who indulged his passion for more experimental sounds. Olympic was a grandstand studio, a former cinema with a suspended floor. You recorded on a four-track analogue tape. Eddie's trick was to record the drums in stereo with the bass and rhythm guitar then bounce those four tracks down to two tracks on a secondary four-track machine – so Jimi could continue adding tracks, finding hyper-textures, while maintaining stereo imagery.

Chas was beginning to feel the cold. Only some of *Are You Experienced* had been done at Olympic with Eddie involved, but almost all of *Axis* had been done there. Jimi felt at home there now, didn't need Chas to guide his hand. He was also immersed in *Sgt. Pepper's*, Zappa's Mothers, *Disraeli Gears* and, most especially, the spectral spirituality of *John Wesley Harding*, Dylan's first album for two years. So completely different from *Blonde on Blonde*, so utterly not what someone like Chas would have advised Dylan to do, yet so truthful to Jimi, so spare and yet limitless, so clearly signposting the right direction home, he wanted more than anything to make something of his own that might one day compare, even a little.

Jimi could not believe that Dylan had actually made the record in less than twelve hours, at the same time as he was wasting studio time fussing over one of Noel's drab, routine songs. During one of the early Olympic sessions, while everyone is still tooling around with Noel's stuff, Jimi tries out a version of 'I Dreamed I Saw St. Augustine' from the Dylan. But it seems too personal to Dylan. Jimi loves the pale-moon melody, the depth of the dream Dylan is describing, but finds he can't sing it convincingly; what Dylan's talking about is just too deep.

Frustrated, he turns to the next track on the album, 'All Along the Watchtower'. Jimi identifying with the opening lines about finding 'some way out of here', but there being 'too much confusion. I can't get no relief . . .'

Noel, turned off by seeing Jimi stop work on his songs, goes to the pub. Not unusual – typical, in fact. Jimi relieved to be left alone to get on with it, dubs the bass himself, then invites his new friend Dave Mason from Traffic to accompany him on an acoustic rhythm guitar, Mitch busking, following the train. Sometime late into the night Brian Jones comes by, sits down at the piano, offers to lay down a colour. Jimi smilingly nods, hey, man. But Brian is so stoned he can't get his fingers to work. Jimi eventually gets Eddie Kramer to lead Brian away. Jimi finishing the track by scatting the lyrics, improvising where he can't quite get what Dylan's singing, the overall mood sounding good. Different enough to the original to have Jimi humming it the next day, a good sign.

As he sat at the table at Noel's family home in Folkestone on Christmas Day – Noel's twenty-second birthday – Jimi was determined that the new year would mark a new way for him to start making the music he wanted to make, fuck Chas, fuck whatever Noel or Mitch wanted, and fuck anyone else who got in the way of that. Hanging out the next night at photographer Bruce Fleming's place, still playing the Dylan, Jimi impressed Bruce and his wife and their friends with his sense of adventure.

'We got to talk a lot,' Bruce later recalled. 'Architecture, painting, all sorts. He was into everything.' Jimi basked in the respect he was now being shown by all these white dudes and their educated mien. Jimi, said Bruce, 'was very radical in his opinions and ideas; a very original thinker'. Jimi was beginning to see that too. Why couldn't Chas see that and let him take his music so much further out?

Less radical and original was Jimi's rapidly expanding appetite for not just acid, but now speed, coke, downers and – quickly coming down the street towards him, ratty black hat tilted, casting its face in deep shadow – heroin.

Back at Olympic the last couple of days of December, Jimi found a new midway path in a musical thumbnail he called 'Have You Ever Been (To Electric Ladyland)'. On the surface the most perfectly manicured R&B song Jimi ever fashioned, as slow and seductive as 'I Can't Stay Away from You' by the Impressions, a single he'd bought that year in America, and at the same time as defiantly far out as he could be without having Chas raise a red flag. Backwards guitar, decelerated drums, a floating fragment of a dream populated by black and white angels, wings spread, riding the same magic carpet he first sang about in 'Spanish Castle Magic', only where that had been a journey in free-fall, this was elevated, heavenly, Jimi crooning in falsetto, '*Right over the love-filled sea*'.

The other number Jimi hit upon at Olympic was almost a salve for Chas – the kind of two-minute pop roar with motorcycle guitars and hell-on-wheels chorus the Animals specialised in – 'Crosstown Traffic'. Jimi laughing at the playback of him doubling the lightning guitar riff on a comb wrapped in tissue paper – a homemade kazoo. Fuck, man, you wouldn't find Clapton playing along to his guitar by blowing through a comb. Zappa using kazoos on *Freak Out!*, sure, but wait a minute here . . .

But it was beautiful – and catchy – and short. A stellar rock song recorded by the original trio – and a definitely maybe hit. Chas went home damn happy that night. Chas not paying attention to Jimi's lyrics about some passing flame with 'tire tracks' across her back – the scars of other lovers? Needle tracks? What kind of big-city sin are we talking about?

Then Jimi goes back on the road. Sweden, Denmark, Sweden again, back to London mid-January for three more long nights at Olympic, Chas chain-smoking at the desk, then a one-night stand in Paris, two scene-stealers with Eric and the Animals. Followed the next day with a flight back to New York, ready for the two-month tour of the US, Jimi shagging it coast to coast, sixty-eight shows in sixty-five days. Even on so-called nights off Jimi hitting the clubs, letting the chicks in for one night, one hour, the dealers and their party friends. Jimi picking up the *Rolling Stone* magazine Great Balls of Fire Award – is that a colour thing, baby? No, man, it's a *groove* thing. Jimi picking up World Top Musician award from *Disc and Music Echo* magazine in London, being told about it just before going onstage at the Will Rogers Auditorium in Fort Worth, Texas – being reminded what *Disc and Music Echo* is. Jimi, back at the Scene in New York two nights later, jamming late stuff with some of the dudes from Electric Flag, Mike Bloomfield and Buddy Miles, losing their shit, man, plus a couple of the English cats from Soft Machine, trying to get it together, and the Tremeloes. *The fuckin' Tremeloes, man!* 'Silence Is Golden'! Come on, man, now that's a trip!

By the time he's ready to begin recording again at the end of April – this time at the newly opened Record Plant – Jimi is in a new dimension. Working out of Studio A, with its outrageous range of enormous Tannoy speakers hanging by chains from the ceiling, emitting sounds louder than anything anybody's ever heard, even onstage, Jimi lets loose, begins to really fly.

'There are some very personal things in there,' Jimi is quoted in the press as saying about 'Burning of the Midnight Lamp' – a track that was released in Britain as a single nine months before but only got to number 18 in the charts. Jimi's first non-Top 10 hit and everything Chas had warned him would happen if he strayed too far down the path of so-called innovation, of would-be experimentation – of wanton wah-wah pedal, me-the-artist-I-strangelove – and tried to sell it to long-haired hippy teens as new-sensation music. Jimi rolling his eyes, already decided it's going on the new album anyway.

'But I think everyone can understand the feeling when you're travelling that no matter what your address, there is no place you can call home,' he continues. 'The feeling of a man in a little old house in the middle of a desert, where he is burning the midnight lamp . . . you don't mean for things to be personal all the time, but it is.'

Chas: 'A fucking harpsichord! What do you need a fucking harpsichord on there for?'

The studio crowding with people, Jimi's people. Noel complaining he has nowhere to sit. 'Yeah, but who are you, man?' asks one freak, stoned halo visibly vibrating. 'I'm the fucking bass player,' Noel scowls. But still no one moves. Just warm smoke and ice in their eyes. Acid fire and low-tide junk: tendrils of cross-thought.

Some chick in a wig: 'I sucked him off in the cab.'

Some head in beard and beads: 'I only handle the primo shit.'

'And Jimi loves it loud . . .'

Jimi cooing over one of the first Scully twelve-track tape machines. This is the future calling. Orders the tech team to take the four-track masters already recorded at Olympic to be transferred over to four tracks of the Scully at the Record Plant. Giving Jimi a whole other eight tracks to play with, mind whirring out of control at the sea of possibilities.

As the days at the Plant turn into weeks and then months, an even newer piece of kit arrives: a sixteen-track Ampex machine, onto which Jimi now orders the masters to be transferred – giving him another four tracks to fuck around with. Jimi almost goes crazy, guitar harmonies, backwards tape effects, endless multi-layered lead parts, multiplying the overdubs into infinity, instruments and voices enmeshed, transported, transmogrified, energy converted. Chas hanging on by his fingernails, gradually losing his shit. Chas lost in a roomful of mirrors, hating it, unable to breathe, his punchbowl spiked. Finally getting up out of his chair after *forty-two takes* of 'Gypsy Eyes', Jimi doubling then tripling then quadrupling the guitar and vocal, split-second perfection. 'Let's do it again, again, let's do it again, okay, that was nearly it, let's do it again, again, okay, that was almost it . . .'

Chas exploding out of his seat, face red and puffed, dripping sweat and frustration. 'I can't stand any more of this! Tell me when you're fucking done – I'm off to my bed!'

Jimi looking after Chas as he storms out of the control room. Jimi getting it alright – just not caring much any more. England was a gas, man. It gave Jimi an out – and an in. He was grateful to Chas for that. But London wasn't New York. England wasn't everything. Jimi was home now, in charge at last. He had earned the right.

'Okay, let's try that again . . .'

Jimi up for three nights, no sleep. Jimi up for five nights, no sleep. Jimi shooting speed, snorting coke, chain-smoking joints, swallowing handfuls of acid. No effect. Jimi living back home in New York for the first time since he made it. Jimi surrounded by starfuckers supreme.

Jimi on a motherfucking roll now, brother. You better look out!

Record Plant co-owner Chris Stone recalling the scene thirty years later: 'I'd go in the control room and . . . Hendrix would be standing at the console, staring at the monitors, burned out of his gourd and just loving every second of it. The man had a constitution like no other. He was like a robot when it came to work. He wouldn't quit. And then, when he couldn't hear anymore, basically, he would stop. Because he listened at such incredibly loud levels.'

Sitting up in bed smoking between nights at the studio, Jimi writing down everything that comes to mind before he forgets it ... UFO-lore, mythology, *I Ching*, astrology, numerology, all the different colours of sound, the blinding spectacle of indoor stars, exploring the interspace between science and nature, astral travel, reincarnation, parallel dimensions, joining the dots, so easy to see now, madly laughing. Crying when the comedowns come, smiling with tears in his eyes, howling. In a fury with Noel and even Mitch now sometimes when their endless bitching is brought back to him. Tripping in front of the TV news, Cronkite with his wet eyes and long dog-face, out in Vietnam talking about the Tet Offensive, about the body counts, about no way to win the war. The ghetto Cronkites yapping on street corners about the Black Power uprising, about student revolt, about the Bobby Kennedy conspiracy, the MLK conspiracy, the Man comin' for your black ass. Fucking Nixon, man. That fucking pig Nixon is gonna be the president. You believe that shit, man?

And now some new shit. Ed Chalpin and his lawyers were back on the scene in a big way. Looking for court orders to stop Jimi releasing records, looking for money and recognition, hand-delivering Xeroxed copies of old contracts with Jimi's signature on them straight to Mike Jeffery.

Mike in a huff, seeing no way out, moving his operations over to New York, to be with Jimi but also to escape the unpaid rent and ripped-off furniture from the London office. Chas has also lost his tie and declared he no longer wants even to manage Jimi, offering his slice fully to Mike for $300,000. Chas going so far as to accuse Mike and Jimi of becoming 'acid buddies' after Jimi made it clear he preferred to stay with Mike rather than go chasing after Chas and his hurt feelings. Chas and his need to control the musical conversation at a time when Jimi is busy inventing new languages. The stress now causing Chas's hair to fall out in chunks. Mike always one step ahead, pushing Jimi back out on the road as the money keeps flying out the door. Jimi complaining he hasn't finished the album yet. Jimi now talking it up as a double album.

Mike laughing at that one.

Jimi, too terrified to stop moving, coming back from the road and dragging people in to help him complete the album at the Record Plant. Old friends like twenty-year-old drummer Buddy Miles, bustin' chops in Electric Flag but whom Jimi had known in the old days of sharing late-night bills with Ink Spots and Wilson Pickett. Buddy came into the studio one night after jamming with Jimi at the Scene, and they laid down the cooking funk rhythm to 'Rainy Day, Dream Away' and 'Still Raining, Still Dreaming', actually the same long, improvised rumble – the Hammond organ comping on the 'Testify' jam from Jimi's 1964 recording with the Isley Brothers – spliced down the middle by the epic thirteen-minute-plus sci-fi trip '1983 . . . (A Merman I Should Turn to Be)'. Jimi and Kathy reincarnated as undersea love-makers, in a future place – 1983 – impossible to imagine outside of *silver blue to bloody red* dreams.

New friends like Al Kooper, the precocious twenty-four-year-old who'd played with Jimi's beloved Dylan on 'Like a Rolling Stone' and *Blonde on Blonde*, and Jimi now coerced into playing jingle-jangle-morning piano on 'Long Hot Summer', Jimi's dope-disguised dissertation on the 'hot' events unfolding on the streets, from New York to Hanoi, that summer. Jimi playing all the other instruments – except for Mitch's roiling drums – even doing the high, sweet-chick backing vocals on multi-track.

'Well everybody's on fire, but its
A-snowin' in a cold blizzard . . .'

Complete unknowns found down the hall, going by the name the Serfs, now butterflying into Jimi Hendrix sidemen: organist Mike Finnigan (white, nicotine moustache, B3 boogie), saxophonist Freddie Smith (black, lyrical, bold), conga player Larry Faucette (black, tall, fast). Or the night Jimi came trucking back to the studio at two in the morning, trailing Steve Winwood and Dave Mason from Traffic, Jack Casady from Jefferson Airplane, and a couple dozen other good, good people from the Scene not yet ready to call it a night. The Airplane had been in town taping a TV show. Traffic had done a show in the Scene's underground basement.

'So we all marched over at closing time . . . He was working on a couple of songs. We stayed most of the night. There were probably thirty people in the vocal booth,' Casady recalled thirty years later. Also present: jazz guitarist Larry Coryell, then being hyped as 'the white' Hendrix. 'All kinds of people there, just partying around.'

It was already past dawn, six or seven in the morning when Jimi, a new rush coming on strong, suggested they lay down a blues. The tapes were rolling. The tapes were always rolling at the studio. They had to be or nothing would ever have got done.

Jimi, so high over the mountain, lays out the swaggering intro to 'Catfish Blues', a riff on the Muddy Waters blues, itself a rebuild of Muddy's earlier 'Rollin' Stone', which Jimi has taken to doing here and there over the past year, see the white folks start to rough and tumble over it as he turns Muddy's deep, mournful blues into a blazing funeral pyre.

Jimi now taking it in an even deeper fire-down-below direction, speaking the words as they flash-fire into his brain.

'Well, I'm a voodoo chile, Lord, I'm a voodoo chile . . .'

The band – Mitch, Jack, Steve – falling into ghost step behind him, shadows taller than their souls.

'Well, the night I was born, Lord, I swear, the moon turned a fire red . . .'

They play without stopping, no single hesitation, for fifteen minutes, slow, ominous, incandescent, hard thunder, blood rain, walking through the fire.

An American negro spiritual for the Space Race, a big-city bluesman's self-mythologising meets American Indian woo-woo. The protagonist, a twentieth-century cowboy, born of third-eye gypsy woman . . . alien African shaman . . . shit-talking drums . . . sexual holocaust . . . the nightly incubus . . . Jimi spirit-walking the vocal:

I make love to you in your sleep; Lord knows you feel no pain
Cos I'm a million miles away
And at the same time I'm right here in your picture frame . . .

'It wasn't just slopped together,' said Jimi, when the subsequent reviews seemed to suggest he was more channelling receiver than astral-plane messenger. 'Everything you hear on there means something.'

'. . . And the Gods Made Love', space-time drum clouds, mountain-divinity voices whispering sweet memory jive . . . Earl King's toothsome R&B bellow. 'Come On (Part 1)', Jimi finally just having fun, echo of the chitlin nights, the cheap clip-on bow ties, the white stiffs dancing, the afterwards fucking in the back of the bus or the hall or just out back, while daddy's not looking . . . another spaced-out tone poem, 'Moon, Turn the Tides . . . Gently Gently Away', an undulating sea of smiling mermaids and heavenly guides towards the new horizon . . . is Jimi saying the journey ends in . . . peace? Even in 1968? With Bobby and Luther's blood still polluting the streets of America? With Nixon hovering like a vulture? With Chas crashing back to Earth and Mike Jeffery now filling that space and Noel all fed up and mutinous, and the girls, the ladies, the chicks, all on his trail, throwing their shadows?

No. This journey ends like this, with the heaven-juddering storm of 'Voodoo Child (Slight Return)', Jimi in full thunder god regalia, full black Jesus spell-casting robes. Jimi feeding on planets and shitting stars as he hurls out his most deathly defiant riff, the words tumbling from his stone visage like holy tablets of fire.

'Well, I stand up next to the mountain
Cut it down with the edge of my hand . . .'

Later. Jimi speaking so quietly, trying his best to explain: 'The everyday mud world we're living in today, compared to the spiritual world, is like a parasite compared to the ocean.' The reporter nods knowingly, uh-huh. 'And the ocean is the biggest living thing you know about. The music flows from the air. That's why I can connect with a spirit, and when they come down off this natural high, they see clearer, feel different things – don't think of pain and hurting the next person.' Yeah, I get it, said the reporter. Then dwindled away to nothing to write his little piece.

The real pay-off, though – the real signpost of the coming apocalypse – comes in his almost offhand cover of Dylan's black-cat-bones masterpiece 'All Along the Watchtower'. The rifling riff, the windswept rhythm, the gathering night, Jimi paints in all the colours Dylan had deliberately drained from his original. Adding some burn, making Dylan actually rethink his own approach, to the point that Dylan would from then on always perform his own song the way Jimi Hendrix had demonstrated how to do it.

Jimi completely unaware of the biblical references in the lyrics, or that Dylan was playing with people's heads – because he was Bob Dylan, and in 1967 he could do anything he damn well pleased and people would forgive him for it or, like Jimi, find new meanings all of their own and not be wrong about it.

Dylan's elliptical lyrics a stronger echo of the Book of Isaiah, Chapter 21, verses 5–9, which state:

Prepare the table, watch in the watchtower, eat, drink: arise ye princes, and prepare the shield / For thus hath the Lord said unto me, Go set a watchman, let him declare what he seeth / And he saw a chariot with a couple of horsemen, a chariot of asses, and a chariot of camels; and he hearkened diligently with much heed / . . . And, behold, here cometh a chariot of men, with a couple of horsemen. And he answered and said, Babylon is fallen, is fallen, and all the graven images of her gods he hath broken unto the ground.

Or as Bobby and now Jimi had it:

All along the watchtower, princes kept the view
While all the women came and went, barefoot servants, too
Outside in the cold distance a wildcat did growl
Two riders were approaching, the wind began to howl.

Two riders now approaching – fast.

CHAPTER TWENTY-ONE

Eddie and Jimi

It was a surprisingly sunny spring morning in London, forty two and a half years after the death of Jimi Hendrix. Eddie Kramer was in town to promote *People, Hell and Angels*, the latest in a staggeringly long line of posthumously released Hendrix albums, this one co-produced with Janie Hendrix and John McDermott of Experience Hendrix LLC, the official family company charged with managing the name, likeness, image and music of Jimi Hendrix's legacy – which Kramer has worked with since its inception in 1995.

Best known for working alongside Jimi as engineer and mixer of all three studio albums made while the guitarist was alive, as well as overseeing the very best of the posthumous Hendrix work, – via his full-time collaboration with the Experience Hendrix organisation – Kramer also famously worked on several key Led Zeppelin albums, the succession of live and studio albums that made Kiss a household name in America in the 1970s, and with a variety of artists as gifted and diverse as Traffic, Carly Simon, Peter Frampton, Brian May, Buddy Guy, John McLaughlin . . .

Wherever he goes and whomever he is working with, though, it's always his time with Jimi that everyone wants to know about. Me included.

On first meeting, over the phone a few years before, Eddie came across as a curmudgeon. After all, he'd had a lifetime of people stopping and asking, 'You know, so what was Hendrix *really* like?' But in person he is a sprightly rock 'n' roll gentleman. As well as the striped pink shirt and jet-black trousers held up with obligatory silver-buckled belt, he was also sporting a purple silk-and-velvet scarf, which he couldn't wait to show off.

'It's made by Lunafinery,' he explained. 'My lovely partner [AJ Newton] and I put this company together and we're selling what we call English gentleman meets rock 'n' roll scarves. They're made from silk and velvet. This one's called Purple Haze . . . duh! And it's got the Eddie Kramer signature on the inside.'

Eddie took off his scarf and we got to it.

What was Jimi like when you first met him?

It was not till January 1967 that I met him. He'd already been in London for a few months and it had already been established that he was the coming man. He'd already had a single out ['Hey Joe']. He'd already played the Paris Olympia and all of that, so I really did know who he was. Everybody knew who he was and what he was doing – turning the music business upside down.

The next thing, I get the phone call from my lovely studio manager named Anna Menzies. She called me up and went, 'Oh, Eddie. There's this American chappie with big hair, and you should do the session because you do all that weird shit anyway.' Because I had this reputation for doing a lot of avant-garde jazz, she thought it would be a good fit, and she was right. We hit it off.

So what was the first session you recorded with Jimi – 'Purple Haze'?

Yeah . . . around there. Because Chas Chandler and Jimi had already recorded some of the stuff – they had done three or four tracks. They'd obviously done 'Hey Joe' and the B-side, and maybe 'The Wind Cries Mary' . . . I can't remember. They'd actually cut a few tracks, but when we started the sessions at the new Olympic Studios in Barnes, in January '67, it was a revelation for him because a) it was a fantastic studio, and b) not only did we hit it off in terms of an intellectual and emotional level, and also a musical level and all that, but we were able to create different sounds for him that he wasn't able to get in the other studios. So we ended up overdubbing stuff on some of those tracks they'd originally cut. Then, of course, we dived right into the new album and started cutting new songs. We virtually finished up the record there at Olympic and mixed it there, obviously.

Can you talk about the creative relationship that you and Jimi developed in the studio?

Well, I think it was a three-way deal, in the sense that there was the band – meaning Jimi, Mitch and Noel, and obviously Jimi being at the forefront of all of that – and then Chas, who was an enormous influence, and me. Chas being the producer, coming from his background as a musician, bass player from the Animals, and changing direction, as he left the Animals, becoming a producer and finding Jimi and blah, blah, blah, bringing him to England and then encouraging Jimi and coaxing him along. And in more ways than one getting him to try to write material, which he eventually did. Because you know, in the beginning Jimi was just doing covers.

It was at Chas's insistence that Jimi write, and then he helped him with the writing process. So in the control room you'd have Chas and me. I'd be getting the sound together, Chas would be saying to Jimi, you know, you should try a different tempo, don't turn the bloody amp up that loud . . . So there's that guidance there. And then there's my interaction with Jimi, which is, what sound are we looking for? He would play something in the studio for me to listen to. I'd run down and have a quick listen through the amp, hear what the drums are doing, what the bass is doing, check that the mics are in the right place – and hear the sound that Jimi was producing there. Then run up to the control room and tweak a bunch of knobs and make it sort of happen for him. Then he would come in and listen and go, 'Whoa, okay! I like that!' So there was always a back and forth, continuously between Jimi, me and Chas. Particularly with Jimi and me, because he would look for what the sounds were.

What was Jimi like in that situation initially? Was he confident? Was he nervous?

Well, you have to remember what Jimi was like as an individual. You've probably read or seen stuff about him as a person. But for me he was this incredible warm character who had a *fantastic* sense of humour. Very biting! Loved to take the piss out of me and Noel and Mitch – and himself, and everything around him. But he was a gentle soul. You know, he was very shy, very softly spoken. It was only when he strapped on the guitar and stood in front of the microphone that he became very animated. But he was such a cool guy. He was the ultimate cool guy, with so much power in his demeanour and his whole being. When he walked into a room you just knew here was somebody who really had his shit together. There was an aura about him that was just undeniable.

Was it this aura as much as his skill on the guitar that intimidated the existing guitar heroes in London at that time?

Well, let's just look at it from our perspective, meaning British blokes. The fact that he was this American geezer who had come over and completely conquered the rock-music hierarchy, flattened them with his playing. From Paul McCartney to George Harrison, the Stones and Eric Clapton – just falling over the geezer. I think at one point Clapton just wanted to give up playing the guitar because Jimi was so fucking good. But it didn't really go to Jimi's head at all, because that wasn't his way. It's just that he was that bloody good. And those of us who were fortunate enough to work with him and see him play, watch this very quiet, shy man just have this incredible metamorphosis into this giant the moment he picked up the bloody guitar and you heard the sounds coming out of that amp. You'd go, holy crap, this is quite something!

It was an incredible musical journey you then went on with him, and in such a short space of time . . .

When you look at the history and the progression of the albums and what he was saying, lyrically, musically, all of that stuff, you really get a sense that . . . *Are You Experienced* starts the ball rolling. Very raw, very in your face, very primitive. Then *Axis* being the next stage of development, where things are a little bit more experimental. You know, I'm expanding the stereo imagery, the sounds are better, etc. And the songwriting is much more experimental too. And then you get the jump, once he gets to the States and we start on *Electric Ladyland* and that complete journey in two volumes. This rambling, marvellous journey that he takes you on, kicking down the doors once again. So each album not only stands alone, it has its own musical segment, but they're all joined together. You can trace the lineage, the way it all sort of joins together. You can see the steps he's taking very clearly. It's a fantastic journey.

And these records were made on what is now viewed as positively Stone Age equipment. No dropping in or Auto-Tune or computers to mix and balance it, just these freaks, freaking out in real time. Nevertheless, by the time you got to Electric Ladyland, the existing technology is almost as much a part of things as the music.

It's a sonic painting, and that's the thing I like to think of as my contribution: this sonic adventure into the land of Jimi's mind. And I was given the freedom to be able to do that. Very rarely would he say no to anything that we came up with. I would sometimes say no to something he was doing because either a) it simply wasn't possible at the time, or b) it just was counter-intuitive. We talked all the time about sounds, and he gave me the freedom to create whatever I could. Just throw the kitchen sink at it, see what works. And quite often things just didn't work. But being given the freedom to create the sounds, as wild as one could conceive of, that was wonderful. And then, you know, work-ing with him, side by side, particularly on *Electric Ladyland*, be-cause we did the mixes together. They were four-handed mixes.

You were literally working together, side by side at the mixing desk?

Oh, absolutely. You have to remember, there's no automation. It's just all hands on deck! I call them performance mixes. We would rehearse them as if they were a live performance. For in-stance, '1983 . . . (A Merman I Should Turn to Be)' is just one straight-through mix. No stopping, no editing. [For thirteen and a half minutes.]

Yet it still sounds utterly futuristic, all these years later . . .

Yeah, it does a bit. He didn't think outside the box, he thought *beyond* the box, out into space, I think.

How much of the recordings were made while Jimi was trip-ping on LSD?

Well, I'm sure it had quite a bit of an influence, but fortunately for me and from what I remember of it – and I do remember it fairly clearly – drugs only played a small role in the studio from what I could tell. I mean, did he smoke grass? Sure. To relax and get himself in the mood? Absolutely. Hard drugs – I don't know. I was never really aware of any of that going on, either on the ses-sion or interfering with the session. But, you know, the fact was that he had to leave and go out on the road. We'd be a week into sessions in New York in '68, and he had to go out on the road and perform. That would interrupt everything. Then come back and we'd get back into it again. Which is why he loved jamming up the road at the Scene club, which was only two blocks away from the Record Plant. He would jam there then bring musicians over to the studio.

And were you open to that situation? Did it help or hinder?

I think one has to look a little deeper and get into the mindset that Jimi had. I look at it from the point of view of who this guy was, who turns out to be not only the great genius I was so fortunate enough to work with, but looking at it from the perspective of all these years on and knowing what I know now about him, and realising what he was trying to do in those days.

He was extremely organised, in spite of the outward appearance of this sort of flamboyant lifestyle and all the rest of that. He had notes on everything he wanted to do. He plotted and planned way in advance of the session. To the extent that, even though it might seem like the result was a casual jam, it was incredibly well thought out in his mind. 'Voodoo Child' being a classic example of that. He would go to the Scene and jam for three or four hours, trying to find the right guys to play with, because he knew what he wanted.

He wanted to have a jam that would represent a specific feel, and when he found the right musicians, he said, 'Right, come on, you guys, let's go back to the Record Plant.' And he would drag them out of the Scene at midnight. Cos we're there from seven o'clock with all the mics plugged in, the whole thing all worked out and everything really together for him when he walked in the door. It was a question of, okay, here comes Jimi, look out, it's twelve o'clock at night. He's figured out who he's gonna bring with him and he traipses down Eighth Avenue trailing twenty people. It was show-stopping. It would stop the traffic, you know? And he would walk into the Record Plant fully aware of what's going to go on, plug in the guitar, Jack Casady on bass and Steve Winwood, and within two takes we got it – 'Voodoo Child'. Because Jimi had done his homework, he had planned and made sure that it was all going to be happening as a jam, but an organised jam. So he knew what he was looking for.

On record, it sounds like you're all having a party in the studio.

Yeah, but that was only a small portion of it. I think Jimi was a very astute . . . I won't say businessman. But I would say when it came to his business that was his business, do you know what

I mean? So that when it came to organising something for a session, yeah, he would experiment and he would sometimes make a mistake, or rather a miscalculation in terms of whether the musician was good enough, and he wouldn't *really* know that until he got into the studio with them. But for the most part, if it was somebody like Steve Winwood, Jimi knew he was going to get something really good, and literally we'd do a run-through and take, and Bob's your uncle.

Another thing was, if Jimi had a track of his own that he was trying to work out, he would work it out and perfect it in the studio. I'm not referring to the jam-type sessions, but the things specific to an arrangement that he was trying to figure out, which were complex, rhythmically and all the rest of it. He would spend take after take after take trying to get it correct, in his mind, his vision of the correct take – rhythmically and the lead part and then another lead part, and yet another lead part. Because at that point [with *Electric Ladyland*] we now had sixteen tracks, and that was a blessing and a curse at the same time.

Sixteen-track studios were then the absolute cutting edge. Was utilising that kind of up-to-the-minute technology a big part of what Hendrix was trying to achieve?

Absolutely. But it was even beyond that. It became the stage. It was like a concert stage in the studio. In the sense that Jimi and I were onstage working on that board. Once we'd got all the tracks and the overdubs and the thing was ready for mixing, that became our concert stage. They were performances mixes, as I said before. This was something that we would lay out and figure out the moves. Not only the moves from a physical point of view, but where the faders would go, what EQ would be happening and the reverbs and panning and all the rest of that.

It would almost be like a play within the play. We would figure out. Okay, you're gonna be on *that* side of the board. I'm gonna be on *this* side of the board. You're gonna do *that*, you'll take care of the vocal moves, Jimi. I'll take care of all of the guitars and the pans and the drums. And then at a certain point we may have to switch. And we would choreograph the moves, and sometimes we would fall over and smash into each other, and we'd fall about laughing and the tape would still be rolling, and we'd scramble to switch it off. It was a lot of fun. But that's the way it was.

How did you and Experience Hendrix LLC find all this 'new' material to keep releasing?

Any project to do with Jimi Hendrix is a labour of love, in the true sense of the words. Since 1993, when we gained all the rights back, Janie, myself and John have tried to give the public the best of what we have to offer, and only put out the very best quality. That's the mantra: only the best quality of stuff. And only the stuff that we feel will make Jimi's legacy shine. If we're working on a project we'll pull a couple of tapes and say, 'Hey, let's transfer this [to a digital file] and put it away.' We're always hoarding, in the sense of, okay, this will be a good track for something down the road.

For *People, Hell and Angels*, John and I put our heads together to figure out what we were gonna do for this next record. We figured it would probably be the last of the studio records. There will be no more studio albums after this. [Another, *Both Sides of the Sky*, would be released in 2018.] We've mined it pretty carefully. So the concept for this record was, okay, what was he doing after *Electric Ladyland*, up until Band of Gypsys? That's a period, late '68 through most of '69. Yes, there has been stuff out from that period. But not quite done this way. We figured we had enough great outtakes, great alternate versions, great performances of various songs – some of the stuff nobody's heard, some of the stuff people have heard but not in this version. You know, earlier versions of songs, later versions of songs.

So that was the mindset. When you think, what was Jimi up to? He was trying to find a new direction, and he wanted to work outside of the Jimi Hendrix Experience, expand his horizons and try different musicians. And that's the essence of the new album.

Were there any surprises as you were sifting through the material?

By the way, this stuff is on eight-track, twelve-track and sixteen-track. So when you go through the tapes and start transferring them, you push the faders up and often go, 'Wow! I remember that! I remember him doing that, but I don't remember it sounding quite like that!' Brought back a lot of memories. That happened, for example, on the track 'Somewhere'. I pushed the faders up and it was like, 'Yeah, I remember that. It was at the Hit Factory.' Jimi called me up in the middle of the night and said, 'Oi, I'm stuck, can you come over and help?' Because in 1969 we were building Electric Lady Studios, I didn't have time to go over and hang. And, frankly, I think people were taking advantage of him. Like, 'Oh, it's Jimi Hendrix – charge extra!' And he wouldn't always have a good engineer, or whatever. So I got a cab over to the Hit Factory and helped him reset the mics and hang for as long as I could. But then I had to get back.

Then there'd be other occasions when I'm not there and somebody else was recording it, the basic track, and then I remember bringing the tapes back to Electric Lady and overdubbing them, and thinking now, yeah, we did that and that and that. And then the conversations [on tape] are wonderful. The ones between Jimi and me are always hilarious. One of these days I'm gonna put together all the little bits and pieces, the little links of conversation, so it's like a documentary. But we won't talk about that right now. [Seven years on from this conversation no such recording has seen the light of day.]

Listening again to the tapes like that, with the faders up, did it give you the opportunity to learn new things about Hendrix and his music, even at this late stage?

That's an interesting question, because the thing you learn is that the genesis of the composition, going back sometimes to the very earliest renditions of it, where the tempo's changed or the feel has changed and there are different musicians involved, it's a totally different trip. You know where he's going with it. You recognise the song yet it's so different. It's got a different edge to it. And that's what makes it so cool. It shows either the very earliest rendition of the song or the latest version of the song.

The wonderful thing about that period, he's trying to figure out what direction he wants to go in now. But in so doing there are all these songs he's working on. They're works in progress, and you can just see him stirring the pot on each one. It's great.

The picture that emerges of that period in 1969 for me is of a figure who was lost, in some way, searching for something new in his life.

I would say Jimi was never lost. Never at a loss for words either. But I think as any truly great artist . . . Can you imagine, he's just done *Are You Experienced, Axis: Bold as Love* and *Electric Ladyland* – three major works. And he'd been touring and doing all the other stuff that you do as an artist. You just need some time to figure out where you're going. You need some chill-out time. But there was never really chill-out time for Jimi. I think he enjoyed going in the studio and letting the tape run and jamming. That was his way of . . . Cos it wasn't like, okay, I've got my beautiful rehearsal studio, I'm gonna bring all these guys in and I'm gonna rehearse. Uh-uh. Because the level of musicianship was so high, it was, 'Might as well go in the studio and turn the tape on cos you never know what's gonna happen.'

How different was it for Jimi working with guys like Billy Cox and Buddy Miles, or the Cherry People, compared to working with the Experience?

Let's just look at Buddy Miles first, cos that would be the first immediate change that you would compare – Mitch was 180 degrees apart, in terms of their style. Stylistically, they were off-the-charts away from each other. Yet there's a specific thing that Buddy Miles did that Jimi loved, which was this deep-forged, heavy fatback feel. Maybe not much imagination, in terms of the rest of it, but it was solid. And for the time that he played with Buddy, it was good. It was something that was necessary for part of his development. And it's interesting too that by the time you get to the Band of Gypsys, the Mitch and Billy thing makes a crossover. But Buddy was fantastic for Jimi to have that kind of a feel. It's a straight R&B feel, which is where a lot of the direction was going.

You famously recorded the 1969 Woodstock festival for the live album and movie version – and in recent years your restored DVD version. What are your recollections of Jimi's performance at Woodstock?

Woodstock was interesting because I think it comes at a point when Jimi's been doing all this experimental stuff and he put this band together, called Gypsy Sun and Rainbows, which only four months later became the Band of Gypsys. This was really an experiment for Jimi. I mean, he treated Woodstock as a big jam, which was wonderful because look at what we got. We got the most stunning rendition of 'The Star-Spangled Banner', plus all these other fantastic tracks. I don't know if you've seen the two-hour-plus version of Jimi at Woodstock that I've done, but it's the full performance, all from a single camera shot from the side of the stage which was found – the entire set in black and white – and it's an object lesson in how to play the guitar. It is just stunning! You can watch what he's doing with his hands and hear this stuff and go, 'It's not physically possible! What the fuck was that?'

Even so, the logical transition from the end of Woodstock – the crowd and all the mud and the fact that Jimi's playing at nine o'clock in the morning – out of this he was like, 'I've got this album I have to do for Capitol [to settle the legal dispute with earlier producer Ed Chalpin] and I'm gonna put this band together,' which was the Band of Gypsys. So he puts this band together with Billy Cox and Buddy Miles, and they play this amazing series of shows at the Fillmore East, in New York, over the New Year's holidays in 1969–70. It was recorded and I mixed it, with Jimi, in fact. I remember him sitting next to me in this little studio called Juggy Sound, I think, on 54th Street in Manhattan, and he's got his head in his arms and he's like, 'Argh! I wish Buddy would shut the fuck up!' Cos you know how Buddy would be going on, you know, 'Whoooh, yeah!', trying to take the spotlight. And at the end of the day Jimi probably figured, you know, there can only be one Jimi Hendrix. But I guess it was a one-off.

And now here comes the change again. The Experience gets reformed right after that and Mitch is back in the band, but Mitch has changed. If you listen to his drumming from the time that he comes back, it's very influenced by Buddy Miles. You listen to the stuff after the fact – particularly on the tracks on this album – and you can definitely hear him change. It's much funkier. It's very interesting. His foot patterns change. Cos I know his music so well and I know how Mitch was playing. But you listen and you go, wait, is that Buddy? No, it's Mitch!

Bill Graham famously talked to Jimi after the first night of the Band of Gypsys' Fillmore shows and told him off for relying too much on the showmanship – all the tricks like playing the guitar behind his back and with his teeth – and not concentrating enough on his guitar playing. Did you agree with Bill at the time?

Yes, of course, no question about it. You have to understand, Bill Graham was one of the great minds of the music business. Tough as nails, loved the guy to death, and he was always right. He knew what to say to the artists. And the artists respected him for that. I mean, he was a tough guy but I loved him, and there weren't many artists who didn't love him, even if they disagreed with him. Because he was right.

Were you someone else who could talk to Jimi frankly about his music? Tell him what you thought was good or bad?

Yeah, yeah. The way it went in the studio was, he would always, always ask me after a take, 'How was that?' And I'd go, 'Yeah, it was good. And how about this and how about that?' And he'd go, 'Yeah, yeah,' and then whoosh! He'd go for it. Then I'd say, 'You sure you want to do another take?', trying to wind him up a bit, use a bit of reverse psychology. 'Yeah, yeah, yeah, yeah, come on, man. Let's go!' And you'd keep doing more until he . . . He would always go until he absolutely had gone to the ultimate, to the end of what he could play. And then he would come into the control booth and listen. Sometimes you'd catch it in the first two or three takes and you'd never get it any better.

Do you have a particular favourite track on the new *People, Hell and Angels* collection?

Well, I have to say, I'm very partial to 'Somewhere', the single. Not because it's the single, just that it came together so beautifully. I just love the fact that Stephen Stills is on bass and Buddy on drums. The three of them just sound so amazing – and Jimi's attention to detail with the wah-wah pedal and the subtle shift in the middle of the song. People hear it and jaws fall down. But pick your own favourites. That's my personal one.

Unlike most of the Hendrix after-death compilations, it's a great album to listen to again and again.

It reveals itself slowly, for sure. But you can say that about all the great Hendrix albums. They're a journey that never ends.

You say this is definitely the last posthumous studio album. But will there be some more live albums?

'Ah. . . yes. Loads. Loads! We're working on two, right now. Can't tell you what they are because I'll have to kill myself, and then have to kill you. Come back from the dead to do it. Naw, there's gonna be some great stuff. Wonderful, oh man, just wait . . . oh! This is from all of his career and not only do we have great live stuff but we have great live stuff filmed – tons. Yeah . . .'

Where were you and what were you doing when you heard Jimi had died?

Let's see, how do I handle this one? Okay, I was in my apartment on 24th Street, in Chelsea [New York], and I went down to get my mail, and there was my green card. I was really happy. I got dressed, jumped in a cab and went down to the [Electric Lady] studio. I walked in and was like, 'What's going on?' Cos everybody was crying. 'You mean you haven't heard? Jimi died.' It hit me like a ton of bricks. And so, you know, that whole day, as you can imagine, was crazy. Television crews and all that stuff coming round . . . it was mind-numbing. But we just had to carry on. It's such a cliché but the show must go on, and I think Jimi would have preferred it that way. We did. We just powered through it.

How did Jimi compare with other musicians you've worked with in your career?

Well, there's Jimi and then there's everybody else. The problem is, when you deal with a person like Hendrix you're dealing with someone who in some people's minds is from another planet. And in some ways they're right, because his talent was so overwhelmingly great, but you could not let yourself be affected by that. You were, but you could not react to the fact that what was happening in the studio was absolutely mind-blowing. Your job was to work with him and make him sound as great as you possibly could, or even better. My job was to be the interpreter of what he was trying to do in the studio, and hopefully I did that. But it was the attitude he had in the studio. The laser-like intensity of his concentration and his power to see the big picture down the road, without letting anything interfere with that till he had reached that goal. There are a few other artists I think I've found that with. Jimmy Page had a similar sort of attitude. They can see the whole thing in their heads and they want to make sure they get there in the end. And it's wonderful.

I think anybody would realise I put Jimi at the top of the pile, and I'm sure Mr Page doesn't mind that. I loved working with Pagey. He was great. He was always an inspiration and a challenge to work with because he was so demanding and clever about what he was looking for. The two of them had a good sense of humour too, which is another thing. Jimi Hendrix's sense of humour was brutal, acerbic, cutting! He used to take the piss out of me and then Noel or Mitch, or anybody. And his comments were like lightning, so fast. It just never stopped. And he was always sending up himself up too. There was a wonderful self-deprecating humour. Making jokes in the studio about the music, or all of a sudden launching into the *Batman* TV theme, just to keep the sessions light. Page didn't quite do that, but he was very funny in the studio. We used to take jabs at each other.

When you're working with other artists now there must always come a point when they feel comfortable enough to sidle up to you and ask what it was like, working with Jimi Hendrix.

It never bothers me, and it's true they do wait for that moment. But it's fine. I love it. What I usually do is bring out some pictures. You know, I've got this huge collection of pictures of Jimi and the Stones and Zeppelin and all that. And that usually sparks another conversation.

Does it ever spark a musical conversation?

It can, but I don't want it to influence what they're bringing to the table. Whoever I'm working with, it's got to be them. I don't want it to sound like we're trying to be somebody else.

Had Jimi lived, where do you think he would have gone next in music? What might he have been doing today?

I think he might have gone into movie soundtracks. Look at the world today and where it's at, in terms of its technology – bang, Hendrix would have been right at the front there. I could have seen him and Steve Jobs hanging out, do you know what I'm saying? The fact that his mind was so open to new technology, he loved it and would have been incorporating anything and everything into what he was doing. But I definitely think the movies, the visual world. Cos I always think about my mixing in terms of a stereophonic painting. I could never even begin to put myself anywhere near Jimi's level, in terms of where his mind was at. His mind was like a kaleidoscopic, genius whirl that took everything in. One could hardly even keep up with him in a conversation, because he would be off on a tangent, talking about stuff. And I'm going, but, but, but I was just over here and you're already over there, you know? He was fantastic. It was always very visual music.

As the guy who has overseen the enormous catalogue of official releases that have been released in the decades since Hendrix's death, can you tell us how there comes to be so much fresh material? And is there still more to come?

'There was hours and hours. Constantly the tape was always rolling, thank God. Over the years we found some *incredible* stuff that had never been heard before. As well as the latest album, we've got a live record coming out as well soon, which is gonna be marvellous ... We have so much stuff still in the library. We have enough to put a new [live] record out every year for the next ten years.'

People romanticise his death. They like to talk about Jimi being so prolific in his lifetime because he knew he only had a short time to get it all down. Do you go along with that?

Naw, it's bollocks. It's all bollocks. No, he loved to record. I mean, *period*. End of story. That was his thing. The studio was his second home, you know? The guy was creating all the time ... If you're a creative soul and you've got a studio at your disposal, you're gonna push the bloody record button, aren't you?

Where would Jimi have gone next with his music if he had survived?

My feeling is that he would have been ... he certainly would have had his own label. Certainly would have been into movies. Certainly would have been into all the wonderful technological things that we are into. The cell phones, the apps, the digital plug-ins. He was so savvy about what was going on around him technologically, he would have embraced all of that. I think he would have been a mogul!

You know, embracing every aspect of sound and music and composing movie soundtracks and producing movies, probably. There's no telling . . .

CHAPTER TWENTY-TWO

Miles and Betty

Miles was a motherfucker, a real *black* motherfucker. When he came to see Jimi at the hotel he wouldn't even walk in the room because some *white* dude came to the door.

Jimi laughed. Jimi was wary. He'd had it up to here with old black fucks in their thirties and forties telling him how it was. Guys with one hit like King Curtis and the Isleys, or cats like Richard with no hit for a hundred years. Old never-went-nowhere dudes full of jive like Curtis Knight, flapping his lips at know-nothing Harlem high yellows.

Now here came Miles with his whole *thing*: Miles the legend, the voodoo master, the seen-it, done-it cat of all time. The Cassius Clay of black-music magic, fuck you up good as look at you. Jimi on high alert.

Jimi had come very late to jazz. Just didn't dig it. Would drop the name Roland Kirk if he had to in interviews. But only because Kirk was a wild young black man who would play two saxophones at once while strutting round the stage like a blind man in a house fire. Roland came on strong the same way Jimi came on strong once he got to London. All eyes on me, baby. And keep 'em here!

Lately, though, Jimi had been quietly tripping on Ornette Coleman, John Coltrane, mixing it up with the crazy classics, Bach and Beethoven, whatever else he came across, buying dozens of LPs at a time on his regular visits to the record stores of whatever town he found himself in. Carrying a portable record player with him on tour, in the car, in the dressing room. Jimi breathing in the fumes, exhaling different-coloured clouds.

Jimi first got an echo of Miles the man through his hairdresser in New York, James Finney. James specialised in black hair. Trained in Frenchy's on 125th Street, Harlem's grooviest beauty parlour (regular clients: Diahann Carroll and Mrs Louis Armstrong). Decided he'd had a gutful of styling negro kinks into swish honky hairstyles and now only worked with his own: plaits, Afros, corn rows, conks. Took Jimi's 'Dylan hair' and made it super-black. Out there, daring, full of come-on.

James gave it a name: the Blow Out. Not the baby-doll blow-outs the mini-skirted white chicks loved. This was a fully male, fully black Blow Out. Like an Afro but blown up like a skyscraper.

Miles saw it, dug it, ordered James to do the same for him. That is, Miles's freaky-deaky old lady Betty saw Jimi's hair, dug it, and told Miles about it, pushing him to wise up and get with it. Lose the Brooks Brothers suits and ties, put some tail feathers to his duds, taking a tender leaf out of Jimi's sexy-sweet cookbook.

Betty Mabry was the real bridge between Miles and Jimi. Betty was a red-hot twenty-three-year-old model with dreams and attitude, a way of just looking at you and sizing you up on the spot. Men were pushovers for Betty. Famous men, so what? She was already on the scene, hosting her own Harlem nightspot the Cellar, had studied fashion and acting and was aiming to be a professional singer.

According to Lester Chambers, his band the Chambers Brothers recorded Betty's funk-soul-sister ode to Harlem, 'Uptown', in 1967 mainly because, 'She wouldn't shut up about the fact she had a tune that was perfect for us.'

At the same time, her then boyfriend Hugh Masekela, the 'father of South African jazz' who'd just had an American number 1 pop hit with 'Grazing in the Grass', arranged for Betty to sing on her own single, 'Live, Love, Learn', which she later disowned as 'so mushy'.

Betty didn't do mushy.

Betty in her thigh-high boots, turquoise chains and box-tight leopard-skin pants knew every musician, hotshot and young would-be somebody in town. Knew enough to know the name Miles Davis at a time when most twenty-three-year-olds had no clue who that was. Knew enough to know the *peep-peep* of 'So What' – Miles's greatest hit from ten years and several lifetimes before – had been buried beneath the avalanche of James Brown's cold-sweat funk, Motown's all-shades zillion-sellers, the white-bread Beatles and all the newly hip white cats that came mewling in their wake. Can you say the Rolling Fucking Stones? Can you say the Motherfucking Monkees?

Betty was the oracle. Knew *every* damn body, black and white. There, in spirit, at Monterey. Channelling acid-Frisco, coco-caine LA, smack-city New York. Flew with the Byrds, out-zapped Zappa, wigged-out Warhol, but fell special for Arthur Lee's Love, Sly and his Family Stone and . . . Jimi Hendrix.

Miles knew none of this shit, only Coltrane, Ornette, Monk . . . the new neo- . . . Stockhausen, Schoenberg, Schaeffer . . . Miles liked to put on the gloves and box. Liked to put down the horn to paint and draw. Liked to snort ounces of coke and fuck bitches in threes and fours. 'After a while it's all just tits and ass,' Miles would shrug and tell you.

Betty was different. 'She couldn't be tamed,' said Carlos Santana, another brown-skinned young guitarist that white America came to lionise, but whom Betty got to first. 'Musically, philosophically and physically, she was extreme and attractive.'

The first time Miles caught sight of Betty, at the club, he patted a barstool and invited her to 'sit on my hand', yukking it up with his badass pals. Betty stared him down cold, walked away slow, trailing his astonished gaze. She wasn't sitting down for some

old-timer in a suit. When Miles offered her a ride home later that
night in his silver Lamborghini, he told her, 'I like little girls.'
Betty spat back, 'I ain't no *girl*.'

Miles wasn't used to that kind of blowback. Miles, with his
thin, high-altitude sound and his black diamond eyes, liked his
women to come with expensive icing on the cake. Like his wife
Frances, who'd been a ballet dancer, one of the original cast of
West Side Story. Frances had the fire but it was all under control.
Frances was ass with class. Or Cicely Tyson, the Harlem model
turned actress – experimental theatre, mainstream movies – two
years older than Miles and cooler even than Frances. Cicely was
so together that she was happy just being Miles's girlfriend. Or
not. Cicely had a lot of famous friends.

Betty was a whole world of different. Betty, said Miles, 'was a
free spirit – talented as a motherfucker – who was a rocker and
a street woman who was used to another kind of thing. She was
raunchy and all that kind of shit, all sex.'

But that was something Miles said after he married her. Before
he married her, Betty was the best thing that had happened to
him in years. Proof – Betty changed Miles's *music*, man. Brought
in the extra voltage of rock, the restless vibration of funk. Betty
showed Miles how to wire his music up again. Make it pulse like
the neon ooze of Times Square.

Betty made Miles listen to LPs she bought by Aretha Franklin,
Dionne Warwick, James Brown – and Jimi Hendrix.

The first album Miles made after hooking up with Betty, in
1968, was *Miles in the Sky*, recorded over three days in May. Betty
was all over that one, from the title – a play on the Beatles' 'Lucy
in the Sky with Diamonds', number 1 the previous summer and
a pretty Betty fave – to Miles opening the door to twenty-five-
year-old electric guitarist George Benson. George had livened up
Brother Jack McDuff's old-school hard bop with his gypsy jazz-
guitar licks and hot-buttered picking. George had since struck out

with his own quintet, but no one outside Harlem knew the cat until Betty whispered in Miles's ear and George got the call to come by the CBS Studio on East 52nd and lay something down on a track Miles called 'Paraphernalia' – geddit?

Jumpy, feel-pulse music, Wayne Shorter's tenor sax drooling all over George's loose-ass guitar. Now Miles could buy it he'd be back for more. Then Betty got him to paint a big psychedelic floating eyeball – Rick Griffin goes to Africa – and use it as the album sleeve. The first sign for furrow-browed jazz freaks that Miles had gone over to the dark side of kids' stuff rock 'n' roll, white long-hair hippy shit. Danger signs that Betty openly encouraged.

'Me and Miles were married in '68,' she cheerily undertoned. 'He got me a limo, and I filled the trash with his suits.'

The key had been when Betty turned Miles on to Jimi's music, something Miles gave unprecedented acknowledgement of when his very next album, *Filles de Kilimanjaro*, released just weeks after their marriage, featured Betty's face on the cover – a self-consciously surrealist eclipsed portrait, at once cool as iced glass and hot as blotter acid, by the Japanese fashion photographer Hiro.

Most extraordinary were the two tracks that bookended the album: opener 'Frelon Brun' (aka 'Brown Hornet'), which brazenly riffed on Jimi's 'If 6 Was 9'; and the closer, the sixteen-and-a-half-minute 'Mademoiselle Mabry', which took 'The Wind Cries Mary' and slowly, insolently transformed it into something more transcendent.

Both tracks recorded just days before Miles, out of the blue, summoned Betty by phone to be married. He had just finished a gig at the Plugged Nickel in Chicago and was feeling righteous.

'He called me from Chicago and said, "Sweetcakes, get your stuff together and come to Chicago, we're getting married."'

For all her wild clothes and up-in-your-face ways, Betty was good for Miles. Betty didn't do drugs. 'I was really into my body and I wouldn't do anything to damage myself. When I was with Miles, he was clean – he even stopped smoking. I had something to do with it, but it was his willpower,' she remembered a long time later.

She would have done the same for Jimi – only Jimi was fifteen years younger than Miles and nowhere near ready to talk about shit like that. Come on, man, be real.

So Betty turned to Miles to fashion her own Jimi-sized fantasy, taking him to her favourite shop, Hernando's in Greenwich Village, 'which had Mexican designs and would custom-make items for him'.

Miles remembered it his way, of course: 'Everybody was into blackness, you know, the black consciousness movement, and so a lot of African and Indian fabrics were being worn.'

With Betty and Hernando's encouragement, Miles started wearing African dashikis and loose, colourful robes. But he knew Jimi was also a regular visitor to Hernando's. So he began looking around at other black hangs, digging wraparound Indian shirts and patch suede pants from a new, young black designer named Stephen Burrows. Stephen made clothes the way Miles and Jimi made music: spontaneously, cutting at all angles, stretching edges off grain, draping as he went. Nothing you could learn from any school. Only from your god or your demon.

Miles tried to do things for Jimi. Show him things in the music, things he believed only he and someone who also had the gift, like Jimi, could see. But Jimi didn't read music, didn't have any of the deep classical training and expensive salon background that Miles had. That was alright. Miles would simply have to show him. Pick up the horn and play and see if he could relate. Miles pleasingly pleased when the boy showed he could pick up instantly whatever Miles played looking down from the heavens of his trumpet – Jimi's guitar sprouting wings, rising sweetly to meet him.

Jimi's atonal electric-city abstraction, Jimi's obvious karma, making sounds off the cuff like some fucked-up Karlheinz Stockhausen to Miles's ears, both men digging deep their love of poisoned noise. One knowing where it comes from, how it can be built, the other knowing nothing of the kind, just blowin' free, man.

Miles giving Jimi some *baad* advice too – introducing him to his personal coke dealer over on the East Side, some cat who wore an amulet around his neck with a lever that released a big spray of coke when you pressed it.

'You get your coke exclusively from this address from now on,' Miles told Jimi. 'Buy it one ounce at a time, you get the best deal.'

Jimi nodding sagely, feeling in his jacket pocket for the money.

Miles giving Jimi advice about having a black band: 'Why you want to play that hillbilly music with those white motherfuckers, man?' Jimi thinking about that a lot, snow-blind on the coke . . . A *lot*.

Miles telling Jimi the best thing was to forget the whitey-pleasing parlour tricks, just stand there and play, man, turn your back on them motherfuckers if you want to, dig?

Then, later, Miles vowing to put together 'a better rock band than Jimi Hendrix'.

Say what, man?

What became the third great Miles Davis Quintet – Austrian keyboardist Joe Zawinul, English guitarist John McLaughlin, American electric pianist Chick Corea, English double-bassist Dave Holland – all *white*. Plus the only black member, drummer Tony Williams.

Say what, man?

Miles ain't turning no back on no audience either, baby. Miles is fly. Dressing high. Coming on strong. The next time Jimi sees Miles he's playing to the tripped-out hippies at the Fillmore West, opening for the Steve Miller Band. *Say what?* The time after that they are sharing the bill at the Isle of Wight Festival, 600,000 rock fans, dig? Miles's album at that time, *Bitches Brew* – the first ever Miles double album – even has a fourteen-minute track called 'Miles Runs the Voodoo Down'. Sound familiar, Jimi?

You bet. Only now it's Miles standing up to the mountain.

Some wise-ass jazz critics accused Miles of 'selling out' to the rock audience. But *Bitches Brew* became Miles's first gold album for over 500,000 sales.

Miles had a new name for it by then, anyway – *fusion.*

Miles had a new name for Betty too – Backseat Betty – after he became convinced that she was fucking Jimi on the side. Miles and Betty divorced soon after.

It was all in Miles's crazy mind, said Betty. Jimi just shrugged. He was always being accused of fucking some dude's old lady. Was it true? What's it to ya, man? Who *wouldn't* want to fuck Betty, man?

Miles was already back together with another on-off lover, Marguerite Eskridge. Betty heard all about it after the couple were shot at five times in his car one night in October 1969. Miles was left with a graze. Marguerite was unhurt. A year later she gave birth to their son, Erin.

Neither Jimi nor Betty ever went near that *baad* black mother-fucker again.

CHAPTER TWENTY-THREE

Mike and the Boys

Tuesday, 11 October 1966. Coddle Chas time.

Mike can't avoid it any longer. Chas's big idea: a golliwog on guitar and a couple of white wankers as his backing group. Whoever heard of such a thing? Oh, you'd get the old American bluesers and rock 'n' rollers coming over, using a white pick-up band. But they were already names you could stick on a poster. Little Richard and Chuck Berry. Has-beens, pay 'em five bob and make a quid.

Chas's guy was different, he said. The black Elvis. Playing the sort of stuff the Stones and the Who were. It was laughable. Who was gonna go for that when they could have the real thing?

I mean, you've got your older American coloureds who were always popular, your Nat King Coles and your Louis Armstrongs, but that was different, old charmers singing proper songs for real people. You've got your Chubby Checkers and your Little Stevie Wonders – novelty acts. One-offs. And you've got your homegrown coloureds. Kenny Lynch singing on *Ready Steady Go!* or writing hits for the Small Faces or Cilla Black. That was fair enough.

But some spade you've never heard of playing electric guitar like Clapton or Beck? Chas had been on the wacky baccy, must have. Or he was trying to get off with that Linda Keith bird. Mind you, you would, wouldn't you? Fancy a bit of posh.

Mike had taken a wide berth when Chas first started foaming

at the mouth about the bloke . . . Jimmy . . . *James?* Wasn't there one of those already? Chas asking for money Mike told him he didn't have right now – not for that rubbish, anyway.

But then Chas changed the boy's name to Jimi to make it sound fash and groovy, and he started to pick up a buzz. Apparently the boy could really play. Good reviews in the music papers. People on the phone talking, and Mike thought, fuck it, better at least tie the cunt down to a contract – just in case.

Plus, what Mike didn't need right now was Chas getting any bright ideas about money he might be due – or think he might be due – from the Animals, now that he'd left the group. Eric had been a pain about it until Mike got him working again, thinking about other things like the *New* Animals. Smart – see? It would make sense to get Chas busy thinking about something else too. If it didn't work it was no skin off Mike's nose, and if it did . . . well, we'll see.

Mike got Chas to bring them all in for a meeting at the Gerrard Street office. Closed the curtains for atmosphere and sat there smoking a cigar as they all filed in, Chas, the boy Jimi and the other two. Gave them a bit of razzmatazz about what he could do for them. Had even come up with a name for them – wait for it – the Jimi Hendrix Experience. You could see they liked that, all sitting there on the couch, grinning. Then he made their eyes really twinkle when he presented them with a 'standard management contract – the same one we have with the Animals'.

Well, they weren't to know. In fact, it wasn't a management contract at all but a production deal they would be signing, with Mike and Chas named as managers and producers. Technically they would be individual musical entertainers known collectively as 'The Jimi Hendrix Experience'. Mike and Chas would take the 'standard' 20 per cent cut, plus further percentages of all future royalties and publishing. The group would get 2.5 per cent of royalties from record sales, shared equally between them – again, all very standard, Mike explained. Which it was – the standard music-biz rip-off. The three boys couldn't wait to get the pen in their hands.

When Jimi and the boys left the room Chas and Mike really got down to business. Not entirely green, Chas foresaw the contractual maze in having Mike as his own manager still, under the terms of his existing contract as a member of the Animals. It meant that not only would Mike be splitting the percentage with him on Hendrix, but he'd also be entitled to his management commission on Chas's personal earnings.

Mike had already seen that one coming, of course, and offered Chas a simple and generous solution. He and Chas would tear up the Animals agreement they had and form their own management partnership together – with the New Animals and Alan Price added to the pool of artists they would manage.

They went to the pub to celebrate. Good old Mike buying, as dear old Chas was still skint. The next day Chas took off with the group for some dodgy gigs in France, and Mike went back to keeping Eric happy making his first solo album – and plotting to get him back with the New Animals.

Two months later Mike phones Jimi out of the blue. Tells him how much he really likes the single Jimi has recorded. That with Mike's contacts it could be a big hit. But first, in order to protect Jimi's long-term future, Mike has kindly arranged for the two of them to see Mike's Mayfair solicitor John Hillman. No need for Chas to be there. Chas is a great guy, but this is more Mike's end of the business. Legal stuff. To ensure Jimi isn't ripped off when he starts to make real money – which he will, if he listens to Mike and does what he says.

The next day, Thursday, 1 December, they meet bright and early at Hillman's office, Jimi still in a daze having not gone to bed till dawn. Jimi is presented with his own individual contract

– separate to the group – to protect him as a performer and all his future income from unnecessary tax.

Mike will now receive 40 per cent of Jimi's gross tour earnings. We are now far beyond the realms of any 'standard' contract. Mike explains that the percentage is set a little higher to cover tour expenses. Hillman explains the Yameta tax-shelter arrangements to Jimi, but Jimi is already thinking of other things. On one level he knows he's being bullshitted. On another he knows this is just how the game goes. He's not stoopid. He knows why Chas isn't there. But if he wants to make it – and boy, does he want to make it – he's willing to do anything these white guys in suits tell him. Ain't it always been the way, brother?

He does mention the Ed Chalpin contract, but Mike brushes it off with a smile. Don't worry, he will deal with it, no reason to get excited. Jimi signs the bits of paper and Mike drives him straight to rehearsals. No need to mention anything to the other boys, he tells him. This is all for your benefit, Jimi. You're the talent. It's your future you have to think about. Jimi knows that part is true. He never mentions anything about his visit to see John Hillman or the new 'individual contract' he has signed. Noel and Mitch are nice cats but Jimi has met a lot of nice cats along the way. Nice don't pay the rent. As for Chas – Mike will take care of that. Mike will take care of all that shit.

That's the way it goes for the next year or so – everything sugar and spice and all things nice. Chas on the day-to-day side, taking care of Jimi, Mike funnelling the dough through to Yameta – and beyond. Oh, Noel and Mitch – especially fucking know-all Noel – bitch and moan about their wages. But when did you ever meet a muso who didn't bitch and moan about money? Write a fucking hit then come and talk to me about money, you little pricks.

Mike hits the ground running in America. Getting a record deal is easy when your guy has just had three straight hit singles in the UK and the whole country including the Beatles are talking him up as the new musical messiah. A deal is made between Reprise Records and Yameta, the contract stating that Yameta will provide recordings 'embodying the performance of Jimi Hendrix or the Jimi Hendrix Experience'.

Mike sitting there in his hotel suite swigging bubbly, looking at an advance of $40,000 on a $150,000 deal, with an immediate promotional budget of $20,000. Again, no need to trouble Mitch or Know-All with this info. They are technically only used as Yameta employees.

More urgent, the suckerfish Jimi signed away bits of his arse before coming to England. They are all waiting with their hands out. Mike throws money at it, hiring a team of top-dollar New York lawyers to buy off various small-time hustlers, pulling a stroke getting back the rights to seven songs Jimi had recorded as a hired gun back in '65.

Keep the boys working – that's the plan. When Noel writes a nasty letter to Mike and Chas demanding to know about the financials, even getting Jimi and Mitch to sign it too – cheeky little sod – Mike laughs it off, throwing them a tight wad of £20 notes. When Jimi tells Chas who tells Mike that he has made a 'verbal agreement' with the boys to split his dough with them on a 50-25-25 basis, Mike laughs so hard he nearly pisses himself. Fucking musos, living in dreamland.

Mike is the one with the really big dreams. By 1968 he has set himself up in swank new offices in New York, now trading as Jeffery and Chandler Inc. As well as Hendrix, the New Animals and Alan Price, he and Chas are now overseeing the careers of a stable of new acts: Eire Apparent, Soft Machine and an American all-chick group, Goldie and the Gingerbreads.

Mike is all about the big picture. With his razor-sharp lawyer Steve Weiss of kick-ass law firm Steingarten, Wedeen & Weiss, Mike decides he can handle American concert promotion too – and save millions on gate receipts. Mike is on a fucking roll!

Then slowly, annoyingly, catastrophically, things start to unravel. Eric Burdon fucks off to another manager, ungrateful Geordie cunt. Then threatens trouble for Mike when he discovers his so-called Yameta nest egg doesn't actually exist. Dear, oh dear, Eric, I don't know what could have happened there. It's a fucking mystery, it is.

Then Jimi starts to go soft in the head, questioning Mike's way of doing things. Even talking about breaking up the Experience. Getting a bunch of blackies in. Fuck's sake, Jimi! You're going to ruin everything!

Jimi is the money tree and Mike badly needs to shake it as 1968 turns into 1969 and all sorts of heavy-duty debts begin to pile up. There is the new Electric Lady Studios that Mike and Jimi are meant to be partners in, but which even Jimi is now aware is his only in name. There had been the initial $300,000 investment – the one written on paper. Then there is the 'arrangement' between Mike and the Mob, who own the land – and now own Mike too if he doesn't play ball. The studio is being constructed on the site of the old Generation Club at 52 West 8th Street. Said to be Gambino turf. Mike is a big man too now and feels he can handle that. Mike still has all sorts of friends in high places in Britain: MI6, army, old pals from up north working off-book, after dark, under cover of cash, lots of cash. What is the Mob next to that? Just less-professional fixers in cheaper suits and with more expensive habits, right? Right?

Mike telling himself whatever he needs in order to keep climbing higher and higher. Whatever you do, don't look down. Mike, taking a lot of drugs to keep it together – to *maintain*. Coke. That's the get-you-out-of-bed stuff. But pills too, get you through those meetings with the suits and the guys in undertaker coats. Weed to help you come down, or the other kind of pills, or both, a bottle of Johnnie Walker Red with ice to help you ease into it.

Even dropping acid with Jimi to show he understands what's *really* going on. Sees the journey for what it really is and still could be; everyone join hands, yeah? Dropping acid with Jimi and talking about making music of the universal mind – something Chas, for all his musical knowledge, refuses to do.

But Mike doesn't have musical talent. He has music in his head, but his soul is all about the money, the spondulicks, the ackers, the bread, the real sound that makes the world go round, am I right, pal? Huh? Shaddup and have another fucking line.

Chas not digging any of this. Chas wanting out, saying so out loud. Until one day he just splits. Mike and Jimi letting it happen. Letting it all come down, just don't crush my high, brother, dig?

But then things get really heavy. Ed fucking Chalpin refusing to simply lie down and die. Planning to cash in on Jimi's crazy fame by releasing the material he had recorded for Ed and PPX in the way back when. Nothing Mike can do about it. Chalpin twisting the knife by insisting Jimi actually *owes* him one more album.

Friday, 28 June 1968. Mike summons Jimi, Noel and Mitch into the New York office for an important meeting. Mike has been busy, he tells them. He has new, much better agreements for all of them to sign. More good news: Reprise has agreed to pay Ed Chalpin a percentage on the Experience albums, putting that particular problem to bed once and for all and a curse on that cunt's name.

Buried in the detail is the fact that Jimi is no longer signed directly to Mike and Chas, but directly to Reprise, for production and recording. Meaning Jimi is now responsible for royalty payments to all sub-producers, vocalists and musicians. That means you, Noel and Mitch. And, by the way, here's some cash to divert you from any further questions, is that cool? Thought so. Oh, and one more piece of business, just sign here as you collect your cash, so that all future earnings owed to Jimi and the group will be sent directly to Mike and Chas, and not to Yameta. Keeps things simpler. Sign here. Nice one.

When *Electric Ladyland* hits number 1 it looks like everything is working out just fine. But Jimi is still talking about breaking up the Experience. Doesn't he get that it's the Experience that is paying for everything? Not just the here and now, but tomorrow too? Tomorrow and the next day and the next fucking day – why doesn't Jimi get with it? But Jimi is so busy listening to the fucking Panthers and the other black scumbags, like that fucking Miles fucking Davis or that junkie groupie Devon Wilson, that he's not listening to Mike anymore. Somebody needs to make Jimi see sense.

Then, to top it off, the mug gets busted on the Canadian border for smack. The *Canadian border* – what kind of punk-ass move is this? Does this crazy motherfucker *want* to be put away for the next ten years?

Sitting around with the boys one night at one of those discreet, private joints in Little Italy, trying to explain what the deal is with his client, someone suggests paying the jig a little visit. Show him who his real bosses are. Mike argues against it. But the boys are losing patience. They are used to running their own singers and entertainers; they don't get this bullshit about 'new directions' in music. They are starting to wonder if Mike is actually up to the job anymore.

Mike, whose nerves are shot from too many nights on the Kool-Aid, is starting to think maybe they are right and a little jolt might be just the thing, bring Jimi to heel. Hearing all about the drug den in Woodstock, they tell Mike they want to see what's going on. Suggest he pays a little visit of his own, taking a couple of the boys with him. Jimi nearly shits when he sees the two limos pull up at the gate of the Shokan House. Mike holding it together just about as one of the boys goes inside with him, shoves Jimi upstairs, sits him on the bed and puts a loaded .38 to his head.

'I'd rather fuck you up with my bare hands but we don't want to mess with that pretty-boy face,' he deadpans. Outside, it's America and a big guy in a hat is enjoying some semi-automatic target practice.

Boom! Boom! Boom!

Terrified, Jimi agrees to do what the fuck he's told and shows up a few weeks later to play at the opening of another Mob-run joint, the Salvation. But he acts all moody, plays a half-assed set and leaves early. The boys tell Mike they've had enough of this ungrateful junkie moolie disrespecting them. Anyone else, they'd have dealt with him by now. While he's still got the potential to make everyone millions they are happy to play along – but only for so long.

They need Mike to reassert his authority, they tell him. So now there's a new game.

They get some of the kids they know off the streets, cheap hoods into breaking and entering, stick-ups, riding shotgun. Tell them to pick up this Jimi Hendrix character one night, throw him around, make it look good. Then let him lose his shit on a bagful of party favours – smack, coke, downers – lock him up with that shit for forty-eight hours. Then arrange for Mike to come to the rescue with his own crew – proper soldiers there on a lark. Scare the shit out of the fucking boogie then have him see it's Mike who saves him.

Yeah, that oughta do it. Mike goes along with it. What choice does he have? And who knows, it might even work. Mike needs a new Hendrix album out in 1970. Everyone does.

But the fucking guy is so stoned he hardly seems to get what's just happened to him. He's no sooner announced the break-up of that money-pit Gypsy Sun and Rainbows than he's talking about *another* all-fucking-black line-up – Band of Gypsys.

Mike tells them relax, he has an idea. Let Jimi do some shows in New York with this latest thing. We'll record them then give the tracks to fucking Chalpin as the album Jimi supposedly owes him. Get things back to normal after that.

Genius! Hey, Mike is back, baby!

Just when we thought you wuz going soft on us . . .

CHAPTER TWENTY-FOUR

Going to Toronto

Pools of blood on Michigan Avenue . . .

Delegates rampaging inside the International Amphi-theatre, CBS News reporter Dan Rather being punched in the gut live on air by security goons. Outside, in the streets, young women being dragged by the hair by crazed cops with lead-knuckled gloves and drawn guns. Tear-gas bombs exploding along Clark Street. Long-haired peace protestors being bludg-eoned and thrown into the backs of police vans. Sirens, screams, shouts, terror in the dark, raw fear, hate.

Jimi smoking a joint, watching it on TV between takes at the Record Plant. Jimi can't believe what he sees at all. After MLK, sure, the blacks tore up the place. After Bobby, you bet the fix was in. But white folks fighting white folks over . . . what? Who gets to lead the Dems against Nixon in the election? What the *shit*, man?

Wednesday, 28 August 1968. Very heavy scenes that night in Chicago, where the Democratic National Convention is taking place. The Yippies – you know, Abbie Hoffman and Jerry Rubin and all those tripped-out cats talking big and handing out free joints and LSD – had announced that they were coming to drive a spike into the whole charade. Jimi dug those cats – he had recently given Abbie ten grand to buy weed that he planned to send through the mail to random addresses in New York. But this was different, they had announced. Not just speeches and rallies and marches this time, they said, they were gonna block roads with stolen cars, dump sacks of powerful acid in the city's water supply. Then they were gonna storm the convention, man! That's right! These wispy-beard freaks with their soft-ass lib values and right-on do-gooding were gonna blow up the whole shithouse!

Ten days before, at a show in Atlanta, Jimi had walked into the gig with a long-legged blonde chick he'd just met. One of the cops hired to protect Jimi pulled his gun and aimed it at his chest. The pig yelled, 'The nigger has no right to have his hands all over the girl!'

Wow. Really? Whoa, yeah.

Promoter Pat O'Day pushed himself between the cop and Jimi, but two more officers stepped forward and also drew and pointed their guns. Pat talked them down eventually, sweat pouring down his back. But the pigs walked off the job in protest. Jimi acting like, seen it all before, brother. 'Fifty years ago, I couldn't have even walked into this auditorium,' he told Pat with a knowing smile. 'And fifty years from now no one is going to care.'

It was laughable. If the Panthers out there having gunfights with the cops couldn't do nuthin', these white hippy cats with their theatre and their poetry and their rich moms and dads had no shot, right? It was actually funny waiting to see what crazy Abbie would do next, after claiming he would use his psychic energy to make the Pentagon levitate. Come on, baby, let the good times roll.

No one was laughing now, though. A tribe of 10,000 anti-Vietnam protestors had hit Grant Park that afternoon. Someone ritualistically lowered the flag. The cops went berserk at the sight of that and rushed in to rescue the flag, beating bloody anyone who got in their way. Horrified, the crowd of hippies, Yippies, students and activists began hurling food, rocks, broken concrete, anything they could lay their hands on.

The chants of, 'Hell, no, we won't go!' turned to, 'Pigs are whores! Pigs are whores!'

They ran to escape the tear gas, but the clouds followed them down into the streets. Vice President Hubert Humphrey, the old-school henchman the Dems were about to elect in place of Dead Bobby, was having a shower in his suite at the Conrad when the fumes engulfed him. He fell out of the stall coughing his guts up, unable to stop sneezing. Humphrey was for the war, God O'mighty, and the kids hated him. All through his campaign trail the under-thirties had been there chanting, 'Stop the war now! Stop the war now!' Then once he had the nomination in the bag, it changed to, 'Dump the Hump! Dump the Hump!'

Fuck Humphrey. Let him get a taste of the gas.

Elsewhere, the protesters, wearing makeshift facemasks from cop-torn shirts, were burning American flags and hoisting the Viet Cong flag instead. Hate running wild on the streets of Chicago. The crowds, bloody, petrified, clustered outside the convention hall, chanting while police continued to attack them.

'The whole world is watching! The whole world is watching!'

Jimi turning off the set and getting back to finishing his new album, the one that would be a double – that's right, baby, a double, like *Blonde on Blonde*, some serious shit. The one he was calling *Electric Ladyland*, after one of his favourite phrases for groupies, whom he called 'electric ladies'.

Everything cool and groovy about the late sixties was defined by the word 'electric'. His favourite East Village nightspot was the Electric Circus: the club's stated aim was to 'play games, dress as you like, dance, sit, think, tune in and turn on'. A trippy mix of head-game light shows, far-out music, freak-show performers, improvisational street theatre, and, of course, speed, acid, coke, dope, chicks, dicks, you name it, Jimi, we love you, man, come on down anytime, alright-alright?

'Everything, you know, is electrified nowadays,' Jimi explained to his many admirers in the underground press. 'We're planning for our sound to go inside the soul of the person, actually, you know, and see if they can awaken some kind of thing in their minds, you know, cos there are so many sleeping people.'

Tom Wolfe's *The Electric Kool-Aid Acid Test* came out that month too. Did you read it yet, man? *Intersubjectivity*, can you dig it, sister? Acid eaters, Ken Kesey, revolution, Hells Angels, Carlos Castaneda . . . Jimi Hendrix, baby!

Asked to describe his new music, Jimi replies in a whispered croon, 'We call it Electric Church Music because to us music is a religion.'

Electric Church Music, man, with Jimi as Our Saviour, alright-alright-alright . . .

America was speeding down the fast lane now. A month after the protesters lit up Chicago, Republican presidential candidate Richard M. Nixon brought his cavalcade to the same city, an evil emperor flashing mocking peace signs. The same month, on the same night that Jimi was making sweet love to his guitar on-stage in Vancouver – dedicating 'Foxey Lady' to his grandmother Nora who was in the audience – the televised Miss America pageant marked the first public blow on behalf of the women's movement.

Didn't you know? Miss America was sexist, racist. Miss America was part of American militarism. Around two hundred members of the group New York Radical Women turned up to make the point. Live on national TV.

They brought a pamphlet written by Robin Morgan, *No More Miss America!* – destined to become a major source for feminist scholarship in the years to come. According to Morgan, Miss America had 'always been a lily-white, racist contest; the winner tours Vietnam, entertaining the troops as a "Murder Mascot", the whole gimmick is one commercial shill game to sell the sponsor's products. Where else could one find such a perfect combination of American values – racism, militarism, sexism – all packaged in one "ideal symbol", a woman?'

There had never been a black Miss America. Miss America was no better than a county fair, the women no more than cattle. To demonstrate, they crowned a sheep as Miss America. These chicks were *baad-ass*, man! They had Freedom Trash Cans, into which they invited women to toss their bras and panties, their baby diapers and high-heel shoes, their steno pads and make-up and girdles – all symbols of the oppression of women. When the New York Radical Women threatened to symbolically burn the Freedom cans, the almost exclusively male media were driven to a frenzy, comparing these acts to sicko draft dodgers burning their draft cards.

Another kind of revolution, brothers and sisters standing tall together, black and white, young and old, right on.

Jimi's face hitting the deck as he opens the box the messenger just delivered with the English copies of *Electric Ladyland*. Different cover, see? The American *Electric Ladyland* was built around a typically triangular Experience group photo with Jimi at the apex of the pyramid, and Mitch and Noel in line below. Dry ice, psychedelic threads, inscrutable poses . . . based on a session with Linda Eastman, rich-girl groupie posing as photographer on the New York scene, soon to capture a Beatle named Paul.

Jimi had handwritten five pages of sleeve notes that he wanted included too, typical sky-head screed written stoned at dawn in some overloaded hotel room in the middle of nowhere new. Typical UFO-chasing Jimi, kite-high love blurb: 'It wasn't too long ago, but it feels like years ago, since I've felt the warm hello of the sun . . .' Page after page of 'border guards' – Mike and Chas maybe – a 'velvet horse' – funky junky – and a 'liquid rainbow' – el-ess-dee, baby. Along with detailed instructions for the record-company suits on how to, why to, when to, where to, in terms of how the whole gatefold thing should be presented.

Dear Sirs,

Here are the pictures we would like you to use anywhere on the LP cover, preferably inside . . . next to each other in different sizes and mixing the color prints at different points. For instance, please use the color pictures with us and the kids on the statue for front or back cover – outside cover. And the other back or front outside cover use three good pictures of us in B&W or color . . . Any other drastic change from these directions would not be appropriate according to the music and our group's present stage. And the music is most important. And we have enough personal problems without having to worry about this simple yet effective layout.

Thank you. Jimi Hendrix.

All this crap the bigwigs faithfully ignore: fucking hippy musicians, man, gimme a break.

Jimi didn't leap for joy when he saw what they did with the sleeve in the US – a much more dollars-and-sense version of what he'd dreamed up – but he could live with it.

The British one, though – *are you fucking kidding me?* This is fucking bullshiiiiiiit . . . COME ON, MAN!

The front cover with the dozens of nudes shocked free-loving, free-spirited Jimi. Yet it was his idea, wasn't it?

'I didn't have nothing to do with that stupid LP cover,' he told American reporters, unsure how to reconcile the wanton chauvinism of the picture with the new dawn of feminism now pervading the counterculture.

'I don't even want to talk about it,' he pouted. 'That album, when it was released [in America], had a picture of me and Noel and Mitch on the cover and about thirty nice new photographs inside. But people have been asking me about the English cover, which seems to have gotten me into a bit more trouble. I don't know anything about it. I had no idea that they had pictures of dozens of nude girls on it.'

In fact, he'd said yes to the basic concept, which had him as the central God figure surrounded by legions of turned-on angels. Then he chickened out the morning of the shoot in London.

The rant kept building. He said he thought it was 'sad the way the photographer made the girls look ugly. Some of them are nice-looking chicks but the photographer distorted the photograph with a fish-eye lens or something. They messed about and although the girls were pretty they came out disfigured.'

What?

'That's mean. Anybody as evil as that dies one day or another.'

What?

'Our scene is to try to wash people's souls. We're in the process of trying to make our music into a religion. It's already spiritual anyway, and we want it to be respected as such. We call our music Electric Church Music. It's like a religion to us. Some ladies are like church to us too. Some groupies know more about music than the guys. People call them groupies, but I prefer the term "Electric Ladies". My whole *Electric Ladyland* album is about them.'

Jimi lost in his dealer's bedspread. Speed jive don't want to stay alive when you're twenty-five. Talking about originally wanting the sleeve to have a shot of tremblingly beautiful German model Veruschka 'leading us across the desert, and we have, like, these chains on us'.

Veruschka, a twenty-one-year-old Prussian countess, real name Vera von Lehndorff-Steinort, had recently gone from the cover of *Vogue* into the most achingly seductive scene in Antonioni's 1967 art-house flick *Blow-Up*.

'She's so sexy you just wanna hmm,' Jimi drooled. But there was no way the record company were picking up that tab. So Jimi wandered off in interviews on some tricked-out acid-consciousness ellipses that got him temporarily off the hook about the UK *Ladyland* sleeve. In London some shops had to put it in a brown paper bag, which only made it even more desirable to the chillum-chewing fans.

Everything Jimi does now vibrating heavily, eerily outwards – inwards – all around. Diggit? The day *Electric Ladyland* is released in America – 16 October 1968 – is the same day that the black American sprinters Tommie Smith and John Carlos, gold and bronze medallists in the men's 200-metre race at the Olympics in Mexico City, take their places on the podium for the medal ceremony wearing human-rights badges and black socks without shoes. In case there is any confusion over what they're saying, during the 'The Star-Spangled Banner' they conspicuously lower their heads and each raises a black-gloved fist.

Intended to be a gesture of solidarity with the Black Freedom movement in the United States, it is instantly beamed around the watching world as a Black Power salute. A symbol of the cop-murdering Black Panthers! Holy fucking shit! Nobody thinks to explain that both men are members of the Olympic Project for Human Rights, an organisation formed a year before to protest against racial segregation in America and elsewhere, notably South Africa.

Nobody in Mexico gives a fuck about that, and the International Olympic Committee shits the bed and orders Smith and Carlos to be suspended from the US team and banned from the Olympic Village. When the US Olympic Committee refuses, the IOC threatens to ban the entire US track team. That does it for the older white guys who run the US team, and both athletes are thrown out of the Games and told to go home – in shame. Lower your heads to that, motherfuckers.

Jimi in LA lying back and grooving on a sunny day at his newly rented mansion in Benedict Canyon – the same palatial hang the Stones had used before – *Electric Ladyland* on its way to becoming his first American number 1, his latest American tour selling out arenas now, selling out the Hollywood Bowl; hanging out with

Eric and Jack and Ginger and all that scene at the Forum, where Cream are playing their Farewell to California concert; jamming later that night at a club in West Hollywood with Lee Michaels, nice young cat on a heavy Hammond organ. Then going home at dawn with his latest blonde girlfriend, this one a former Playboy Bunny now working as a cocktail waitress at the Whisky a Go Go, named Carmen Borrero.

Carmen was that rare jewel: a beautiful blonde Puerto Rican. She went well with the new millionaire's crash pad, the three limos on twenty-four-hour standby and, at all of his shows, the unlimited cocaine, Johnny Walker Red, gold Jose Cuervo tequila, bins full of weed, assorted types of acid, mushrooms, mescaline, lab speed, reds, ludes, and – way back of the shop, backstage of the backstage – heroin, brown sugar, horse.

The Beast. The Witch.

The good stuff, pretty mama . . .

If 1967 had been Jimi's military-jacket period and 1968 his magic-hat period, 1969 would be the year of the beautiful bandana, the expanding headband, the moment his new halo-crown would finally fit snugly onto those crushed-velvet corkscrew curls. The year of really feeling his power now that he had broken free of the bloodied chains of his childhood, the poverty and self-denial of his early twenties, the self-loathing and the pissy little games. Now it was time to shrug off the easy-going, sweet-talking honorary-white act he'd been putting on for the easily fooled rich folks in London.

Now it was time to show what Jimi could really do. He felt it. Chas gone, even as he still talked about him. Kathy gone, even though he told her he still loved her. Noel on his way out, Mitch doing as he's told. Jimi stretched out by the pool at his new million-dollar-baby manse high in the Santa Monica Mountains. Carmen, all over him like a cheap suit.

'My initial success was a step in the right direction,' he took the time to explain to yet another writer. 'But was only a step, just a change. Now I plan to get into many other things. This year we're really going to make it in a big way. Above all, our records will become better, purely from the point of view of recording technique. We haven't been happy with a single one! Our producer up till now, Chas Chandler, hasn't had the right feel when he turned the wheels in the control room. Before, sometimes I'd finish a thing and somebody else would come along and goof it, in the cutting of the record or in the pressing, they'd screw it up.

'In the future we'll take care of that detail ourselves, together with Dave Mason who has quit Traffic to spend time on this, among other things. He thinks in a different way, he's got new ideas in recording techniques and a good ear for new sounds. I know exactly what I want to hear. I'm going to take Buddy Miles and Paul Caruso into the studio. I want to write songs and produce stuff. And Noel's going to take some people in by himself too.'

Speaking to the same reporter, Noel, who now had his own side group, Fat Mattress – groovy name, right? – backed Jimi up on this, though being Noel couldn't help having a dig too: 'I wanted to work with Fat Mattress because that was giving me an outlet for writing. And I thought I should co-produce, cos I got ideas, but Jimi wasn't letting me do it.'

Poor fucking Noel, man. Not even second banana. But look how far it took him, not being a bass player. Not being a singer or a very good songwriter. Getting his fizzog on the cover of Jimi's number 1 American album yet barely being on five of its sixteen tracks. Touring the world, sleeping with all the chicks who couldn't get to Jimi, crème de la crème stuff, man – and getting *paid*. When you could have been a milkman instead – in fucking Folkestone. Let's hear it for Noel.

Jimi's mood blackening as the early weeks of 1969 turn into mudslide . . . chicks hitting the doorbell in the middle of the night; sometimes he minded, sometimes he didn't; Carmen coming down the stairs to find him banging them on the floor ... the joint full of musos, famous and otherwise; Eric Burdon stopping by on acid; Paul Caruso, an old acquaintance from the East Village days, blowing on his harmonica at the drop of a coke spoon. LA vagabonds of no fixed abode loading up on the hospitality, eventually helping themselves to some of Jimi's guitars, stage clothes – even a book of Jimi's poesy and lyric ideas, dream fevers and sonic doodles ... Jimi, drunk and on acid, flipping the fuck out! Blaming Paul Caruso, punching him in the gut and chasing him out of the house, throwing shit at him. Paul running for cover in West Hollywood, seeing Noel in the Whisky, telling him what had just happened. Noel, unmoved, squinting through his granny glasses, telling Paul, 'Bash him in the face. He's got it coming.'

Two days later Jimi, hi-hi-hi again and falling over drunk, putting on a show in front of Eric and Noel, playing the wounded soldier, accusing Carmen of fucking Paul Caruso, of wanting to fuck Eric, of being in on it, all you fucking people in on it. I FUCKING SEE IT ALL! Throwing a half-empty vodka bottle at her – hitting her in the face, just above the eye. Noel shouting, 'CALL 911!' Carmen in the ambulance, lying about what's just happened so they don't call the cops, the medics warning her she might lose the eye.

'You know, Noel may have saved my life one time,' Carmen would recall a long time later. 'Jimi was a very jealous man, and when Jimi would drink liquor, he could become very violent. Anyway, this one time he threw a bottle across the room, and almost took my eye out. Noel rushed me to the hospital ... You see, Jimi had a side to him that nobody really knew ... I've got the scars to prove it: one over my ear (a pretty good cut there) and my eyebrow covers the scar over my right eye where he threw a vodka bottle and it hit me and broke – just because he thought that Eric Burdon was making eyes at me.'

Back on tour in Europe. Jimi and the band dragging it across Sweden, Denmark, West Germany, France, Austria ... not easy places to score in 1969 ... Jimi boozing heavily, risking all to get shit flown in from London ... voted Performer of the Year for 1968 in the early February issue of *Rolling Stone* ... then back to London and Kathy and whoever, you know ... two shows at the Royal Albert Hall, the second one filmed ... living back at the Brook Street pad, flitting between Olympic, laying down tracks, and hanging out at the Speakeasy and Ronnie Scott's ... jamming with Roland Kirk, jamming with Jim Capaldi and Dave Mason ... hitting the launch party for the new Mary Hopkin ... voted Top World Musician by *Disc and Music Echo* ... back to the Speakeasy, jamming with Kwasi 'Rocky' Dzidzornu ... jamming with the Gods ...

Flying first class – alone, no Kathy, duh – back to New York. Jamming in a club, out of his gourd, with the Buddy Miles Express ... back to the Record Plant, laying down whatever comes into his head, using all his sweet time, go right ahead ... chicks dripping from the dimly lit walls, dudes blowing smoke up his ass ... back in LA at the end of March, hitting the Palladium on Sunset, getting up and jamming with Delaney and Bonnie ... hitting the Sound Factory studio on Sunset for a party for Donovan ... back in New York in April, swinging by the Record Plant by night to record ... what? Rehearsing for another tour during the day, supported by Fat Mattress – yaay! Raleigh, Philadelphia, back to New York and the Plant ... Memphis, Houston, Dallas, back to New York and the Plant ... back to LA for the Forum ... shagging it up the next day to San Fran for the Oakland Coliseum ... morning flight the next day back to New York and the Plant.

Sixteen more dates in May booked, Mike Jeffery pulling the money levers, beginning with the giant Cobo Hall in Detroit then flying direct to Toronto early the next day for the big show at the Maple Leaf Gardens ... 9.30 a.m., Jimi stopped as he tries to go through Canadian customs. Busted for carrying a big fuckin' bag of heroin – and hash. Released much later that day on $10,000 bail. Making the gig with just minutes to go.

Jim fucked. Fucked. FUCKED. Smuggling smack into Toronto? That's mainlining jail time, brother. Straight to hell.

Jimi onstage that night, keeping it together reasonably well considering the shitstorm that is about to rain down on his head.

Jimi leaning gently into the mic during a tender, bare-bones version of 'Red House', singing, '*Soon as I get out of jail / I wanna see her . . .*'

CHAPTER TWENTY-FIVE

Electric Family

'*A*re you high, Jimi?'

Crowd noise. Hendrix trying to talk, but it's hard for him to concentrate. Again, from somewhere near the stage: '*Are you high, Jimi? Are you high, man?*'

Jimi *was* high. Now he is low.

Woodstock, around eight o'clock on Monday morning, the sun hiding behind cloud. Nine hours late onstage. Ninety per cent of the crowd already gone home: the rest either waking up or struggling to stay awake.

The young promoters – panicked by the thunderstorms, the half a million overrun, the lack of toilets, food and water, and freaked out by the deaths (three), the births (two), the miscarriages (four), the hundreds of acid casualties – had scrambled and offered to interrupt the show and squeeze Jimi on at midnight on Sunday, but Mike Jeffery, who could only see headlines, insisted that Jimi as the headliner must *close* the show.

The young promoters – so busy distributing handwritten leaflets warning the crowd to stay away from the 'light-blue acid', offering sage advice like 'don't run naked in the hot sun', so busy setting up 'bad-trip tents' – nodded their stoned heads and agreed. Whatever Jimi wants, man.

Jimi, who hadn't slept in nearly seventy-two hours, shrugged and hunkered down for the night in a tent with his new band,

Gypsy Sun and Rainbows, smoking a ton of dope, snorting coke, dropping acid, drinking wine and playing acoustic guitars haloed by rippling percussion. Summoning the jinn.

Around dawn, Jimi decided it might be cool to do a couple of acoustic numbers in his actual set but was told no way by the promoters, backed by Mike. They wanted Monterey all over again. The guitar on fire, the waggly tongue, the smash hits ... Jimi tried to explain, No, man, I'm into a different scene now.

It isn't different-scene Hendrix the promoters have booked to close the festival, though. It isn't different-scene Hendrix that Mike Jeffery wants anybody to be talking about.

As Jimi and his new six-piece line-up shuffle onstage, the announcer introduces them: 'Ladies and gentlemen, the Jimi Hendrix Experience!'

Jimi keeping it together, torn between two worlds as he has been all year. He smiles and says, 'I see we meet again. Hmmm ...' The crowd liking that, cheering, hooting, waking up.

Jimi has to make it clear, though, whatever Mike or anyone else wants now.

'Dig! Dig – we have to get something straight. We get tired of the Experience every once in a while ...'

The crowd not really listening, just pleased to be communing with a legend.

'So we decided to change everything around and call it Gypsy Sun and Rainbows. Because, for sure, it's nothing but a band of gypsies ...'

No crowd reaction at all. Jimi continues on anyway.

'We have Billy Cox on bass ...' Splashes of applause.

'From Nashville, Tennessee, we have Larry Lee playing guitar over there ...' Smaller splashes.

'We got Juma playing congas over there ...' Bigger splashes.

Jimi joking, 'Excuse me, Mitch Mitchell on drums ...' Instant name recognition, anticipation, real applause.

'Then we got Jerry Velez on congas too.' Splash, splash. Everyone happy now, though: Jimi about to start playing – at last.

Jimi leaning in, telling it: '*Well, I travel at the speed of a reborn man . . .*'

Jimi *was* low. Now he is high. In 1969 it changes hourly.

He'd been down about Cream calling it a day. Felt like he'd been left as the last soldier standing. Eric had told him it was happening at the show in LA. Everybody wants to quit sometimes on the road, man. Then you get home, feel the empty space and change your sweet mind.

But that wasn't what happened to Cream. Jimi had heard different, that they were going to make another album. So he was bummed on New Year's day in New York, when he was back at the Record Plant laying down some more things he just had to get out of his head and onto tape, and Eric told him on the phone, 'No, man, we're done.'

Flying back to London the next day for *Happening for Lulu*, a big-deal Saturday early evening show, going out live on BBC1 before the *Six O'Clock News*. Freckly twenty-year-old singer Lulu in her sexy mini-skirt and husky blonde voice intro-ing them so sweet: 'They're gonna sing for you now the song that absolutely made them in this country – "Hey Joe".'

The plan is for Lulu to sashay on at the end of the number and duet with Jimi on one of her hits, 'To Sir, with Love'. But Jimi and the boys have been in the dressing room tucking into a giant lump of hash that Mitch has brought along, making like chimneys.

Just about holding it together as they start to play, Jimi, who has zero interest in playing his two-year-old hit, fools around with it for a minute, then waves the band to a crashing stop with his guitar and says to the tea-time millions gawping at home: 'We'd like to stop playing this rubbish and dedicate a song to, uh, the Cream . . .'

Mumbles something about Eric, Jack and Ginger and goes into 'Sunshine of Your Love' – Cream's big American hit based on a chunky bass riff Jack Bruce came up with after being inspired by one of Jimi's early London shows.

Cue middle-management panic from the BBC floor staff. The show is meant to finish exactly on time so they can segue into the news. But Jimi don't care, baby. Jimi's got his groove on.

'We're being put off the air,' he chuckles as the floor manager frantically jumps up and down, waving for him to please stop.

But Jimi don't care, baby, and just keeps going. Cut to Lulu's face, close-up, eyes wide with naughty-child delight.

Jimi finally brings it to a close with a *looong* wind-down outro.

Cue posh, wooden BBC-announcer voice: 'And now, with apologies for the slight delay, the *Six O'Clock News* . . .'

Jimi and Noel and Mitch sniggering back to their dressing room, very, very stoned, Lulu skipping behind them.

Jack Bruce, who watches the show from home, phones Jimi the next day. 'I told him how shocked I was when he went in "Sunshine",' Jack told this author years later. 'He was asking all about the farewell shows Cream did at the Albert Hall [in November 1968]. He was in America when we did them so couldn't be there. He was very interested to hear how we filmed and recorded them, knowing they were our last shows. Then he told me how he was doing two shows at the Albert Hall the next month. I don't know if he was thinking about making them his farewell shows – sort of end of the Experience shows, anyway – but he was very interested in wanting to know what it felt like. What we were all going to do now we didn't have to think about being in Cream anymore.'

In fact, Jimi has already spilled the beans in an interview with *Melody Maker*, how he and Mitch and Noel want to 'explore different scenes'. They won't be breaking up permanently, he was quick to stress, it was more to allow Noel to get his own group,

Fat Mattress, off the ground, while Mitch was now involved with an outfit called Mind Octopus.

Jimi would also be 'doing this and that'. The Experience would become more 'like a band of musical gypsies moving about everywhere'.

April 1969, back in New York. Far from breaking up the Experience, Jimi is about to begin rehearsals with Mitch and Noel for another high-profile American tour, under pressure from Mike Jeffery, who is now living and working out of a large steel and glass building in Manhattan and in need of heavy dough after buying out Chas's half of the management deal while supporting his star client through six months mostly off the road. Never mind the two all-night sessions he has recently recorded with the British jazz pair, guitarist John McLaughlin and double-bassist Dave Holland, and the tough-nut young black drummer Tony Williams, all members of the new 'electric' Miles Davis group.

If Jimi wants to spunk away his time making worthless noise with jazz musicians – not even *real* jazz like the kind Mike used to have in his clubs, but this fucking unlistenable head-shop electric-soup shit – that was his lookout. But when Jimi is also walking around being the big man, carrying fat rolls of five-hundred-dollar bills tucked in his boots, giving hand-outs to every broken-down beat on the street he once knew, expecting Mike to pay the rest of the bills, then it will be Mike who makes the big decisions about who Jimi tours with, *capeesh, Jimbo?*

Jimi is up and down with it. He knows he needs money to keep his new no-problem-baby lifestyle. But the craving to go beyond what Mitch and Noel were capable of doing with him was beginning to take over. Quincy Jones had tried to finally get Jimi and Miles together in the studio. They'd been circling each other long enough, sharing clothes, sharing girlfriends, sharing coke dealers. It was time to get real.

Jimi agreed on condition that Miles cut the personal shit. Miles agreed – on condition that Jimi pay him $50,000 cash on the day. Jimi agreed. Mike just laughed and told him to fuck off. There was no way he was laying down fifty gees for some coked-up fucking has-been like Miles Davis to come and make even more unusable instrumental nonsense. Jimi was quite capable of doing that on his own at no extra cost. Mike laughing as he says it, Mike's new yes men laughing right with him.

Instead, Mike books more time at the Record Plant, and Mitch and Noel dutifully show up knowing Jimi may or may not show too – and that even when he does it will be with his getting-bigger-every-day entourage. One night it's Devon plus another couple of girlfriends, and some cat named Mark introduces himself as 'Jimi's dealer', laying out fields of snow for everyone to ski down. Another night it's Devon and Mark again, only there are now six other chicks, different from last time – nobody knows their names or cares – plus some cat carrying bongos, says he's Jimi driver but when the Man found out he played the bongos he said to come by the studio too.

Drunk chicks picked up at the Scene falling over, slurring their words; street kids who won't stop laughing nervously, posing with switchblades disguised as steel combs. Jimi ignoring them, pushing Mitch and Noel to do take after take after take after take, until they walk out and don't come back. Till the next time.

In the middle of this, Mike has organised an interview and photo session for Jimi with *Life* magazine. Mike is over the moon. Never mind the dime-store hippy long-hairs that read *Rolling Stone* with a roach clip in their hands, *Life* was for rich grown-ups. *Life* was class. The Beatles got *Life*. Dylan got *Life*. Harry S. Truman and Winston Churchill got *Life*. Jimi on the cover would be like crowning him the new king of American rock.

Life, Jimi! Don't fuck this up!

It would be months before the issue hit the newsstands, in

October, but boy was it worth the wait, thought Mike. *Life* was known for the quality of its photography and illustrations, and the Jimi Hendrix cover was intense and beautiful.

Under the heading 'An Infinity of Jimis', the cover came in an ornamental gatefold, shared with a ballet shot, portraying Jimi in a 'roomful of mirrors'. The photographer was Raymundo de Larrain, a Chilean aristocrat who liked to go by the questionable title of the Marquis de Larrain. A brilliant, wildly extravagant fashion designer in his youth who would later marry into the Rockefeller family with a bride forty years his senior, the 'Marquis' took pictures of Jimi that were outrageous, exquisite, fit for a golden god.

Quoted directly, after a brief introduction, Jimi's words were equally ornamental, similarly ostentatious, if not entirely grammatical.

'Pretend your mind is a big muddy bowl,' they begin portentously, 'and the silt is very slowly settling down, but remember your mind's still muddy and you can't possibly grasp all I'm saying.'

Okaaay . . .

'Music is going to break the way. There'll be a day when houses will be made of diamonds and emeralds, which won't have any value anymore and they'd last longer in a rainstorm than a wooden house. Bullets'll be fairy tales. They'll be a renaissance from bad to completely pure and good, from lost to found. The everyday mud world we're living in today compared to the spiritual world is like a parasite compared to the ocean and the ocean is the biggest living thing you know about.'

Uh-huh.

'One way to approach the spiritual side is facing the truth. People who make a lot of money, they get sadder and sadder 'cause deep down they feel a hurt. So they go and buy a prostitute on Saturday and go to church on Sunday and pray down on the ground in a little saltbox, hearing another man who has the same problems preach, and the collection plate keeps going around and around. That man thinks he's found religion but he gets hurt more and more because he's not going toward the spiritual side, which is the way the atmosphere is . . .'

It goes on like this for several more paragraphs. All 'atmospheres . . . through music . . . a spiritual thing of its own . . . like the waves of the ocean. You can't just cut out the perfect wave and take it home with you . . .'

More and more: 'the race of man . . . people living in cement beehives . . . big ego scenes . . . Look at the pimps and the congressmen . . .'

Thankfully, Jimi could 'explain everything better through music . . . preach into the subconscious what we want to say . . . going into another world . . . this natural high . . . think of getting your own thing together . . .'

And on and on. 'Like my mind will go back in the days when I was a flying horse . . .'

Concluding, finally: 'A musician, if he's a messenger, is like a child who hasn't been handled too many times by man, hasn't had too many fingerprints across the brain. That's why music is so much heavier than anything you ever felt.'

Wait . . . *a flying fucking horse?*

Mike didn't bother with the gobbledegook words, he just looked at the stunning gatefold cover, the beautiful pictures inside – fucking arty! Then ordered fifty copies to give to people, American record-business people he wanted to impress, powerful agents like Frank Barsalona, big-league concert promoters like Bill Graham, and some behind-closed-doors faces he also needed to put on a show for. What they called old moustache Italians – original-generation wise guys. New York's finest.

By the time the *Life* cover hit the streets, though, Jimi was already in a very different place. The summer had been heavy. Super-heavy. The Toronto bust was fucked up, man. Jimi denied it, of course – he would *never* do smack. Claimed some chick in Detroit the night before had given him the stash in a glass jar with a yellow lid, which he had just slung into his tote bag without thinking. Didn't even look inside to see what it was, you know the scene, fans were always giving you little gifts, dig, and Jimi had had a cold, just assumed the chick was laying a little cold remedy on him, okay?

Sure, baby. A glass jar with three tightly wrapped cellophane packs of white powder in it. And a small metal tube smeared with a dark resin. Coulda bin anything, am I right, brother? How was Jimi to know?

Then there were all the other rock stars getting busted around that time. Jagger and Richards, Jones of course, Lennon and Donovan, cats from the Dead, the guys in the Airplane, Clapton . . . all getting hassled. Musicians being hassled by cops went all the way back, right?

But the Stones and the Beatles, Donovan and the Dead – that was all about weed and acid. What Jimi was busted for was *scag*. The real nasty shit the cops would nail you for, big time.

For all Jimi knew, the cops had planted it on him. Nobody really believed that, but it got Jimi the sympathy vote in the underground press. But when others began whispering in Jimi's ear, speculating over whether Mike Jeffery might be involved somehow . . .

Jimi's antennae began to twitch. He'd been tipped off in LA that some FBI spooks were now paying close attention to him, their lights flipped when they received intel about Jimi giving bread to the Panthers. Staking Abbie Hoffman was one thing. Hoffman and his ilk were never going anywhere real. But Huey Newton and Eldridge Cleaver and the gang – that was the big leagues. Better watch your fucking back, boy.

It was true. Jimi had been trying to find a way to connect ever since some hard-ass, heat-packing Panthers invaded his dressing room at the Fillmore West, ordered everybody out and started calling him out for being 'a white nigger'.

Six months before the Toronto bust, an interview with Jimi had come out in radical youth-culture magazine *Teenset*, head-lined jimi hendrix, black power and money.

Jimi talking about black *militancy*, quoted as follows: 'Then get your Black Panthers . . . I know it sounds like war, but that's what's gonna have to happen, it has to be a war if nobody is going to do it peacefully . . . You have to fight fire with fire.'

Mike shit the bed when he was told about it. *What the fucking fuck, Jimi? You wanna kill your audience stone dead overnight?*

The Feds took it even more seriously. But the Feds, led by Evil Edgar, didn't grasp the fact that no self-respecting American black kid would be caught dead reading crapola white hippy jive like *Teenset*.

Anyway, none of this rang any bells for Jimi. He knew where the gear came from, what it was. He'd been carrying all kinds of shit in his hand luggage for *years*. Of course, what someone like Mike might do with that information was another thing. Lately things had become more and more *complicated* with Mike. He'd been warning Jimi for months that he was messing with the rules, fucking around with Miles Davis, with the Black Panthers, with changing the group, even. Could the smack bust be Mike step-ping up the warnings? Summer of '69 paranoia said anything was possible. Jimi snorting gram after gram of the primo gear, direct from the Aztec mountains, chain-smoking good Califor-nian grass, Devon and Carmen and Mike and Mitch and whoever in his face twenty-four seven.

At a preliminary hearing in Toronto in June, Judge Robert Taylor set Jimi's trial date, on two counts of possession, for 8 December. Relieved not to be facing charges of smuggling and/ or trafficking as well, Jimi paid the $10,000 bail and flew back to New York.

*

Woodstock was supposed to cure Jimi of his ills. Mike was now able to demand $100,000 for a Jimi Hendrix Experience show, but the tour had been up and down. A shit night in the San Fernando Valley, where Jimi did the whole show with his back turned to the audience, then blamed it on some 'bad-news people backstage' – another surprise delegation of angry black radicals demanding money for political actions who left Jimi shaking. Talking about it to the writer Sharon Lawrence, he said, 'I don't *feel* black. It's the Indian part that I mostly pay most attention to.'

A cool night at the Seattle Center arena – Jimi's hometown – where he and Carmen, both tripping heavily, got a young autograph hunter to drive them around in the early hours after the show, Jimi showing Carmen some of the places that had meant something to him when he was growing up.

Everywhere he went he always left his doors open, all kinds of people streaming through them. When Jeanette Jacobs showed up in New York, she recalled, 'He would say to me, "What do you want?" And I would say, "What do you mean?" And he'd say, "In the next room you can get anything for free." I asked who they were, and he said they were fans trying to get him stoned. Not to hurt him, but to turn him on. There was anything you could think of – uppers, downers, white lightning, purple hearts, take your pick.

'You wouldn't believe it. They really thought he could take it all at once. It's a drag to think that the people who loved him would have killed him. Not intentionally, of course. He was an idol, maybe a genius, and they thought he could take everything. He enjoyed experimenting, but I never saw him take anything except acid. I know he snorted, cos everybody snorts something. [But] I've never seen a needle on Jimi.'

One of the best nights came when Jimi jumped up with the Buddy Miles Express, who were on the same festival bill, joined by Eric Burdon and a new band, Earth Mother. Jimi wailed for over two hours, improvising freely with them all. 'It was as if Hendrix had broken through to the most profound musical dimension available to mortals,' drooled the arts editor of *Los Angeles* magazine.

Then, at the end of June, the Jimi Hendrix Experience played its last-ever show, headlining the Denver Pop Festival, at the Mile High Stadium. Jimi, tripping, as he was at almost every show now, was off his game again, unusually bitter, changing the words of 'Voodoo Child' and spitting into the mic, '*Gonna make a lot of money and buy this town / Gonna buy this town and put it all in my shoe . . .*'

Anger and recrimination already filled the ninety-five-degree Colorado air. A large crowd had rioted outside the stadium, demanding it be made free. Then, when Jimi mumbled something about this being 'the last gig we'll ever be playing together', the 17,000-strong crowd inside the stadium rioted too. Armed cops started shooting tear gas into the crowd and Jimi sardonically remarked, 'We see tear gas – that's the sign of the Third World War.'

Sickened, Noel Redding decided he couldn't take anymore and flew back to London the next day. He'd been surprised – devastated, he said – when a backstage visitor had asked before the show what he was going to do now that the band was over. Noel claimed he knew nothing about it. Ah, man, that Noel. He knew. *Everyone* knew. Laying on the guilt trips all the way to the end of the road.

Mitch, a born pro from his stage-school days, waiting to see which way the wind blows, knowing enough not to rock the boat. Observing the vibe, talking of some project with Roland Kirk. Roland Kirk, man! Hey, man, check Mitch out! Mitch saying all the right words but still having to get on the plane home now that the tour was over.

The same day that Noel took off for London, Jimi flew back to

New York and checked into the Hotel Navarro on Central Park South. The Navarro was the new place for the rock elite to hang, and Jimi was hoping for a better scene. The day after that he got a phone call from London: Brian Jones had been found face down at the bottom of his swimming pool, dead at twenty-seven.

Major downer. Then more paranoia as whispers reached New York of Jones being taken care of, dig? Brian had been telling Jimi since the start how the others had it in for him. How they were always plotting against him. How they wanted him gone.

Jimi sitting up all night in his suite at the Navarro, snorting coke, on the phone to London, to LA, on the phone to Mike, telling him, 'Look, man, I gotta get away, dig?' Then regretting it. Jimi not wanting to confide in someone he doesn't completely trust, and Jimi doesn't trust anybody anymore, not really.

Jimi snorting coke with Carmen, snorting smack with Devon, talking about a new kind of band he wanted to put together. Something like a modern orchestra, but one for the intergalactic generation to come, the ones who heard music as colours, dig? Took in *both* sides of the rainbow, you understand what I'm talking about?

First call is to his old army buddy Billy Cox, to come and play bass. Invited on to NBC's *The Tonight Show Starring Johnny Carson* less than a week after Brian's death, Jimi comes over twisted, chewing non-stop on Black Jack liquorice gum. With Johnny ducking the whole deal on the advice of 'close friends' in fear of even the slightest whiff of any Panther association, the show is guest-hosted by Flip Wilson, a thirty-five-year-old black comedian making himself sound even older by trying to sound hip. 'I can dig it,' he says as Jimi wanders off down some internal galactic highway about music being religion.

Finally, Jimi wanders over to the stage where Billy Cox – who arrived in town just forty-eight hours before – is waiting to make his first public appearance as a Hendrix band member, along with Ed Shaughnessy, forty-year-old drummer of *The Tonight Show* house band. Ed is ex-Basie, Goodman, Dorsey, session man for Quincy, Gillespie, Etta, Billie . . . Ed knows his shit, baby, and the band cooks!

Jimi dedicates the performance to Brian Jones. 'This is Billy Cox, our new bass player,' he says, 'and here's this thing called "Here Comes Your Lover Man Out the Window, I Can See Him".' But the take is abandoned after Jimi's amp blows up. Cue more live-broadcast chaos.

Three nights earlier, Mike had booked Jimi onto Carson's big rival, *The Dick Cavett Show* on ABC. Thirty-two-year-old Dick is infinitely cooler than Johnny. Dick would have Groucho Marx sitting next to Salvador Dalí if he could. Marlon Brando opposite Bobby Kennedy if he could. A month later he would turn that night's show into a Woodstock special, with Joni Mitchell, Stephen Stills and the Jefferson Airplane all performing.

Jimi appears in a blue-dragon kimono, starts talking about how, with his new group, 'We plan for the sound to go into the soul of the person.' Then gets up with Cavett's in-house group – Billy hadn't arrived in New York yet – and performs a sketchy, improvised version of 'Hear My Train a Comin''. Elastic guitar stretching in and out, the studio boys popping behind him, Jimi riffing on the putting-this-town-in-his-shoe lyric, only turning it this time into, '*And if you make love to me one more time girl, I might even give a piece to you* . . .' Then ending it with a little something for the straights in the studio audience, lifting his immaculate white Strat to his face and picking out the last pearly notes with his teeth. Laughing in the face of all the lies. Smoothy Cavett hip to those trips digging it special, right on.

After that Jimi split the scene completely, leaving the city behind for his seriously groovy new pad in the countryside. An eight-bedroom mansion set in ten acres of glorious mountain woodlands in the tiny hamlet of Shokan, just a short drive from

Woodstock. The pad came with riding stables, horses, a large out-door swimming pool, and a live-in cook and housekeeper.

Mike, who had recently begun renting his own luxury country villa a few miles away, had actually found the place for Jimi. Suitably wowed, Jimi moved his whole new 'electric family' up there with him.

The rent was $3,000 a month (around $21,000 fifty years on) but Mike told Jimi it would be worth every cent if it meant the musician could now fulfil his artistic vision in peace, away from the hourly distractions of New York.

This was Mike-speak for getting his prize asset out from under the runny noses of several competing interests for Jimi's attention. If it had just been the viper groupies and the endless drugs, the desperate hangers-on and ravenous music-biz vultures waiting to pounce – like that bastard Alan Klein had just done with the Stones, first cutting Loog Oldham off at the legs financially then buying him out completely, in exchange for a million dollar advance to the band – that would have been more than enough for Mike to try to deal with.

But Jimi was now involved in all sorts of shit that Mike didn't feel he could control anymore. Hell, Mike was now involved in all sorts of shit he didn't feel he could fully control anymore. For Jimi it was mainly the fucking Panthers. Mike was savvy enough to see that Jimi didn't really give a shit about those guys. He just couldn't handle being shamed by them for not being black enough. Being called 'white nigger' by gun-toting American blacks dug into Jimi worse than anything Mike had ever seen. So Jimi had ponied up some big dough, more than once, had paid lip service to the brothers in the press. Had even rid himself of his white band.

But it was never going to be enough for the black radicals. They weren't stupid. As soon as they saw how fucked up Jimi was about the whole thing they just doubled down and squeezed him for more. More money, more of his time, more publicity . . . Fuck those people!

There was more to it, though. Jimi had become one of the most famous black musicians in the world – to an almost exclusively white audience. The bigger he got, the whiter they became. Mike had ordered Jimi's American label, Reprise, to quietly research which black American radio stations played Jimi Hendrix records. The answer came back: none. When asked why, it came back: our listeners don't regard Hendrix music as black music. Fuck, man. Who's going to tell Jimi?

Hence Mike's desperate opposition to Jimi breaking up with Mitch and Noel. His insistence on them keeping it together for those big-money shows throughout the spring and early summer.

At the same time Jimi was going through a revolution of the head. It wasn't just a white or black thing to him. He knew the places he wanted his music to explore now stretched way beyond the cosmic guitar rock that Mike wanted him to continue making. That meant bringing in cats with real musical muscle and imagination. And that meant raiding the jazz and funk and experimental-electronic realm. And that meant mainly black or mixed-blood cats like he was. Plus he needed people he could really trust. And that meant black or mixed-blood cats too, though not exclusively.

People like Billy Cox. Billy could really play, not just hit the right notes like Noel. Billy would always be grateful to be by Jimi's side, another thing you couldn't ever say about Noel.

People like Larry Lee from the band he and Billy had in Nashville all those years before, whom Jimi also had flown up to the new country mansion. Gerardo 'Jerry' Velez, a white Bronx drummer and percussionist Jimi had got to know in the old days and recently became reacquainted with through jamming in the New York clubs. This would be Jerry's first-*ever* professional gig – another reason for him to stay loyal to Jimi. And, finally, another ace in the hole, Juma Sultan, an African-American conga player from California, then doing African drum circles on Woodstock village green. Juma was a veteran of the Haight-Ashbury scene, Be-Ins and freak beatitudes, who also had connections to the New York scene, through which he had appeared on a couple of jazz albums. He now found himself parachuted into a world he'd never imagined.

'Jimi was a very eclectic person,' recalled Juma. 'Not only was he brilliant in terms of music, but his concepts and ideas were pretty advanced, I would say.' Mike Jeffery 'was a whole other character. He wasn't interested in the music. He was interested in the money.'

For Billy Cox, what Jimi was doing was about more than trying to make some kind of musical breakthrough; it was about trying to find his way back to Earth again, to when things were real.

'Yeah, without doubt. 'We'd go to amusement parks when we were up in Woodstock – we bought bows and arrows and rode motorcycles and horses. We had a good time.'

Larry Lee 'was kind of a jokester. So Jimi finally had guys around him that *knew* him. Guys he trusted and guys who were the same age.' Billy was actually a year older, Larry a few months younger. 'Therefore he had a chance to relax and really be Jimi.'

They would jam for hours on end, often outdoors in the cool, head-clearing mountain breezes. Music that would unwind over a period of hours, very few vocals, just an ever-evolving musical mesh, diving deep then resurfacing. 'Letting the music tell you where it wants to go,' said Billy.

Jimi was also building a new coterie of friends away from the music. Jimi more uncomfortable than ever with whatever biz-wizardry Mike was advocating. Rebuffed by Chas on those late-night phone calls to London, during which he would beg Chas to come back and help him take back control, Jimi now looked for support wherever he could find it.

People like Deering Howe, whom Jimi had met after hiring his private yacht for a party. Deering was one of those old-money cats, educated at the finest schools, a product of one of the largest family fortunes in America, but you'd never know it from meeting him. A trust-fund kid with zero interest in business, a lifelong passion for the blues and a good-times rock 'n' roll lifestyle, Deering was cool, far out, fun and super-intelligent. As he said, 'Part of the attraction for Jimi was that I came from money and there was nothing I wanted from him.'

Deering was on the scene but not *of* the scene. That's why Mick Jagger liked hanging out with him. Why Jimi dug being at Deering's groovy Fifth Avenue penthouse jingle-jangling on acoustic guitars and getting high on the super-good stuff.

The same with some of the new women in Jimi's life, like Colette Mimram and Stella Benabou, who co-owned a far-out boutique in the East Village. Jimi loved going there, buying fringe leather jackets, kimonos, turquoise bracelets, Moroccan antiques, getting to know other people that hung there like the German painter Mati Klarwein – whose spiritual father was Dalí, he would explain – soon to become known for his expressionistic album-cover art, and John Edward Heys, who founded America's first overground newspaper for the gay community, *Gay Power*. Scenes that would merge with other scenes, as Devon Wilson, Betty Davis, Carmen Borrero, Billy Cox and others became part of the same Jimi-orbit.

Mike Jeffery had bigger fish to fry. Jimi was now booked as headliner – show-closer, no less – for the forthcoming Woodstock festival in August. To Mike it was just another big open-air gig – easy money. Mike saw Michael Lang, the twenty-four-year-old promoter, as just another long-haired kid, used to own a head shop in Miami's boho Coconut Grove. Lang had done a decent job promoting the Miami Pop Festival that Jimi had headlined the year before. Mike saw this as more of the same, sold them on

the Jimi Hendrix Experience – figured Jimi was living in the area
with a bunch of musos anyhow, didn't matter who he turned up
onstage with. Get in, do the gig, get out again. Count the dough.
Happy-hippy days.

Then, three weeks before the show, with no drummer but a
loose invitation to Mitch to come back and jam, Jimi took off. Va-
moosed. First to New York to party with his pal Deering, who was
flying off for a vacay in Morocco, where Colette and Stella were
waiting for him. Then, goddamn! To Morocco with Deering!

Mike went *insane*. Threatened to do all kinds of bad shit to
Deering when he came back – *if* he came back. No one knew what
Jimi's plans were. Just that Deering had been jibing him about
spending some of the pile of cash he'd made on having a little fun
– without asking anybody's permission first. Deering would get
his own high-powered lawyers to fix it with the Canadian authorities to waive the don't-leave-town restriction they had put on him
as a condition of his bail – no need to bother Mike, haw-haw-haw.

Come on, man, let's just fucking go!

So they did.

Arriving in Casablanca in late July, Jimi hired a chauffeur-
driven limo and began letting himself go, travelling to Marrakesh,
Mohammedia, ending up in Essaouira, where everybody checked
into the Hôtel des Iles. Still paranoid, he thought he could see
mysterious men following him around. But he thought that
everywhere he went now. As it was a last-minute thing, he only
had a couple of thousand dollars in cash on him – but enough to
live like a lion god in Africa, man.

For once he didn't even have a guitar, except for the acoustic
Deering brought along. Mostly, Jimi just loved the idea of stretching out, no Mike up his ass, no people on the payroll waiting on
him for direction each day, no starfuckers – all with that same
smile that says, I'm ready to eat shit for you, Jimi.

He and Colette shared a little scene together; nothing heavy, just sweet and serene, loaded up on pure, unfettered straight-from-the-bazaar Moroccan gold. The whole thing lifting him in ways he hadn't felt since he first set foot in London. Maybe since for ever . . .

Only one bad omen: Colette's stepmother, a second-sight tribal elder who worked for the King of Morocco. Colette couldn't wait to take Jimi to meet her. The old gal told Jimi he had a 'forehead' – a sign of great artistic vision. Then she read him his Tarot. The first card out of the deck was the Star card – of course, everyone purred. The second card was the Death card – and Jimi freaked.

Take it easy, Jimi, the Death card in the Tarot can mean different things – transition, rebirth, new beginnings. Too late – Jimi will spend the next year telling everyone how he won't see thirty. Or how he only has six months to live.

Told off by Colette for being negative, he responds, 'It's not negative. It's just the way it is. I'm sorry. I'm not ready to go.'

Onstage at Woodstock, stupefyingly early, that dreary Monday morning three weeks later, it's a whole other thing. Gypsy Sun and Rainbows – and Mitch – come on and begin to blow. Good energy undulating out towards the bare-bones crowd. It is a bringdown how few people there are left to feed off. Pale dry mud for ground, white tired sky above, crowd thinning out quickly just beyond the stage, stoned stragglers adrift.

They rattle through looong versions of 'Hear My Train a Comin'', 'Spanish Castle Magic', 'Red House' . . . doleful, rambling, bodies being dragged from the river, Jimi making up the words. Make like an eagle on a new slapdash thing called 'Jam Back at the House', then another jam thing they don't even bother to title, bringing some poise and moxy, but it all disappears into jazz-to-Jupiter zzzz.

Some hits thrown in, crumbs on the blanket: 'Foxey Lady', 'Fire', 'Purple Haze' . . . bent, twisted versions, coiled and uptight.

It's the supernova shit like 'Izabella' that brings out the new band's best efforts, but in the porta-studio truck next to the stage, Mike is directing Eddie Kramer, who is mixing the sound, to lay the focus squarely on the money – Jimi and Mitch and Billy. As close an approximation of the signature Experience sound as they can get. Juma all bent out of shape for a long time after over him and Larry and Jerry being kept out of the mix, but watcha gonna do when you ain't the one paying the bills?

'Voodoo Child' is laid like a plan to bring the whole wang-dang-doodle to a suitably lid-flapping finale. But it goes on and on . . . nearly quarter of an hour, ending badly, disjointedly, Jimi actually lifting the damn guitar to his lips at the very end, chewing out a few last completely unnecessary notes, the crowd reacting Pavlov style, like all crowds will always do.

Into the real wholly unexpected climax.

Jimi had started playing snatches of 'The Star-Spangled Banner' on tour during the end jam of 'I Don't Live Today', an ironic top note to his song about growing up part-Cherokee. But the idea had grown until it became a stand-alone highlight of the show. Now, in the morning mildew of Woodstock, it becomes a stoned aftershock to the whole American experiment. Whitey on the moon but the black ghettos just kept growing. The anti-war protestors constantly parading but the body bags kept coming back from Vietnam. Jimi had seen the future like the Star Gate sequence at the end of 2001: life through different-coloured filters; death through duplicate negatives, the universe a starburst in your brain.

Jimi conducting the feedback and distortion like a general aiming his rockets, sending in his bombers, the air shrieking with jets, the sky lit up with napalm flare, the excruciating cries of war babies as bodies are ruptured and faces peeled off.

Yet somehow, at the end, Jimi's amulet guitar offering thin rays of hope, glimpses of the corporeal. Crowd completely agog.

Three weeks later, back with Dick Cavett, Jimi uncomfortable as Dick teases him about the 'controversy' over playing the national anthem. 'I don't know, man,' he says, 'they made us sing it in school . . . it was a flashback!'

When Dick makes a joke about the hate mail Jimi will receive because of his 'unorthodox' rendition of the sacred song, Jimi wakes up, pulls a face, that less-known fierce side of him coming through even on TV now.

'I didn't think it was unorthodox,' he says. 'I thought it was beautiful.'

A tight, exhausted smile as the studio audience breaks into spontaneous applause.

He flashes a peace sign then an inverse peace sign, then, 'I think it's the last job we'll do until we take a rest.'

CHAPTER TWENTY-SIX

Jimi and the Boys

There must be some kind of way outta here . . .
It got dark after that. Jimi a virtual prisoner in the recording studio, still dreaming of a life outside of what he is now, wishing for Gypsy Sun and Rainbows to help him make that move, to pick up its own speed, burn off the excess whiteness of his image, his music, his whole deal. The way Jimi saw it, anyway.

Mike Jeffery not at peace with any of this, scheming in the shadows, looking for a way to force Jimi back to a place where he can be controlled, forcibly if need be. On a trip back to London he has dinner at Annabel's with Don Arden. Don has never forgiven Mickie Most for stealing the Animals from him, or Mike for his part in it. He spends the evening regaling Mike with horror stories of how he has dealt with those who have crossed him.

Having his men pick up Robert Stigwood by his arms and legs and threaten to hurl him over the balcony of his office in Cavendish Square, after the Australian theatre agent tried to steal the Small Faces from under Don's nose.

'His whole body went limp and he shat himself,' laughs Don. 'Shit running down his fucking cowboy boots. It was disgusting but he never bothered me again, little queer rat.'

Or his most recent escapade: a personal visit to Cliff Davis after Cliff tried to take the Move from under Don's nose.

'I took the cigar out of his mouth and drilled it into the middle of his forehead,' Don tells Mike proudly. 'He struggled, of course, but I was too strong. I wanted to see if I could actually penetrate his forehead with that thing. Eventually the crushed embers of the cigar fell down between his knees and burned a hole right through his trousers. I started to laugh.'

Mike and Don sitting there, yukking it up together, knocking back the Cristal bubbles. Mike getting Don's message loud and clear: don't you ever try to fuck me on a deal again. And the other part of the message: actions speaks louder than words. Mike leaves Don that night, his head full of plans for everyone.

More trouble waiting, though, when Mike gets back to New York: Ed Chalpin, the ghost of Curtis past – has come to cash in on *his* prime asset. Talking serious dough, plus percentages, cuts from existing albums, backdated, future recordings, concert tours, name it – full-spectrum nightmare.

Mike starting to see Jimi more as an alley cat that shoulda had its balls cut off long ago – a fucking tart signing his name to anything for a few dollars, don't care where it comes from. Mike bringing in the heavy-gun legals and being told there's no way out, this guy Chalpin has paper, he will need paying.

Jimi saying, 'No way, that ain't right,' and complaining about all the money it's costing him already now that he's practically living at the Record Plant. Talking about having his own studio, like, yeah, why not, man? Mike taking that one onboard and starting to join the dots in his mind, starting to turn on to the idea as he sees how it might become money, maybe *serious* money, hmmm.

Jimi, meanwhile, making the kind of racket with his new all-black band Mike knows he will never be able to sell. Ten- and twenty-minute shit, not even a chorus sometimes. Even Mitch is being sidelined. One day he's in the band, the next it's some other cat. More faces from the old days showing up, like keyboardist Mike Ephron, whom Jimi hasn't seen in a million years. New faces being brought in like drummer Ali K. Abuwi – some dude

Juma Sultan introduces to Jimi, like, yeah, man, come join us, hey, that's far out.

Then Jimi making arrangements to have Buddy Miles flown in, first-class everything. Buddy can *really* play the drums, Mike keeps hearing. 'As good as Mitch, Jimi?' Who knows, but Buddy is black, right?

Mike warning Jimi that it's all going to blow up in his face. Jimi ignores him, hanging out with Devon and Carmen and Colette and Deering and Buddy and whomever they happen to hook up with, doing blow, gobbling acid, staying up for five days straight, a little valium to help that crash, a little white horse.

On days when he allows himself to think straight, Jimi now openly talks about losing Mike, finding someone new and more in tune with what he's doing. When some 'old friends' steal some contracts from Mike's office and show them to Jimi, he is freaked out to read about gigs for which Mike had told him he'd been paid $10,000, had actually paid Mike $50,000. Worried what Mike might do if he found out Jimi's people had broken into his office, Jimi tells them to shut up about it; he'll take care of it when the time is right.

Mike's words about everything blowing up in Jimi's face came true when he and his band of payroll gypsies roll up in September for a gig in Harlem. That's right, *Harlem.* Benefit for the United Block Association – money for the brothers struggling to survive – free street-festival vibe. Also on the bill, righteous mother-fuckers like Big Maybelle, J.D. Bryant, Maxine Brown, plus Sam & Dave's *backing band.*

Can you dig it? Jimi says he can and shows up with the Woodstock line-up of Gypsy Sun and Rainbows, ready to play for free. His first gig to a genuinely all-black audience since his days playing in bars for *bupkes*, he can't wait to see what the people make of where he's at now. Quietly carrying hopes that this might persuade some of the closed-minded programme directors at

America's black radio stations to open up to the idea of playing some of Jimi's new music on their shows.

They had tried to do the show at the Harlem Apollo – make it a proper historic occasion. But the Harlem Apollo didn't want Jimi. Said there would be too many white people there. White people taking drugs, dancing naked and disrespecting the place – that's the image the name Jimi Hendrix summons in their minds.

Fucked up about it, Jimi goes ahead with the Harlem show anyway. He'd been hearing about some Mob-connected hoods who were scamming people about a Hendrix Experience concert in Harlem that Jimi knew nothing about until he saw some guys in the street actually putting up a poster for the show. Jimi lit into the guys but one of the mobsters behind the scam was on the scene suddenly, flanked by two of his soldiers. All three pulled out their pieces and aimed them head high at Jimi. Told him to back the fuck up and split or else. Jimi did as he was told.

Mike *hates* the idea of the UBA show. He's had enough of these black hustlers in Jimi's face day and night about not having any white people around. But for Jimi the UBA show is a symbol of where he's at now – a message to the universe. Affecting nobility, he tells the *New York Times* about his visits to Harlem, 'Sometimes when I come up here people say, "He plays white rock for white people. What's he doing up here?" Well, I want to show them that music is universal – that there is no white rock or black rock.'

Five thousand of the bored and the curious show up on the day, but the whole gig goes to shit almost immediately. Standing watching the show with Carmen, Jimi gets heavy static for having a blonde girlfriend, being called out for bringing a 'white bitch' to Harlem. In the fight that breaks out Carmen has her blouse ripped open.

Hours of this bullshit until around midnight, when Jimi and the band crowd onto the tiny street stage – Jimi dressed in *white*, motherfucker.

A bottle is thrown at the stage before a note is played. It smashes into an amplifier, shattered glass flying. The band digs in but people start throwing eggs. *Eggs*, motherfucker. Then people start leaving. *Walking away.*

Desperate, he sticks to first principles and gives the thinning crowd stoic versions of 'Fire', 'Foxey Lady', 'Red House' . . . the blues finally coming through and bringing a spark of warmth from what's left of the crowd. But then Jimi risks his ass and does 'The Star-Spangled Banner', and it's back to honky square one. He almost saves the day with 'Voodoo Child', scraping the bottom of the barrel by announcing it to the restless crowd as 'the *Harlem National Anthem*'.

Nobody calls it that. Most people in Harlem have never even heard it before. The show finally grinds to a halt with fewer than two hundred people still hanging around in the street.

Looking in the mirror, back in his suite at the Nevada Hotel, Jimi jokes to Carmen that he is looking old, that his hair is starting to fall out, his chest hair and pubes turning grey. He is laughing. Pretending to.

Mike hears all about the Harlem wig-out and thinks, what a fucking waste of time and money. Jimi could have been badly hurt. Could have been killed. And for what, to prove he's fucking black? Things were getting badly out of whack. Something would have to be done.

Four nights later Jimi is back on the Cavett show, again with the whole Gypsy menagerie, playing a looong improvised jam built around a new thing Jimi has come up with called – Mike *thinks*, it's hard to tell because Jimi mumbles so much now – 'Machine Gun'. Close your eyes, wish for it hard enough and this could be something from the *Electric Ladyland* album. Jesus, Mike thinks, that seems such a long time ago now. What the hell is Jimi doing with all these fucking wasters telling him he should go African, baby, go more jazz, like Miles, dig, go somewhere new and more, you know, *black?* How the fuck is he supposed to sell that to Jimi's *white* fans?

Something would definitely have to be done – and soon.

Twenty-four hours later Jimi is dragged out of a club, bound and blindfolded, thrown into the back of a car – and taken.

Wait. Say that again, man?

Mike had been dealing with gangsters all his life, of one sort or another. From duck's-arse-haircut spivs in the old army days to hard-case Geordie 'businessmen' in the Newcastle clubs. London music-biz mavericks like Don Arden held no fear for Mike, either. He wasn't about to become entangled with Ronnie and Reggie Kray, but he had watched their relationship with New York mobsters grow as the twins moved into West End nightclubs.

In America, the record business and the Mafia had been hand in glove since the days when sixteen-year-old Louis Armstrong received his first wages for playing the trumpet at a tavern owned by Henry Matranga, leader of the Matranga family, one of the most powerful crime syndicates of the early twentieth century.

Since the days when Frank Sinatra's Sicilian uncle Babe Garavante, a Morettis crime-family member, was convicted of murder after driving the getaway car at an armed robbery in 1921.

Since the days when Frank was JFK's go-between for Sam Giancana, a leading figure in the Mob's Chicago Outfit.

Since the days when the Mob ran all the big-shot Las Vegas entertainers like Frank, Sammy Jr., Deano, Liza and Tony Bennett.

Since the days when Frankie Valli was connected to the Genovese family. 'I don't think anyone who was in the entertainment industry in the sixties can say they've never rubbed shoulders with the Mob,' said Frankie with a shrug.

Since the days when Morris Levy – a Jewish record-company chief with lots of Italian friends – ran Roulette Records, a front for the Genovese family.

Roulette – where there were no handles on the inside of the doors.

Roulette – where Yardbirds manager Simon Napier-Bell went for a meeting in 1966 and found Morris with his hands round the throat of one his producers, lifting him off the floor and screaming, 'You fucking black cocksucker! You promised to make me a hit record and you screwed up!'

The cocksucker in question was Mickey Stevenson, who'd written 'Dancing in the Street' for Martha and the Vandellas and had just had a hit with 'What Becomes of the Brokenhearted' by Jimmy Ruffin.

Since the Mafia grasped the income potential of the new generation of 'heavy' rock bands and became involved in the management of groups like Vanilla Fudge and Humble Pie.

In 1969, Kinney National, an investment syndicate headed by Steve Ross – real name Steven Jay Rechnitz – bought the ailing Warner Bros. Seven Arts film studio and record business for $400 million, with Ross installing himself as CEO. Steve was a suave, easy-going operator who had no problem hobnobbing with the Mob. The fact that he now de facto ran Reprise, Jimi's American label, meant Jimi – and Mike – now had their own long-distance ties to the mob. And vice versa.

But the game was already in play long before that. The Mob controlled record distribution across America. Of the more than six thousand radio stations then jamming the air in America, over four thousand had playlists under Mafia control, who would 'promote' their records by supplying DJs and producers with coke, prostitutes and, when that didn't work, suitcases full of cash.

In 1969, Jimi Hendrix was the biggest-selling act on Reprise. But he hadn't released a new album in a year. What was going on? Mike kept being asked. Not by Steve Ross – but by people who knew people.

Salvation was a club in the Village that had been taken over by

John Riccobono and his Mafia partner Andy Benfante, working on behalf of the Gambino family. When the joint ran into trouble with the licensing laws, its days as a high-end disco were over, and club manager Bobby Wood decided to make it over as a live-music venue. It was Bobby who gave John the idea of having Jimi Hendrix play the club's relaunch night.

Mike ran it by Jimi, who said no. It didn't make sense. Jimi had been a regular at the club for years. He still went there now, especially if he was looking to score, maybe late at night on the fly.

But Jimi dug in. Sure, he was a regular face at the club. Bobby was a coke-hound too and they would share bottles of bubbly, drinking straight from the bottle. Bobby boasting when stoned of his wise-guy connections. But Jimi wasn't down with doing some party-favour gig, no matter how much it paid or who it was supposedly for. He was still at the Shokan house at the time, doubling down with Gypsy Sun and Rainbows. He tried to explain to Mike: he just wasn't in that headspace right now.

But when Mike went back and told Bobby Wood, and he told Riccobono, a decision was made to pay Jimi a visit.

Mike didn't give a shit about whether Jimi played Salvation. He needed to keep the Gambino people reassured that if he and Jimi built a recording studio on a site on their turf it wouldn't draw the wrong kind of heat because of all the drugs. They owned the local NYPD but the FBI sniffing around was a different ball game. And the Gambino people also needed Mike to understand that if he got their blessing there would have to be 'an arrangement': protection money.

Mike understood everything. Two limos arrived unannounced at the Shokan house one morning in September: Mike in the first, John Riccobono and Andy Benfante following close behind. Mike and John went inside the house and took Jimi upstairs to talk to him. Andy stayed outside and set up a target on one of the trees. Juma watching all this wide-eyed through a window, seeing 'this guy pull out his .38 and, pow! pow! Bullseyes every time while the conversation with Jimi is going on.'

Looking back on that day years later, Riccobono said, 'I don't remember needing a gun to make Jimi Hendrix play for us. He liked Salvation because he could get drugs there.'

Jimi did the show. What a scene! A punch full of Quaaludes, beautiful models walking around naked, Riccobono later claiming that Jimi had tried to get the gangster to shoot speed with him. 'It was like Rome!' Anybody tried to cause trouble, said Riccobono, he had his men 'drag them into a backroom and beat them within an inch of their life. That's how I kept the spirit of peace and love going.'

For Jimi it was a king-hell drag. The amps didn't work properly and the crowd was not remotely interested in Gypsy Sun and Rainbows or 'Izabella' or back-at-the-house space jams. There was a moment of intensity as he duelled with Larry Lee, then Jimi put down his axe on top of one of the malfunctioning amps and walked off.

He was back there a few nights later, though, 'doing my own thing'. When a couple of razor-faced guido kids sidled up and began rapping about some primo charlie they had on tap and would Jimi like a taste? Being such a coke connoisseur, how could Jimi refuse?

'We'll take you there, man. We gotta a limo outside . . .'

That's when they snatched him. Threw him in the back and pointed a gun at him.

The first Mike hears of it is the following morning. A phone call to the office, saying Jimi is dead unless his management contract is handed over today. The office phones Mike. Mike is very cool. He calls Riccobono, who makes some calls of his own.

'It took me and Andy two or three phone calls to get the names of the kids who were holding Jimi,' Riccobono later wrote. 'We reached out to these kids and made it clear, "You let Jimi go or you are dead." These guys were morons. They let Jimi go. The whole thing lasted maybe two days. Jimi was so stoned he probably didn't even know he was ever kidnapped.'

The whole thing was fake-bizarre. The day after the so-called kidnapping Mike and John and some other heavies with guns took a limo up to the Shokan house, where the wannabe wise guys had said they'd left Jimi.

When Mike gets back to New York later he tells everyone of his heroics, rescuing Jimi from the evil clutches of the bad guys. Good old Mike.

What is Jimi to think, man? It was true, these young cats had loaded him up on grade-A gear and driven up to the Shokan house and put him upstairs to bed. But, yeah, baby, there were guns – 'men in trees with guns', as Mike put it.

Bobby Wood is found dead soon after with five bullets in his skull.

What *is* Jimi to think, man?

Two weeks after that Jimi called time on Gypsy Sun and Rainbows. He brought the guys to the Nevada Hotel, where he was staying, and told them the project was 'on hold'. Billy Cox, who was the most freaked out, looking to get back home at every opportunity, was told his spot was safe in Jimi's next band. Mitch was told that he was still 'part of the deal', though Jimi had already said the same to Buddy Miles. Jimi didn't really know what he was going to do now. He also told them that the parallel idea Jimi had allowed to grow in their minds – a loose cooperative of musical equals that Jimi had dubbed Heaven Research Unlimited – would also have to be 'put on hold'.

They should talk to Mike about getting whatever bread they were owed.

CHAPTER TWENTY-SEVEN

Jimi's Next Trip

That last year was bad to the bone.

It started well enough for Jimi, showing off his new line-up, Band of Gypsys – Billy on bass, Buddy Miles on drums – with two shows a night either side of New Year's Eve at the Fillmore East. But even that came at a price when the venue's owner, Bill Graham, chewed Jimi's ass out after his first set for being 'a shuck'.

Jimi, acting hurt, asked Bill what the fuck? Had he seen how crazy the crowd had got?

Bill shakes his head, tells him straight: 'You did an hour and a half of shuck and grind and bullshit that you can do with your eyes closed, lying down somewhere. But you forgot one thing. You forgot to play.'

Jimi *pissed*. 'You gonna give me advice now on how to play?'

Bill coming straight back at him: 'Jimi, you're the best guitar player I know, and tonight for an hour and a half you were a shuck. You were a disgrace to what you are.'

'Fuck you, man!'

Jimi is not a fighter, never mind the year in the army hiding in corners. Bill is from Russian Jews and a tough motherfucker who saw action in Korea and came home with the Bronze Star (for heroic service) and a Purple Heart (wounded in action). You do not want to mess with Bill.

It is New Year's Eve, the last night of the sixties. Back in San Francisco, Bill has his band Santana booked to celebrate at the Fillmore West. Over at his other San Fran showcase venue, Winterland, he has Jefferson Airplane supported by Quicksilver Messenger Service.

Bill had special handbills printed up with quotes from several of his most famous musician friends. On the East Coast that includes, from Roger McGuinn of the Byrds, 'It's a groovy thing to look forward to the future and hope that things'll be better.' And from Bill himself: 'My hope for the new decade – may the dove rest.'

And from Jimi: 'All the hang-ups of 1969 – kiss my behind.'

Bill sees all the love-love-love shtick for what it is. Jimi is no different to Mick Jagger or Bill himself when it comes to ensuring he gets the best deal, even if it means shitting on thy neighbour. Bill recalling the time Jimi ordered the stage lights stay on during Janis's set when Big Brother opened for the Experience at Flushing Meadows. Janis came off in a rage, her performance ruined. Jimi came on, lights dimmed, made a big deal of being seen wiping his nose on a Confederate flag, and took the place apart.

Bill recalling the story of Jimi telling Jim Morrison to fuck off when drunkie Jim tried climbing onstage with junkie Jimi at a club in New York. Yelling, 'Hey, Jimi, do you know who I am? I'm Jim Morrison of the Doors.'

Jimi looking down at him like he'd just stepped in dogshit. 'Yeah, I know who you are,' he sneered, 'and I'm Jimi Hendrix.'

Bill seeing Jimi shit all over Chas, hearing the real reason the big Englishman finally walked was because Chas had caught Jimi schtupping his old lady – in his own bed. Come on, man. That's not cool. But Jimi dug blondes special. Everybody knew that, right? Jimi couldn't help it if these chicks just lay down for him, right? Sure, buddy.

Bill seeing Jimi after he got back from Altamont, where he'd witnessed the killing of the black kid, Meredith Hunter, beaten and stabbed to death by the Hells Angels. Jimi with that deep, centuries-old anger in his midnight eyes.

Bill seeing Jimi flying high again after the court case in Toronto goes his way two weeks before Christmas. Jimi standing in court, trying to look straight-guy inconspicuous in his blue pinstripe suit bought specially for the occasion, acting righteous, smiling for the press cameras, playing the wronged man, telling the judge he had 'outgrown dope'.

That's right, sir, it must have been one of my crazy fans put that evil substance in my bag without me knowing, could happen to anybody . . . yes, sir!

Bill Graham is the last white man in the world who will ever tell Jimi the truth – for Jimi's sake, not anyone else's. Bill is probably the last *person* who will ever tell Jimi the truth.

After they've shoved the furniture around and cursed each other some more Jimi finally gets this.

'You're right, you're right. I'm sorry,' he tells Bill.

The second set that night is completely different, Jimi just *playing*. Channelling the cosmos through his guitar, letting the music do all the talking, no jive, just music, sweet music. Saving all the party tricks for the encores. Because encores are meant to be corny, right?

Bill hugging him as he comes offstage. 'The most brilliant, emotional display of virtuoso electric guitar I have ever heard,' says Bill.

Hello, 1970.

It's downhill from here.

Listening to the live tapes that Eddie Kramer has recorded from the Fillmore, Mike Jeffery is happy because he feels he is delivering a pup to Ed Chalpin. No discernible hits, just a rambling live album of eye-rolling funk and dirge-blues, Jimi not even singing half the time. Just Buddy Miles doing his boring soul thing. Even

Billy Cox joining in on one thing. You didn't know Billy could sing too?

He can't. Fuck you very much, Ed.

Six tracks, only four written by Jimi – the other two by Buddy, for chrissakes! Wait until Ed hears about that! And only one of those – 'Machine Gun' – of any real Experience-level quality as far as Mike can tell.

Win-win, he tells himself. Especially now that Jimi has got that shit out of his system. He hopes. Actually phoning Mitch and Noel long distance on New Year's Day, while the bunch of gyppos are onstage, telling them both: 'Be ready.'

Then dismay as Jimi comes out of Bill Graham's office, happy like it's going out of style. Jimi talking about putting together the *real* Band of Gypsys album, once Ed gets his. Jimi all excited about this other fucker who's now on the scene – Alan Douglas.

Mike doesn't even see Jimi as black anymore. He just sees all the black faces crowding round him day and night. All of them whispering in Jimi's ear, telling him to ditch his white band, start making black-and-proud music, asking him what his honky manager has done for him lately. Telling him things he doesn't need to hear. How even his white fans see only a cartoon version of a black man when they think of Jimi doing his thing: super-spade, the hippy-generation Stagger Lee – a right-on racial stereotype of a hypersexual black man who is high all the time. Even seeing his thunderous, improvised wild-is-the-wind music like that. Not serious like the Beatles or Dylan. At best an actor, at worst an Uncle Tom, only he don't even know it, dig?

Alan Douglas – another fucking leech. Not black this time – Jewish. One of these types who spends all night telling you what he did for Duke Ellington, Charlie Mingus, Bill Evans, Eric Dolphy . . . Oh, who didn't this cunt know?

Equally at home on the Left Bank or in the Village, see? But scratch the surface and you've got another schemer, a mini

Morris Levy, from whom Douglas had learned the ropes at Roulette before passing himself off as some kinda new-age hipster,
got a special way with the *shvartzes*.

He'd been introduced to Jimi at Woodstock, while Jimi was
off his head piloting another flying saucer, and hypnotised Jimi
with his endless talk about how he'd brought Miles back from the
dead. How he dug special what Jimi was doing with the new all-
black band he was working with. How Jimi was going in the right
direction. Just needed a little help maybe from Alan to focus in
the studio. Jimi buying all this shit like he always did.

Well, okay. Let Jimi waste his time with the fakes and the wannabes. But then he heard about how Alan was now 'advising' Jimi
about the business side.

You what? *You fucking what?*

Seeing Douglas turn up day after day at the Record Plant those
first weeks after the Fillmore shows. Douglas and that other fucking big mouth, Buddy Miles. Both of them telling Jimi they know
what's best for the music, for him, for them. Especially them.

Even Mike could hear the good side of what Jimi was trying
to do. He just couldn't stand the extras. Douglas sitting there at
the desk, vibrating like a kike Buddha while Jimi spun the tapes.
Some good, catchy stuff hidden among the druggy jams. 'Ezy
Rider' a possible single. Some nice gospel-type thing called 'Earth
Blues'. The finished version of 'Machine Gun' a real keeper even
at twelve minutes, even with Buddy singing along. The moody
'Who Knows', Buddy trading parrot-fashion vocals with Jimi,
funky and low but with edge. Other lightning-in-a-bottle stuff that
convinces Mike that Jimi still has it, like the one called 'Crash
Landing'. All this stuff ready to be improved once Buddy is finally
ousted and Mitch can come back in and put a bit of fucking life
into it.

Because I'm telling you now, that fucking Buddy has got to go.

Buddy going on and on, telling everyone how this new thing

is going to be Jimi's 'finest moment'. Bad-mouthing Mitch. 'He was a great drummer, but he never contributed anything to Jimi.'

Wow.

It got better. Buddy telling Jimi to call Steve Winwood and get him to join the Gypsys as well. *Buddy telling Jimi*. Mike having to listen to Buddy, a big evil-looking fucker of twenty-two who would later serve time at San Quentin, explain how he is 'co-leader, and I'm a perfectionist. A lot of people might not like my attitude, but I get the job done.'

Mike knows he has to fix this, and fast.

He gets his chance just a few weeks later at the so-called Winter Festival for Peace show at Madison Square Garden, a fundraiser in aid of the Vietnam Moratorium Committee – a big-deal hippy anti-war thing organised by Peter Yarrow of Peter, Paul and Mary. All kinds of do-gooders on the bill: Harry Belafonte, Dave Brubeck, Judy Collins, Richie Havens, a ton of others all standing up for peace. Seven hours of it.

Mike stifling the yawns as he goes backstage before the show to give Jimi his pep talk – a couple of heavily laced tabs of acid he tells Jimi will give him superpowers. Jimi doing what he always does when handed free drugs: gobbling them straight down.

It is somewhere around 3 a.m. by the time Jimi's Band of Gypsys amble onstage. Jimi talks to the crowd, no one really listening, just excited to see him in the flesh, waiting to hear him play. But Jimi is having trouble getting it together.

Somebody yells out for 'Foxey Lady' and Jimi turns his laser beam on them, rambling incoherently, nastily about the 'Foxy lady sitting over there . . .', pointing, 'with the yellow underwear stained and dirty with blood'.

What'd he say?

They finally ease into 'Who Knows', but after a while Jimi is playing less and less and Buddy takes up the slack, scatting his vocals. Jimi tripping onstage is nothing new. Jimi tripping on-stage is *normal*. He starts to recover, making the guitar spit and roar.

The number finally fades after thirteen minutes. Followed by another long wait while Jimi, silent, tries to get the guitar moving again.

They try 'Earth Blues', or is it 'Message to Love'? Maybe both? Jimi can't quite recall the words, his guitar starting to drift and roll. Maybe it's deliberate, Jimi trying out some new shit. Yeah, man. Like, dig.

Jimi tripping onstage is *normal*. But this is starting to sound . . . like the band is trying to sick something up. The number goes on too long, Jimi going on too long. Buddy and Billy looking at each other as Jimi just fizzes out. Sits down on the stage, the guitar still echoing.

'That's what happens when you're in touch with space,' Jimi mumbles. 'Never forget that, never forget that . . .'

Buddy covering. 'We're not . . . uh . . . *quite* getting it together . . . So just bear with us for a few minutes and we'll try to see if we can do something together.'

Wasted, Jimi staggers off the stage, muttering to himself. Back to the dressing room, where he collapses. Jimi out, man. That's all.

Johnny Winter, a long-time Jimi jam-pal, is freaked out by the whole thing. Hanging backstage, he tells people that Jimi was in bad shape from the moment he arrived that night, sitting on the couch with his head in his hands, not speaking to anybody.

'When I saw him it gave me the chills,' said Johnny. 'It was the most horrible thing I'd ever seen. He came in with this entourage of people and it was like he was already dead.'

As Jimi lies on the couch retching, Mike goes up to Buddy and tells him, 'The trip's over.'

Buddy will never play onstage with Jimi again.

Mike tells Billy the same. There's a plane ticket waiting for him back at the hotel.

Buddy later mouthing off about Mike giving Jimi some bad-shit acid on purpose. Fucked the whole thing up deliberately. Mike's new way of dealing with Jimi when he stops doing as he's told.

Buddy talking all kinds of shit because that's just Buddy, am I right?

Ah, man. Everything turning into a bad trip after that – *everything*.

A week after the hammer blow of the Garden charity fiasco, Mike arranges for *Rolling Stone* to send a photographer and journalist to his Manhattan apartment where – ta-da! – he has Jimi and Mitch and Noel lounging on the floor in front of one of those new fake fireplaces, waiting to be interviewed about the reformed Experience.

It's a puff piece, Jimi acting coy when quizzed about his association with the Black Panthers. 'Listen, everybody has wars within themselves. We form different things and it comes out to be war against other people and so forth and so on.'

Waving away the reasons behind why the Band of Gypsys had been prematurely retired. Buddy had too much, uh, 'earth' in his playing. Yes, man, we see.

The piece went on.

Does that mean he doesn't relate personally to the Panthers?

'It isn't that I don't relate to them . . .' he said, and then trailed off in contemplation.

Does he mean he doesn't feel part of what they're doing?

'I naturally feel part of what they're doing. In certain respects. But everybody has their own way of doing things. They get justified as they justify others, in their attempts to get personal freedom. That's all it is.'

Hendrix is with them, then?

'Yeah. But not the aggression or violence or whatever you want to call it. I'm not for guerrilla warfare.'

Mitchell hunched up his shoulders monkey-like and said, 'Gor-illas?'

Funny, ha, yeah. Mitch making monkey noises.

What about what he told the court in Toronto? Was it true he had outgrown dope?

'Oh yes, it's true, it's true. I don't take as much. That's what I was trying to tell them.'

It's a cringe-fest. But Mike gets the message out: Jimi Hendrix and the Experience are back in business. A week later Noel is out and Billy is back in. No one really notices. The Jimi Hendrix Experience announce the imminent release of a new album, *The Cry of Love*, along with a world tour – to begin in April at the Forum in LA.

What's happening, Jimi? That bad acid Mike slipped you still giving you flashbacks?

What's happening is that Jimi is starting to wake up. The smack bust, the Italian bad guys at his house doing target practice, the kidnapping, the Madison Square Garden mind-fuck . . . Jimi starting to blame *himself* for getting in this mess, starting to maybe see it Mike's way. Especially after Mike lays out the plan – a written agreement for Jimi to sign for US, European and Japanese tours that will gross up to a million dollars, half for Jimi, the other half shared equally between Mitch and Noel or Mitch and Billy, Mike don't care who.

That's a lot of bread just to hold it together for one more year. Jimi knows Mike's contract will be up for renewal at the end of the year – that's the time to finally take a stand. Everyone he talks to privately says so – even Alan Douglas.

Mike has also made Jimi read the bits of paper he has signed on his behalf, which state that Jimi now owes Reprise *four* albums (two per year, neither of which had appeared in 1969 or so far in 1970). Plus the $250,000 cash advance paid by Reprise towards the construction of Electric Lady Studios. Plus the bread-and-butter stuff: the $15,000 bill owed to the Record Plant; the $5,000 per month for limos and drug-bust lawyers. And, hey, Jimi, you know you're gonna have to raise a little sand when the taxman comes calling soon too, right?

Jimi even feeling quietly that he's the one getting something over on Mike. Leaving one of the meetings without having actually signed the papers. Getting Mike to agree that Billy should be in the reformed Experience, not Noel. Even Mitch doesn't want Noel back in now. Noel is fucked up, man. His wife is on the lam and Noel is blowing what was left of his bread on drugs. He's even been kicked out of his own band, Fat Mattress.

The US tour runs from April to June, when the Band of Gypsys album that neither Jimi nor Mike is making one dollar from is released – and hits the Top 5 in Britain and the US. Jimi staying upbeat, knowing that on those days off in June he will be able to get into *his* new Electric Lady Studios for the first time. Well, Mike's new studio, in partnership with his other 'silent' New York partners. But still, hear me, brother, in my own new place. See me shine.

Three days of studio joy then back on the road. Sticking to the script – 'Foxey Lady', 'Purple Haze', 'The Star-Spangled Banner' – with some throw-the-dog-a-bone songs from the still unreleased *The Cry of Love* album.

Festivals – a Fourth of July show at the 'Second Atlanta International Pop Festival' in Atlanta. Billed as the Woodstock of the South, over 300,000 people show up. Mike getting it all filmed. Mike getting as much as he can of everything filmed now in preparation for his next big idea – movie-making. Back in May, Mike had included a stop on the tour at the Berkeley Community

Theater: two shows that Mike paid to be filmed, and which he would later release as the concert movie *Jimi Plays Berkeley*.

Film and big-money shows, that's Mike. The giant Sports Arena in San Diego. Sick's Stadium in Seattle. New York pop festival at Downing Stadium on Randall's Island. Then Mike's special treat – two shows on the island paradise of Maui, at the Haleakala Crater on Rainbow Ridge, both filmed.

Man, but Jimi is dog-tired, his spirit low, his mind running out of fresh moves. The kind of tired no amount of naked chicks in the room can fix. The kind of tired no magic combo of acid, coke, pure lab speed or sheer nerve-burning adrenalin can touch.

He begs Mike, tells him, 'No, please. Postpone the Maui trip.'

But this is Mike's hot tip. There's no backing out now. Maui has been Mike's special place since going there for the first time on a Hendrix tour in 1968. Now he flies out there every chance he can get. Mike boasting of owning an army field phone in case the office needs to call him urgently while he is meditating on the side of a volcano.

On those rare nights when Mike and Jimi still got stoned together, he would talk of some day building a musician's retreat and studio on Maui. Now, in 1970, his dream is to produce a Jimi Hendrix documentary concert film there entitled *Rainbow Bridge*.

Mike so convinced the idea is a winner he personally kicked in half a mil in US dollars to get the project off the ground. Talking Mo Ostin, the new president of Reprise, into putting up a further $450,000.

Mike formed a company to handle the deal, which he called Antah Kar Ana Incorporated. And Reprise owners Warner Bros. would distribute. It didn't matter how tired Jimi claimed to be. The fact is, on Mike's advice, he'd signed a contract for the movie-distribution rights in exchange for an advance towards completing Electric Lady.

But the more Jimi learned about *Rainbow Bridge* – an 'answer' to the movie *Easy Rider*, which had caused such a commotion the previous year and featured Jimi's 'If 6 Was 9' on the film score, but which director Chuck Wein saw as too negative a depiction of the hippy nation – the less he wanted to do with it. It sounded exactly like the kind of white college-kid hippy fantasy that Jimi now desperately wished to distance himself from.

Mike put his foot down. Chuck Wein, alumnus of Warhol's Factory, would deliver something radical *and* profitable. Jimi told to act – to *act*, motherfucker – in supposedly improvised scenes with black New York model and actress Pat Hartley. Jimi loading up on weed and wine to get him through the skin-crawling embarrassment of pretending to be some sort of wandering occult minstrel.

Man, it fucking sucked. The only minor nod to credible action the seventeen minutes of the Jimi Hendrix Experience playing at an open-air concert in front of a crowd of hippies, pieces of which flare up at the end of the movie.

When Chuck Wein returned to LA with more than forty risible hours of film it was obvious the original budget would need to be doubled. Mike didn't have it. So he told Warner Bros. to dip into Jimi's future royalties. But the Jimi Hendrix Experience hadn't released a new album or single in nearly two years, and the label told Mike no.

Fuck no. So Mike pledged more of his own money – that is, did his own dip into 'future' Hendrix royalties. Tour money. In this case, as many sacks of cash as could be carried out of the Honolulu International Center, on the Hawaiian island of Oahu, two days after the second bullshit Maui show.

There is one last, brief moment of light over three weeks in August when Jimi is able to get back into Electric Lady and record some of the real music he's felt building inside while he's been jumping through money hoops for Mike.

Secretly encouraged by the success of the Band of Gypsys

album, Jimi had abandoned the idea of having the so-called
The Cry of Love album released as some sort of Jimi Hendrix
Experience item. He'd given Mike everything he wanted, been
a pretty good guy, most of the time. Now it was Jimi's turn to
reassert hisself.

His plan was to take the hundreds of hours of tapes he'd ac-
cumulated – with Juma and Larry and all those cats, along with
whatever he and Mitch and Billy, with the help of Alan Douglas,
and even Eddie Kramer, hell, maybe even some bits and pieces
done with Noel on the fly – and turn them into a grand musical
statement. Another double album, like *Electric Ladyland*, but this
time something more thought out, more fully realised. A set of
sonic tapestries he planned to call *First Rays of the New Rising Sun*.

No need to bother Mike about it. If everything panned out the
way Jimi really hoped, Mike would be gone by the end of the year
– and that would be the time to release what he now envisaged as
his greatest work. So *far*, anyway – after that the sky was the limit,
baby. Wait and see!

Yeah, well, these are the stories Jimi comforts himself with
as he sits on the plane heading out of New York City and back
to London at the end of the month. He spends three days at the
Londonderry Hotel on Park Lane, in the Park Suite, doing press
interviews. One for *The Times*, the *New Musical Express*, *Melody
Maker*, *Disc and Music Echo*, *Record Mirror*, *Music Now*, one for the
German papers *Bild am Sonntag*. Talking about what a blast it's
going to be doing the Isle of Wight festival. Talking about whatever comes out of his mouth.

'If I'm free it's because I'm always running,' he tells *The Times*.
'It's all turned full circle,' he says in *Melody Maker*. 'I'm back right
now to where I started. I've given this era of music everything. I
still sound the same, my music's still the same and I can't think
of anything new to add to it in its present state . . . When the last
American tour finished earlier this year, I just wanted to go away

a while and forget everything. I wanted to just do recording, and see if I could write something. Then I started thinking. Thinking about the future. Thinking that this era of music – sparked off by the Beatles – had come to an end . . .'

Then, at night, hitting the Speak with Billy, jamming with Stephen Stills and telling him how he can't wait to get the Isle of Wight and all these other bullshit festival dates Mike has lined up in Europe out of his life so he can get back to . . .

'What, exactly?' asks Stephen. Jimi laughs, says he'll try to think of something before they meet again.

Jimi has phoned ahead, to someone he met at a show in Düsseldorf eighteen months before. Nice blonde chick named Monika. Comes from a good family, was once a champion ice-skater. Not your usual groupie chick but someone Jimi can talk to. They had a scene, and a few weeks later, when Jimi did the Albert Hall in London, Monika was there too. Low profile. Fading if Kathy came into view. Only ever a phone call away, though, whenever Jimi needed a change of scene.

Monika gets to London first, books a hotel apartment at a place called the Samarkand in Notting Hill. Somewhere Jimi can get away from it all for a few hours. The chick is a little strange, a little heavy, but Jimi can dig that. He has never felt stranger, his life never heavier than right now, when things are supposed to be so much better than ever before. Monika comes with him to the Speak. Monika comes with him wherever he wants to go. No fuss.

Flying the next day by helicopter from Stapleford Aerodrome in Essex to Bembridge Airport, on the Isle of Wight. Driving to East Afton Farm, where it is just another fucking day in Crazy Town. Same festival hassles, bullshit about who goes on first, last, in between, equipment breakdowns, amps picking up radio signals, drug deals gone wrong, dropping the same acid, having the same trips, everything so much less than before. The world no longer new and strange and far out . . .

Jimi coming on in the early hours – late-late-late again – with, it seems, a deliberately strangulated version of 'God Save the Queen'. But this is not Woodstock. Jimi vamping on the national anthem, no following wind at all. Just another gimmick, like playing the guitar with your teeth – what it comes across like, anyway.

The show is off. The new numbers – the raunchy 'Dolly Dagger', dedicated to Devon, the spectacular 'Freedom', dedicated to one and all, the mood fracturing with a stray 'Room Full of Mirrors'. The out-front sound being blown around in the wind.

They finish with the crowd pleasers – 'Joe', 'Purple', 'Voodoo'. But end with another new one, something built on a riff stretching all the way back to Jimi's army days, when he and Billy tried to outdo each other on their little practice amps. Something called 'In From the Storm'.

'I just came back today / I just came back from the storm . . .'

The band eventually winds it way to the end and a ghostly Jimi tells the near half a million people there, 'Thank you very much. And peace and happiness and all the other good shit.'

Slumped in his dressing-room caravan after the show, the lax security letting anyone and everyone in to gather round him, Jimi is without words. Just sooo damn fuckin' tired. Someone offers him a joint, an open bottle of wine. He smiles but waves them away. Jimi has to split now. The chopper is waiting to get him back to Southampton Airport for the early bird flight to Stockholm, where he has another gig that night. Jimi losing it as the crowd cries out for the hits. 'Fuck you! Fuck you! You come up and play guitar!'

Then another gig the next night – outdoors this time – in Gothenburg. Same deal. A crowd bored with the new shit, demanding more of the old shit. 'This song is dedicated to all the girls who get laid,' Jimi announces sarcastically, before giving in and playing 'Foxey Lady'. Then grinning, 'And, erm, all the little girls back there with those little yellow, orange, pink and turquoise panties that they keep throwing on the stage. It's close to Mother's Day. Anybody that wanna be a mother, come backstage.'

Asked by a Swedish newspaper reporter about the $5,000 contribution he had made to the Martin Luther King Memorial fund two years before, Jimi snaps, 'Would you rather I gave it to the Ku Klux Klan? In the USA you have to decide which side you're on. You're either a rebel or like Frank Sinatra.'

Confessing: 'I'm tired of lying down and I feel mentally hollowed.'

Then another gig the next night, in Aarhus, Denmark – Jimi sleepwalking off after three songs. His new girlfriend for the tour, Kirsten Nefer, is shocked to see Jimi 'staggering' and 'acting in a funny way'. Telling her, 'I don't want you to see me like this.' Backstage, the venue's manager, Otto Fewser, catches Jimi as he 'collapsed into my arms and we sat him upon a chair. He was cold – cold fever – then they asked for cocaine. "We have not cocaine," I say. Hendrix could not play more.'

'I'm not sure I'll live to be twenty-eight years old,' Jimi tells another interviewer the next day. 'I mean, at the moment I feel I have nothing more to give musically. I will not be around on this planet anymore, unless I have a wife and children – otherwise I've got nothing to live for.'

Chas – Chas! – appearing as if in a fever dream at one of the shows, comes away disturbed. 'He was wrecked,' Chas tells everyone. 'He'd start a song, get into the solo section and then he wouldn't even remember what song they were playing at the time. It was really awful to watch.'

Then another gig, forty-eight hours after that, in West Berlin. Travelling by train to the so-called Love and Peace Festival on the Isle of Fehmarn, off the northern coast of Germany in the Baltic Sea. Billed as the European Woodstock, it turns into a mini-Altamont. Hells Angels have ransacked the production office and given out free tickets to everybody. Machine-gun fire fills the stormy air.

Overrun by all the bikers, battered by storms, plagued by cancellations from big-name acts like Emerson, Lake and Palmer, the festival has descended into chaos, violence and arson by the time Jimi finally arrives onstage around 1 p.m.

Walking on to boos and jeers and shouts of '*Hau ab!*' – German for 'go home!' or 'get lost!' – Jimi is shocked. He tries to smooth things over, telling them, 'Peace anyway, peace.' But the booing grows louder, Jimi walking to the front of the stage, arms outstretched. 'I don't give a fuck if you boo, as long as you boo in tune, you mothers . . .'

Hit by force-five gales, murderous rainstorms, Jimi ends the set with 'Voodoo Child', his voice against the hurricane: '*If I don't see you no more in this world / I'll meet you in the next one and don't be late, don't be late . . .*'

The guitar still bucking the heavens, he shouts, 'Thank you. Goodbye. Peace!'

Taking off from the wrecked festival site by helicopter straight after the show, to make a connecting flight from Hamburg – home to London.

Jimi, fuuuccckkked, man.

But not as fucked as Billy, who had his drink spiked with acid so strong his brain is blown for days then weeks then months afterwards. Billy is having a fucking breakdown. The decision is made to get him on a flight back to the US pronto.

Driving in from Heathrow, Jimi heads straight for the Samarkand, where Monika is quietly waiting, reading Jimi's interview in that week's *Melody Maker*.

She likes the bit where he talks so positively about the future.

'Something new has got to come and Jimi Hendrix will be there,' he tells the writer Roy Hollingworth.

'I want a big band.' Smiles. Still talking about his beloved big band. 'I don't mean three harps and fourteen violins. I mean a big band full of competent musicians that I can conduct and write for. And with the music we will paint pictures of Earth and space, so that the listener can be taken somewhere . . . They are getting their minds ready now. Like me, they are going back home, getting fat and making themselves ready for the next trip.'

Monika is ready to make that next trip with Jimi, she is sure. And so is Mike.

He'd heard about Chas's 'surprise' visit to see Jimi on tour. Yeah? Well, you can fuck off too, matey. I know your lousy game.

He'd got wind of Jimi's little plan to walk off into the sunset with Alan Douglas. 'Alan Douglas is scum!' Mike had screamed in Mo Ostin's office when confronted with what everyone knew Jimi was about to do. 'I will never let him get his hands on Hendrix!'

Heard too about Ed Chalpin, not happy with making a million off the Band of Gypsys, now coming to London to sue Jimi's UK labels, Track and Polydor – and take yet more of what was rightfully Mike's.

Mike sitting puffing on a big, fat fucking cigar, squeezing his brandy glass so tight it nearly breaks in his hand, sweating, talking late into the early hours on the phone.

Pursued for the money he'd taken from Warner Bros., Reprise and the Italian boys to keep building Electric Lady Studios. Crushed by the shambles of the *Rainbow Bridge* fiasco. Unable to sleep at night, knowing that when the deal goes down and Jimi does finally leave him in the shit, Mike will not be able to come back from it – he begins to think about the two-million-pound insurance policy he has recently taken out on Jimi.

All those drugs, all those crazy people he always surrounds himself with. Mike had seen what happened to Brian Jones, asked himself what he would do if Jimi – God forbid – is found face down one day at the bottom of a swimming pool? Not so hard to imagine, is it?

Meditating on his Maui hillside, with his new girlfriend Melissa, a very spiritual girl who always sees the good in people,

Mike begins to seriously rethink his priorities. Always the kind of man to think several steps ahead. Never one to let anything – anyone – get in his way. Mike comes up with a plan.

Ready to make that next trip with Jimi too.

EPILOGUE

Monika and Uli

Monika never got over it. The rest of her life defined by her proximity to the crucifixion of her black Jesus. Her fate: to be stoned by the unbelievers, until she too lay dead – her fall from Earth likewise wreathed in 'suspicious circumstances'.

She lied about her part in Jimi's death. She lied about her part in Jimi's life. She lied about her life after Jimi's death. Told herself the same stories over and over, no one really listening, except for the other believers. The ones that came after the Departure, desperate to hear the 'message' she told herself Jimi had made her promise to send.

Became a recluse, painting pictures of a god-like figure clad in scarlet-and-gold robes and planet-sized hair, a guitar-like wand casting its spell over thankful legions of third-stone disciples.

'I never go out and socialise,' she told the tabloid reporter who door-stepped her a year before she chose to leave this plain to join Jimi in the next. 'I'm just working on my art. Jimi gave me a very heavy burden. I had to promise, really promise, that if he died I'd spread his message. It is a lonely life. But if I'd not met Jimi my life would have been very ordinary.'

Poor, sad Monika, the crazy, fucked-up chick Jimi crashed his plane into. The lone survivor whom no one believed, whom everyone blamed, whom everyone made fun of, scorned, hated, declined.

Of all the chicks, hundreds of them, the one Kathy came for. Because of the upside-down fantasies: the backward fairy tales, the slurred ideas and sick-making beatitudes. The claims that she was the only one Jimi finally revealed his true purpose to.

Kathy had heard it all before. Monika was hardly the first chick-on-a-trip to think she knew something more about Jimi. But when Monika began bad-mouthing Kathy in an interview, Kathy brought out the heavy guns and took that bitch to court – and won. Got a High Court order in London ordering her not to repeat her allegations that Kathy was an 'inveterate liar' for accusing Monika of playing a decisive role in Jimi's death – the too-many-sleeping-tablets version. Kathy petitioned the judge to jail the cow, but the judge was no pushover and let poor, deluded Monika go free.

Two days later Monika was found dead in her Mercedes in the garage of her house in Seaford, East Sussex, drowned in a toxic miasma of carbon monoxide. Verdict: middle-aged blonde suicide. The whispers started immediately: Monika had been killed. Like all the others: by forces unknown.

Night moves. Stray gazes. Bumps. Baby, just you shut yo' mouth . . .

The only one who ever really understood was Monika's husband, Uli Jon Roth, himself a Hendrix devotee and heavenly guitar messenger. Like Monika, Uli was German. Like Jimi, Uli could play histrionic guitar. He started young, making his name in West Germany in the mid-seventies as the guitarist in the Scorpions, destined one day to become Germany's biggest international rock stars.

Uli had left by then, though, to become stardust in his own musical omniverse, Electric Sun. This was Hendrix as depicted in Monika's idolatry paintings. Grandiose, serene, earnest, beautifully presented. Uli even dressed like Jimi, even though it was now the eighties and bell-bottom jeans and LSD-length hair were outlawed, laughed at.

Monika's soft-psychedelia paintings adorned all the Electric Sun album sleeves. Uli wrote songs with Monika sometimes too. Always the same one: how Jimi hadn't forgotten Monika, how death could not separate them, how they lived and loved still in their dreams. Uli playing them, so sad, his eyes closed.

> *Death brings us apart*
> *Our timeless love always grows*
> *Because you are my other part . . .'*

When Monika killed herself, Uli had already split for his own dreamscape forest dwelling in the hobbit hills of Wales. He still loved her, but she had decided long ago that she only had room in her broken heart for Jimi. Uli understood. When she died he announced that he was dedicating all his future works to the memory of his lost bride.

NOTES & SOURCES

Much of the 'truth' in this book is gleaned from my investing in the following books. Not all of them are worth reading, but they all contain jewels. For die-hard Hendrix people, I recommend the Harry Shapiro and Caesar Glebbeek book. For great insight info, hard facts, and big etceteras, it has it all. For readers of wider interests, I suggest you just dip in. There's some very beautiful ugly stuff here. You'll know it when you see it.

Brown, Tony. *Hendrix: The Final Days* (Omnibus, 1997)

Burdon, Eric. *I Used to Be an Animal, but I'm All Right Now* (Faber & Faber, 1986)

Carr, Ian. *Miles Davis: The Definitive Biography* (HarperCollins, 1998)

Comfort, David. *The Rock & Roll Book of the Dead* (Citadel Press, 2009)

Conrad, Joseph. *Heart of Darkness* (Wordsworth Classics, 1995)

Constantine, Alex. *The Covert War Against Rock* (Feral House, 2000)

Cross, Charles R. *Room Full of Mirrors: A Biography of Jimi Hendrix* (Sceptre, 2005)

Dannen, Frederick. *Hit Men: Power Brokers and Fast Money Inside the Music Business* (Vintage, 1991)

Davis, Miles, with Troupe, Quincy. *Miles: The Autobiography* (Macmillan, 2012)

DeLillo, Don. *Underworld* (Picador, 1998)

Ellison, Ralph. *Invisible Man* (Penguin classics, 2001)

Ellroy, James. *Blood's a Rover* (Century, 2009)

Emerson, Keith. *Pictures of an Exhibitionist* (John Blake, 2003)

Etchingham, Kathy. *Through Gypsy Eyes: My Life, the Sixties and Jimi Hendrix* (Victor Gollancz, 1998)

Faithfull, Marianne. *Faithful* (Penguin, 1994)

Foulk, Ray and Caroline. *The Last Great Event, with Jimi Hendrix and Jim Morrison: When the World Came to the Isle of Wight, Volume II, 1970* (Medina, 2016)

Ginsburg, Allen. *Howl, Kaddish and Other Poems* (Penguin Modern Classics, 2009)

Glatt, John. *Live at the Fillmore East & West* (Lyons Press, 2014)

Goodman, Fred. *The Mansion on the Hill: Dylan, Young, Geffen, Springsteen and the Head-on Collision of Rock and Commerce* (Jonathan Cape, 1997)

Hendrix, Jimi. *Starting at Zero: His Own Story* (Bloomsbury, 2013)

Hendrix, Leon. *Jimi Hendrix: A Brother's Story* (Thomas Dunne, 2012)

Hoskyns, Barney. *Small Town Talk* (Faber & Faber, 2016)

Houghton, Richard. *Jimi Hendrix: The Day I Was There* (This Day in Music Books, 2018)

Kerouac, Jack. *On the Road* (Penguin Modern Classics, 2000)

King, Jr., Martin Luther. *The Autobiography of Martin Luther King, Jr.* (Abacus, 2000)

Knight-McConnell, Kathy. *Curtis Knight: Living in the Shadow of Jimi Hendrix* (Star Books, 2010)

Lawrence, Sharon. *Jimi Hendrix: The Man, The Magic, The Truth* (Pan, 2005)

Lefkovitz, Aaron. *Jimi Hendrix and the Cultural Politics of Popular*

Music (Palgrave Pivot, 2018)

McGowan, David. *Weird Scenes Inside the Canyon: Laurel Canyon, Covert Ops & The Dark Heart of the Hippie Dream* (Headpress, 2014)

Mitchell, Mitch. *Jimi Hendrix: Inside the Experience* (St Martin's Press, 1993)

Murray, Charles Shaar. *Crosstown Traffic: Jimi Hendrix and Post-War Pop* (Canongate, 2012)

Napier-Bell, Simon. *Black Vinyl White Powder* (Ebury, 2001)

Potash, John. *The FBI War on Tupac Shakur and Black Leaders* (Progressive Left Press, 2008)

Redding, Noel. *Are You Experienced: The Inside Story of the Jimi Hendrix Experience* (Da Capo, 1996)

Roberts, Jon. *American Desperado: My Life – from Mafia Soldier to Cocaine Cowboy to Secret Government Asset* (Crown, 2011)

Seale, Bobby, and Shames, Stephen. *Power to the People: The World of the Black Panthers* (Abrams Books, 2016)

Shapiro, Harry, and Glebbeek, Caesar. *Jimi Hendrix: Electric Gypsy* (St Martin's Press, 1995)

Thompson, Hunter S. *Hell's Angels* (Penguin Modern Classics, 2003)

Tingen, Paul. *Miles Beyond: The Electric Explorations of Miles Davis, 1967–1991* (Billboard, 2001)

Walker, Michael. *Laurel Canyon: The Inside Story of Rock-and-Roll's Legendary Neighborhood* (Farrar, Straus and Giroux, 2007)

Welch, Chris. *Hendrix: A Biography* (Music Sales, 1983)

Williams, Richard. *Long Distance Call* (Aurum, 2000)

Wolfe, Tom. *The Electric Kool-Aid Acid Test* (Black Swan, 1989)

Wright, James 'Tappy'. *Rock Roadie: Backstage and Confidential with Hendrix, Elvis, the Animals, Tina Turner and an All-Star Cast* (Thomas Dunne, 2009)

X, Malcolm. *By Any Means Necessary* (Pathfinder, 1992)

Plus . . .

Boyd, Joe; Head, John; and Weis, Gary. *A Film About Jimi Hendrix.* (Warner Bros. 1973)
The Sixties (TV miniseries, CNN, 2014)

Thousands of newspapers, magazines, YouTube clips, and my own meetings and interviews with Chas Chandler, Noel Redding, Mitch Mitchell, Kathy Etchingham, Eddie Kramer, Robert Wyatt, John McLaughlin, Billy Cox, Uli Jon Roth, John Entwistle, Jack Bruce, Jimmy Page, Don Arden, Peter Grant, and a great many others over the last forty years.